Paths to Teaching the Holocaust

PATHS TO TEACHING THE HOLOCAUST

Tibbi Duboys, Editor
School of Education
Brooklyn College of the
City University of New York

SENSE PUBLISHERS
ROTTERDAM / NEW YORK/TAIPEI

A C.I.P. record for this book is available from the Library of Congress.

ISBN: 978-90-8790-382-4 (paperback)
ISBN: 978-90-8790-383-1 (hardback)
ISBN: 978-90-8790-384-8 (ebook)

Published by: Sense Publishers,
P.O. Box 21858
3001 AW Rotterdam
The Netherlands

Printed on acid-free paper

For the teachers from whom I've learned so much

Ariana David, my daughter and

Alexandra, my daughter of Blessed Memory, who is sweet sixteen forever,

For Fannie Duboys, my mother,

And for Gil, who knows "it is not given unto many" . . .

TABLE OF CONTENTS

ACKNOWLEDGMENTS

The contributors to this book were, in the main, unknown to one another before a week-long workshop for teacher educators cosponsored by the American Association of Colleges for Teacher Education and the United States Holocaust Memorial Museum in Washington, D.C. I thank both agencies for their splendid hospitality and willingness to listen to our comments and suggestions. We who participated found fertile bases for professional discussions that sometimes extended beyond the work day. Although this volume began with those conversations, the views here are solely those of the writers, as neither sponsoring agency has been connected with this publication.

This volume is graced by the mutual respect of those who participated in the project. I offer special thanks to the dedicated scholars whose contributions are presented here. It is a great privilege and honor to work with these brilliant teachers and writers. I hope I have done justice to their efforts.

The editor offers great personal and professional thanks to Dr. Gilbert Klajman, who weighed, measured and corrected language and ideas in his inimitable way. I am most grateful to him for his clarity of vision, and patience in seeing this through to completion.

TIBBI DUBOYS

INTRODUCTION

There is a glaring absence of Holocaust curriculum in the years immediately following World War II. European populations had come through social upheavals that massively dislocated their lives, and people needed to rebuild society after prolonged human devastation, loss of morale, and destruction of the physical infrastructures caused by war. Even countries beyond the theaters of war were deeply affected by the social and economic difficulties it engendered. The end of the Second World War in 1945 marked the culmination of social crises that had begun with the First World War in 1914, followed by the Great Depression. The accumulation of stress and social upheaval over a period spanning nearly two generations fueled the desire of many people for a return to normalcy. To listen to survivors or to teach about the Holocaust threatened the hoped-for social and emotional stability, the comfort of engaging in the simple routines of an ordinary life. An unwillingness to listen to them was surely an additional source of pain inflicted on survivors, who felt they were met by disbelief or impatience when they spoke of the atrocities they had witnessed. Their experiences were so unprecedented as to stretch the limits of credibility, and the horror so great that many listeners recoiled. (Szwajger, 1990; Holczler, 1991).[1]

In the years since the end of the war, the scope of events during the period of National Socialism has produced a body of literature in the form of historiography, memoirs, fiction, poetry, art, and philosophical analyses. All these present questions about the legacy of the period and its effect on the latter part of the 20th century and beyond.

Educators are especially concerned with the events of the Holocaust, as we are always in search of methods and processes to make the past knowable and meaningful to students. We seek ways to make events of the past part of the tapestry of human experience, and to teach about the connections between ourselves and others.

In the US, a number of states currently mandate teaching about the Holocaust as part of the required curriculum. The curricular specificity of these mandates varies greatly, and in part these variations reflect differences in the views of professional historians of the Holocaust. Thus, one issue concerns which aspects of the Holocaust should be addressed, and how to teach them. There are those who view it as a singular event in Jewish history, while others view it in a universal context (Schweber, 2004, p. 146-150). As examples of these curricular differences: California mandates a curriculum that identifies both specific topics and content details while New York State's mandate (Ed. Law of 2000) identifies the Holocaust as yet another topic required to be taught, among such others as The Underground Railroad, the Irish Potato Famine, and the slaughter of Armenians.

T. Duboys (ed.), Paths to Teaching the Holocaust, xi–xvi.

The questions and events embedded in the Holocaust can lead teachers to the slippery slope of teaching morality and character education (required by some states) issues are addressed by Leah Stambler in her essay. It should be noted that her university is in Connecticut, a state that mandates character education.

The decision to extensively name topics to be taught, as did the creators of curriculum in California indicates the moral lessons embedded in those topics, and the posture the learner should take as a result of learning the curriculum. Thus, in their focus on Christians who helped Jews, the implication is rescuers are to be emulated, while Nazis are to be excoriated (Schweber, 2004, p.148). In states with fewer prescriptions, the policy of teaching Holocaust is adapted in classrooms in ways that vary. At issue are the community and the political climate of the venue in which such curriculum is taught.

Controversy about whether the Holocaust is a unique or a universal topic has engendered passionate discourse. Some say the Holocaust is and should be connected to various other acts of genocide (International Association of Genocide Scholars). Yet others think the Holocaust is unique, (Yad Vashem) and should be considered independently of other histories, other times, or other groups. For them, the Holocaust is specifically about Jews, and the task of such a curriculum is to help those who are not Jewish to identify with the victims, who were. They recognize that the Nazis targeted others, such as Roma or Sinti (often called Gypsies), Jehovah's Witnesses, homosexuals, trade unionists and Communists for victimization. For the latter group, the essential reality is that the intention to annihilate totally was directed only toward Jews and Roma.

When teaching our own students, we may focus upon the cultural, historical and ethnic identities of the children whom they teach. While that is often a good way to invite students to identify with others, and to make unknown people more real to learners, care should be taken not to compare different histories. It is essential to look at the overarching human violations and injustices embedded in all stories in which people are oppressed.

There are elements of uniformity in histories of many oppressed peoples. Oppressors make their victims fearful. Oppressors humiliate and overpower their victims. Oppressors deprive victims of the freedom and the dignity they previously enjoyed. Oppressors think they gain by their oppression of others, and most often feel superior to those they oppress. Oppressors vandalize and discredit the cultures of those they oppress and aim to destroy. The curriculum we create or focus upon should, it seems to me, draw upon the fundamental injustices that exemplify the histories of all groups of people who have been oppressed and victimized by others. In the following chapters, various scholars have approached issues in different ways. In their compelling chapter, Parks and Spector show the mere reading of Holocaust literature by students does not positively affect their views of others. The research they undertook using Discourses of identity and techniques of critical literacy offers an approach to bringing about such attitudinal change. Faithful to the view that teaching is a highly personal set of activities, Duck invites teachers to personalize and prepare for the difficult work of teaching the Holocaust and other genocides and offers several models of teaching that he has refined over time.

Helen Bond's research encompasses the Need to Know, and offers both passion and urgency in her work. In her view, children need to know beginning in the elementary grades, and add to their body of knowledge throughout their schooling.

The points of view of various scholars may differ in the following work. Sometimes their views may have only slight differences, but others may be diametrically opposed. Contributions by Spalding and Garcia find that travel and movement out of the classroom offers an opportunity to see events of the past in a more personal way. The reader is invited to find the view and method that best suit his or her needs.

All of the contributors agree that teaching about the Holocaust is important. Increasingly public and vociferous denial by some groups of the veracity of the accounts of what happened during the period of National Socialism underscores the need to teach this material now. Teaching in pursuit of knowledge of historical truth is important. Most teacher educators agree history and literature are an integral part of social reality. This is borne out in the very fine chapter by Marian McKenna, whose work addresses global citizenship using service learning and literature. Jan LaBonty, interested in literacy, provides a number of books for use with middle school learners, as well as some that have been used in childhood education classes.

The contributors to this volume also think that teaching the Holocaust now is important. In an historical sense, the Holocaust is a contemporary event, and there are living witnesses to much of what happened between 1933 and 1945. However, each day the number of people who can bear witness, who can serve as speakers, as resources, is rapidly dwindling. The youngest who may personally remember any of the events are currently in their late sixties 60's and early to mid 70's and beyond. Those who are older will inexorably be dying at increasing rates. In the not-too-distant future those who were directly involved as victims, bystanders or perpetrators, will no longer be available to add to the already documented body of knowledge.

Finally, teaching about the Holocaust enables educators and students to see the personal dimensions of what occurred, rather than numbers and statistics alone, which tend to depersonalize historical events. In the following essays, teachers will find challenges with respect to materials and their use. Teachers will be encouraged by knowing that the material provides the vehicle through which to meet standards for which they are responsible. Teacher accountability, and achievement by students may be clearly met in various disciplines within Holocaust curriculum.

Issues in the Holocaust mandate questions about one's own personhood and that of others. They entail confronting ourselves, perhaps to visit a place within us which we have not previously acknowledged. It may comfort us to think we would have taken the moral high road when we examine events of the past, but we might also be impelled to consider our own darker side. Would we offer assistance to others if they were in danger? How much assistance? What if we were told we too would be punished if we offer aid to those who have been identified as "the enemy?" What political considerations might people take into account while making such decisions?

How does diversity in our society affect responses to these questions? How are many children in our country who are poor, or children and youth of color, and often English language learners, perceived by others? Are the responses of some people vastly different from others based upon social class, ethnicity, gender or other identifiable characteristics? What encounters do children and youth have with people outside their immediate neighborhoods? Knowing others outside the boundaries of one's daily life is important for a variety of reasons. One hopes learners will conclude even people who are different from us share qualities of personhood in ways they may not have known. The skilled teacher can then make connections about things we share even with those, who at first glance seem totally unrelated to us and to our lived experience (Duboys, 2006).

Many children are familiar with the language of discrimination and that which is "unfair." "What would I do if none of the friends I have were allowed to be seen speaking with me?" "How would I behave if I were ordered to shun others?" Many children may have been rejected by a friend, and can describe the feelings they had when that happened. In all likelihood the disagreement or misunderstanding was solved over time. But in the National Socialist era children were enjoined from ever having friendships with children who were Jews no matter how close they had previously been. Such an issue, and there are others, can be taught even to young children (Paley,1999).

The ethnic diversity in American classrooms should most naturally lead us to curiosity about others. Sometimes we find we have stereotypic notions of "them" that need to be confronted. All of us have histories that are legacies of a past that cannot be redressed. But we can, in schools, focus on the need to include others, if only for the reason we would not want to be excluded from society.

Studying the Holocaust compels us to examine the quintessence of stereotyping. All Jews were lumped together because they were Jews. There was an elaborate system of labeling people based upon the number of Jewish grandparents they had. Some Jews converted to Christianity in the hope of being accepted in the society determined to reject them. They found that conversion did not matter if it had not taken place before a certain date, and that date got earlier and earlier to be considered acceptable.

A focus on Jews in particular can be related to children and youth who may sometimes feel despised and excluded from society. They do not fit the "norm" of what is considered beautiful, or smart, or admired. There is a further connection in the fact that for Jews during the Holocaust, what they were, what they did, how they behaved was of no moment. The intent was to rid all of Europe of Jews. Ultimately, two thirds of European Jewry was murdered. Among those killed were artists, poets, actors, scientists, doctors, teachers, lawyers, postal workers, clerks, as well as thieves and drunkards. They were targets only because they were Jews. Never before in human history had there been the intention to eliminate an entire group of people. Never in human recorded history had children and youth been a particular target of such aggression, humiliation and murder. Nazis thought that if children were killed, no one would remain to bear witnesses or to reproduce. It is not a quantum leap, but a tiny step to substitute the word "my" group for the word

"Jew" as a way of inviting learners to identify with others in a plight they have not experienced.

In a perfect world, we would truly find value in the diversity that is everywhere around us. The Holocaust exemplifies the opposite of what educators strive to achieve, as it illustrates the ultimate exclusion and the genocide so readily born of the lies and hate that preceded it.

In working with students who are preparing to become teachers, or when working with in-service teachers, when the curriculum entails the story of others, discouraging comparison of one group to another is important. The issues embedded in the Holocaust, unique to Jews, are now part of world history, and should not be compared with any of the other abuses we human beings are so practiced in inflicting upon others. The Irish potato famine, the colonization of Puerto Rico, the slaughter of Armenians, the history of slavery in America, the treatment of Native Americans, are but some examples of damaging and horrific experiences of various groups of people. But each is incomparable. To compare them is to trivialize each saga, each life lost, each act of resistance by victims of oppression. The focal question is not, "Who suffered most?" We might more usefully consider how we can do better. We should, it seems to me, teach about the insidious way in which hate has often led to violence. Merely knowing facts about the past will not in itself prevent its recurrence. More consequential is how we learn – the questions we ask ourselves and the choices we make in response to them that impel us to see and analyze events of the past with different eyes. What aspects of personhood were violated? Which principles of fairness, decency, respect, justice?

In learning stories of past oppression, we might also consider how these stories are connected to us. To know about the brutality which people have inflicted on others does not insulate us from inflicting similar or even worse treatment in future. The ability to introject lessons of the past, to identify with others, is more likely to make such knowledge change our responses and attitudes. Facts, numbers and even an understanding of technology do not complete our understanding that social studies are about people and their lives. Deep knowledge and human judgment are indispensable guides toward more peaceable conduct. Our technology has already led to creating bombs that can kill people and leave buildings intact. I hope teachers will help students raise questions about the value of technology at the expense of human life, questions that offer choices that allow students to refuse to act in a way that is damaging and oppressive to others. One hopes students will find oppression so vile, they will refuse to be perpetrators or bystanders in quite the same way they would refuse to be victims. For that, students will need a keen sense of social justice, and the belief that acting upon our convictions and working with others of like mind is a powerful tool in bringing into being the goals we value.

Tibbi Duboys,
New York, December 2007

NOTES

[1] References are cited at the end of chapter eight, “Resistance.”

FOREWORD

The word "Holocaust" evokes images of brutality, human devastation and uniqueness in the long history of the Jewish people.

In the many anti-Semitic regimes before the Holocaust, Jews were oppressed in many ways, and often forced to convert to Christianity. There were options, however difficult. They could go into exile and face many hardships that come from being a stranger in a strange land. During the terrible period of the Nazi regime, and particularly during the dark and oppressive war years, there was no option for Jews. If one was successful in surviving by going from one place to another, it was usually to similar or worse conditions in a new place and form. Jews were subject not only to Nazis, but to the collaborators of each country as well. The Nazis, with help from their supporters, exploited anti-Semitic feelings that had been cultivated for centuries previous, which enabled them to cause cultural genocide of a scale that was unprecedented in human history. It culminated in the destruction of Jewish culture on the European continent.

I am a child survivor of the war, and was later trained as a historian. I have dedicated my professional life to introducing Holocaust studies in the United States and to bring back to life my hometown of Eishyshok in Lithuania. My aim was to make the subject relevant to Americans for whom the life of the Shtetl and the life of Jews in Europe was a completely unfamiliar subject.

I was the first person to introduce the subject of Holocaust Studies in schools and universities. In addition I set about to publicize the importance of teaching Holocaust studies. As a result, I opened the First Center for Holocaust Studies in Brooklyn which later merged to become the Museum for Jewish Heritage in Manhattan. President Ford visited my Center on October 12, 1976. During that meeting I was able to suggest to him the building of a Holocaust Museum in Washington, D.C. The idea later came to life as the United States Holocaust Memorial Museum in the time of President Carter, who invited me to be a member of his "President's Commission on The Holocaust." This helped to bring to the American public the importance of Holocaust studies. In trying to make my material relevant for students, I used the medium of my own experience and pictures of people to bring to attention the human aspects of a vanished way of life In that way my hometown became a prototype of all that was decimated.

As a professor, I have always known the importance of context when we learn new information. Depth of knowledge is strengthened when we can identify with the lives and the stories of others. It took a number of years and a great deal of travel and money to gather the photographs that now comprise my famous exhibit: "The Tower of Faces" in the United States Holocaust Memorial Museum in Washington, D.C. The photos show how real people lived in the Shtetl before the conflagration. There are pictures of people enjoying the moment in which these photographs were taken. Americans and others can well understand the pleasure people take in their families and surroundings. There are photos of more and less

T. Duboys (ed.), Paths to Teaching the Holocaust, xvii–xix.

observant Jews, some pictured observing religious festivals. (In those days, even more secular Jews were somewhat orthodox.)

Some are professional photos, many taken by my grandparents, who were Eishyshok's photographers. Few people owned their own cameras in the 1920's and 1930's or were skilled in the technical aspects of developing the film. Part of my work today as a historian of the life of my town is the collection of photos and historical material and the connection of the families of Eishyshok.

In my book *There Once Was a World – The 900 Year Chronicle of the Shtetl of Eishyshok* I document the lives and joys of the people of my town up the point of our decimation on September 25 & 26 of 1941. It is extraordinary to consider 900 years of history eradicated in those two fateful days.

In my TV Documentary "There Once Was a Town," I take survivors back to the town in 1979 to meet those who oppressed them. In addition to my own town, I am currently involved in publicizing the story of the children of Transnistria and the history of the Teheran Children. In addition, my students and I collected Hasidic stories and published them in my work, *Hasidic Tales of the Holocaust,* which has been translated into many languages.

Remembering through education is vitally important. I know that my dear friend and colleague Prof. Tibbi Duboys agrees with my philosophy in her scholarly work contained within this volume, which I highly recommend to every scholar and teacher of the Holocaust.

Today, many Holocaust heroes (every survivor is a Hero!) of the last era are gone. Soon, it will be hard for a child to point to a relative or friend and say that he knows someone who lived through that terrible time.

It is only through making the material of Holocaust education relevant for today's students that we can avoid pitfalls for the future! We must, as Jews and other minorities, deal with the world neither afraid nor daunted by the challenges of living and valuing our traditional cultures. The message of the Hitlers in every generation is to cling fast to our identity and not to hide in fear. This was the message of Hanukkah and it is a message that is relevant for the Holocaust as well. Where, as Jews have always done traditionally, people live in a moral and upright way, so too in every generation, in every place and in every time, there are those who seek to extinguish the light of law and order. They would replace peace with terror, murder and other acts of criminal activity, which they seek to justify to the world by putting evil in clothes of righteousness. We see this pattern in the acts of genocide that have followed the period of the Holocaust.

In this way, we can realize that learning from the past will help our students in the future to cope with the challenges with which they are faced. In fact, this can apply to everyone in every place that hate against groups of people exists.

As a pioneer in the field of Holocaust Education, I have long been teaching undergraduate and graduate courses at Brooklyn College where I met Tibbi Duboys when our interests and departments crossed paths. A special program at Brooklyn College made it possible to cross-list graduate courses in Judaic Studies and in Education. Prof. Duboys and I taught six graduate courses in our years together. I can speak with great authority about the success of our work together, the effect the courses had on the personal and professional development of our students, and the ongoing need to continue to learn and to teach about the Holocaust.

This little volume offers material and processes that remain dear to me. I think it is an important addition to the study of Holocaust education for several reasons. *Paths to Teaching the Holocaust* addresses the need to contextualize and carefully structure curriculum in an age-appropriate way. In addition, it brings together the work of scholars of different backgrounds, interests and philosophies.

To teach about the Holocaust and to focus upon survival against all odds, is an honor to the memory of our comrades so cruelly cut down in the flower of their lives and who cannot speak for themselves. Holocaust denial is increasingly visible, and it is vital to learn and to teach young people and make relevant to them the events that preceded the war so that they can see these processes at work in world events today.

In educating our students we hope to stimulate interest in their own vanished pasts and in the beautiful and amazing stories of those who survived. Teach about the success of the living and the beauty of our way of living proudly wherever we are, in whatever country or time in which we each live. My father always told me to "choose life!"

Dr. Yaffa Eliach
Eighth Day of Hanukkah
New York City, 2007

LLOYD DUCK

GETTING READY TO TEACH THE HOLOCAUST

A Teaching Styles Approach for Personalizing History

> The teacher's understanding and acceptance of himself is the most important requirement in any effort he makes to help students to know themselves and to gain healthy attitudes of self-acceptance.
>
> --Aruthur Jersild, 1955

> The parent or teacher should make it his first business to know himself; for most surely he will transmit his moral character by inspiration to his child in just such proportion as circumstances allow him to have any influence, and the child has any sensibility.
>
> --Bronson Alcott, 1836, in Peabody's *Record of a School*

PERSONAL PRELIMINARIES

Teaching the holocaust requires deep personal and emotional preparation. How comfortable do you feel teaching about any issue dealing with morality, especially those involving social injustice and murder? Can you express your stand on a moral dilemma with friends or colleagues—calmly but with certainty and comfort? If so, you are probably ready to design and teach a lesson based on these issues.

If, on the other hand, you become too passionate to use coherent phrasing and too prone to blush, you need to get in touch with your own feelings about the matter and accept those feelings before you can verbalize them to others. The two quotes above are from educational pioneers who knew how crucial it is for teachers to know themselves and accept their own viewpoints before offering any instruction. The same personal preparation and self-acceptance are necessary before teaching about the Holocaust and other genocides. It parallels the advice I typically give to teacher licensure candidates when they first attempt to teach lessons based on moral dilemmas.

As a participant in the Holocaust Institute for Teacher Educators at United States Holocaust Memorial Museum, many experiences and topics of conversation reminded me of Jersild's and Alcott's wisdom—but none more than the events of one afternoon when, during breaks from presentations and analysis of source materials, we were encouraged to visit exhibits on our own. I began walking through the museum's new exhibit on the Lodz Ghetto and was struck by the

T. Duboys (ed.), Paths to Teaching the Holocaust, 1–12.

personal memorabilia—old shoes, discarded soup bowls, pictures of children who didn't have enough to eat, the story of the family who grew their own vegetables and were in an "ecstasy of eating" when Nazis came to harvest new souls for the death camps. The father exclaimed, "Why should we go out? Let them come and take us!" But there was a new ecstasy in being left behind because the soldiers glanced hurriedly through the windows and, in the dimness, saw no one inside.

As I was absorbing these scenes, I overheard two other visitors talking—an elderly man and a young woman. The young woman was obviously an intern at the museum, and she was helping the elderly man—no longer as mobile as he once was—with details about getting back to the entrance, getting a meal, and getting a ride home. As I listened to his measured speech, I realized the elderly visitor was a survivor of the Lodz Ghetto (and the very experiences memorialized by the exhibit we were visiting)—like those children in the photos and newsreels who hadn't had enough to eat, who feared toil in the cramped city factories, who thought working "in the countryside" would be better, not knowing that working there would mean crematoria! I had the great privilege of hearing his recollections and observing him re-live his days in Poland and at Lodz—and I didn't want to disturb the moment. I listened silently and unobtrusively—knowing if I introduced myself I would be forcing him to serve as a "guide" to Lodz, rather than reliving the experience authentically for himself. I chose not to inject the distraction of my presence and interest into his reverie, and remained anonymous.

We three approached the part of the exhibit showing Mordechai Rumkowski, the Jewish leader who "ran" the ghetto for the Nazis; we saw his stern but caring face and heard his speech: "Brothers and sisters, hand them over to me. Fathers and mothers, give me your children." (The elderly guest exclaimed, "They have his *voice*! I *knew* him!") Rumkowski felt he had to "amputate the limbs to save the body" (Berenbaum, 2006, p. 80). He may have believed that by sacrificing the children he was saving adults in his community, but he was wrong. Rumkowski discovered the truth in August 1944 when he was deported to Auschwitz and murdered there (Berenbaum, 2006, p. 81). The elderly visitor softly explained an outcome of his experience to the youthful intern. In Rumkowski's day he was a little boy with blond hair and blue eyes. He survived the horrors; his parents didn't. The power of my museum experience only deepened as the afternoon progressed—through the "Daniel's Story" exhibit (Matas, 1993) and then visiting a display and account of Father Niccacci's sacrifices in Assisi (Pettit, 1993, pp. 61-87) to engage in Jewish rescue efforts.

How much emotion and empathy do I still feel for my fellow museum visitor who survived Lodz? (With each recounting of the experience, my emotional commitment is reinforced.) But more than that, can I talk about my emotions regarding Lodz and this guest *appropriately* during a lesson on the Holocaust for a group of high school students? Can I come to the place of being able to talk coherently and effectively *about* my emotions—rather than re-living them during the lesson? That's the kind of personal preparation, and self-acceptance, I mean when getting ready to teach the Holocaust.

About a month after this experience at the museum, our granddaughter Grace had to be tested for leukemia. (My emotional commitment here is so great that I have begun to recommend grandfatherhood enthusiastically to everyone I know, in spite of the fact that it is not an academic achievement.) The possibility of losing my 2 ½ year old granddaughter—so full of life and questioning, so insightful beyond her years—made me think again of the Lodz Ghetto and the terrifying specter of losses it symbolized. I re-read James Whitcomb Riley's poem about a little girl, "Life Lesson" (Stuart, 1999, p. 58):

There! little girl; don't cry!
They have broken your doll, I know;
And your tea-set blue,
And your play-house, too,
Are things of the long ago; But childish troubles will soon pass by.
There! little girl; don't cry!

There! little girl; don't cry!
They have broken your slate, I know;
And the glad, wild ways
Of your school-girl days
Are things of the long ago;
But life and love will soon come by.
There! little girl; don't cry!

There! little girl; don't cry:
They have broken your heart, I know;
And the rainbow gleams
Of your youthful dreams
Are things of the long ago;
But heaven holds all for which you sigh.
There! little girl; don't cry!

Joy about the report of excellent health for our granddaughter jolted me with additional questions. How much empathy do I now feel for parents and grandparents who heard Rumkowski's speech ("Give me your children. . .") and who ultimately realized that "life and love will [not] soon come by" for their cherished ones? How do we teach students to avoid assuming it is "acceptable" to wait for heaven, that "holds all for which you sigh," rather than doing what we can *in the* present to address social injustice? Because of this personal development experience as a grandparent I now feel an added layer of emotional commitment to the Lodz Ghetto inhabitants. This new and deeper commitment has served to underscore the importance of being able to talk appropriately about that emotion when teaching lessons that are affective, rather than giving way to reliving the emotion in class. How does one fully prepare to personalize history without succumbing to some debilitating pitfalls of reliving an emotion with students? How might one avoid too much passion and non-coherent speech?

TEACHING WITH THE AFFECTIVE AND PERSONAL IN MIND

What Are Affective Lessons?

Affective lessons are those that incorporate moral dilemmas and controversy—as well as the cognitive elements of facts, concepts, and generalizations. In such lessons, students take positions on moral issues and use the cognitive elements of subject matter to analyze and support those positions. Affective lessons typically focus on death, justice/injustice, and personal choice-making as a way of motivating students to explore aspects of the subject matter. Such lessons begin with the affective—and ultimately expect students to use cognitive skills in developing rationales for their positions on issues. In fact, lessons that begin with the affective also must incorporate cognitive analysis (Duck, 1994; 1996). That is why the question of teachers being able to talk appropriately about emotional issues in a classroom—rather than succumbing to reliving their emotions—is so crucial for preparing to teach about any affective issue. Teachers must be able to model rational thought processes and cognitive decision-making for their students.

What Does It Mean To Personalize History?

Personalizing history involves teaching with an affective emphasis; it means attempting to have students understand and experience at least some of the full emotional power of an historical event. It is a key to motivation and engagement for students immersed in the sophisticated media of today's popular culture. A teacher's time is typically consumed by thinking of ways to engage students with personalized history. The following example illustrates two attempts at personalizing history.

Several years ago I worked with an intern in an alternative high school; some of her students resided at the facility, and some came for the day—but all had been arrested and were in legal difficulties. The intern had to teach them a world studies curriculum—and the next topic was CHINA. She knew she had to depart from the typical curricular emphases on philosophy, religion, culture, and current international relations difficulties. She brainstormed about basic ways to capture their attention and engage them. What about introducing the topic this way? Bring in a highly decorated piece of porcelain and ask, "Why do we call this plate CHINA?" She wanted students to consider what parts of Chinese culture are captured when we call such plates CHINA. She even wanted to use humor to attract their attention with the following joke: How do you feel about Red China? It looks great on a yellow tablecloth! (Most, of course, didn't quite understand the humor.) These ideas incorporate only the cognitive emphasis.

The intern's attempts yielded limited successes—until she decided on a way to personalize history more deeply, using an affective emphasis. When teaching World War II, she invited an elderly neighbor who had fought in the Battle of the Bulge. He came with much paraphernalia, including a captured helmet, a dagger or two, a few other weapons—and a commercially produced video on Battle of the Bulge. His frequent pauses to comment on video segments, his direct descriptions of "crashing" in a glider with equipment to be used in battle as the preferred way to enter the conflict—not as a paratrooper who was an easy target on the way down—and his engaging personal accounts had students' attention riveted. The class was all but reliving the snowstorms of 1944-45 with him. They asked question after question, and the guest was obviously delighted to tell his story. Students were indeed experiencing the emotional power of an historical event—and they probably will never forget the impact. The power of personalizing history through affective lessons comes mostly from the fact that emotional processes of the brain take precedence over cognitive processes. Affective lessons, therefore, help assure that information and insights get into long-term memory and last there (Tileston, 2005). Fortunately, the same emotional power and benefits of affective lessons can be attained using historical documents and images, such as those from United States Holocaust Memorial Museum, when direct witnesses no longer exist.

How Do You Know When You're Emotionally Ready to Teach about the Holocaust and other Affective Issues?

This chapter begins with quotes from Bronson Alcott (Louisa May's father, a well-known nineteenth century teacher and reformer) and Arthur Jersild. Their perspectives are early expressions of a continuing tradition that advises blending personal and professional growth to emphasize lifelong learning (Alcott, 1836; Peabody, 1836; Jersild, 1955). It is a tradition that insists teachers are whole people—with both affective and cognitive sides, each of which can be productively *and educationally* expressed in the classroom. Students need to see teachers who are models of rational decision-making about social justice issues and who can act on those decisions to contribute as responsible citizens in a democratic community. We need teachers whose thinking and acting don't exhibit a "disconnect" to student observers (Mitchell & Weber, 1999; Intrator & Kunzmen, 2007; Robinson & Curry, 2007). Adolescents appreciate the honesty of living out the values one expresses—or "walking the talk," as they are fond of saying. And for teachers, the satisfactions that come from making personal and professional growth complementary are obvious to those who accomplish this feat—because work and play can merge in satisfying ways (Mitchell & Weber, 1999). Teachers who accomplish this don't experience a "disconnect" between thought and action. They have renewed power to live their ideals. Blending the richness of work life and personal life can become a powerful key to maintaining energy well into years of aging (Graves, 2001).

And what are some practical means teachers can use to reach this blending of personal and professional growth? How can they ready themselves to share their whole selves—both cognitive and affective aspects—comfortably *and educationally* in classrooms? How can they know when they are ready to teach about the Holocaust or other affective issues?

Steps toward Emotional Readiness.

1. If you are beginning in the profession, mentally rehearse how you will introduce yourself to students on the first day of class by sharing learning experiences that gave you a zeal for studying the discipline you are teaching. As you gain experience in the profession, think especially about ways you can explain your positions on some affective issues in your subject matter when you first meet a group of students. It will probably be more comfortable for you to talk about these affective issues as a way of introducing yourself and explaining to students how the discipline you are now teaching has enriched your life—and can enrich their lives, as well (Duck, 2000).
2. Make conscious efforts to blend your plans for professional and personal growth. As mentioned above, this blending can allow students to perceive your genuineness and can underscore your credibility with students as a model for rational and moral behavior. Students need the power of such teacher models for bolstering their courage to turn knowledge about moral behavior into moral behavior. For instance, one of our former science education interns had decided, as a fourteen year old attending summer camp in New Mexico, how to blend his personal and professional growth. He watched another youth in fragile health mature physically and emotionally to the point that the young camper could willingly climb a tree even with a heavy backpack digging into his shoulders. The future science teacher knew at that moment how he would blend his personal and professional development: he would keep learning about and experiencing outdoor education, and he would make outdoor education a focus of his science teaching (Duck, 2000). He was convinced he could use the power of outdoor education to motivate all students, including the physically challenged.
3. *Talk with a friend about moral issues in a lesson you are planning to teach.* Do you feel comfortable talking publicly about these issues? Remember that the lighter your skin, the more likely you are to blush if you feel uncomfortable—and you won't be able to intellectualize yourself out of this reaction. Students can use your display of discomfort as occasions for "button pushing" or other kinds of challenges that could perhaps sidetrack your instructional goals. Can you verbalize your positions rationally and with passion at the same time? Can you gain credibility by showing that you have strong feelings about affective issues but that you are able to analyze those feelings cognitively and reach productive solutions? And can you, at the same time, encourage students to analyze their own feelings—through productive discourse in the face of diverse responses and possible disagreements?
4. *Share your personal positions on moral issues with students only when you are ready*—not when you are surprised by questions which you are not prepared to address. It is quite acceptable to say, for example, when someone asks about your position on legal and illegal immigration, that the question is an important one and that we will be considering it in a

later lesson or unit. Be certain, however, that if you publicly share this intent, you do make the question central to the context of a later lesson and indicate why this issue is important.

5. *Create a support group of those interested in teaching lessons with an affective emphasis*—those lessons, such as ones about the Holocaust that involve deep moral questions. Support group conversations should focus on successes, not just on concerns. A good discussion format would be to have participants share <u>three</u> things they liked about a lesson, <u>two</u> things they learned about themselves from teaching it, and <u>one</u> thing they would change if they were offering this lesson again to a similar group of students. Support group dialogue in this format can spark brainstorming about new and more effective ideas for instruction. Building on successes is more likely to yield new successes.
6. *Remember that students learn differently, but affective issues embedded in a lesson make it more likely that students will be engaged and learn.* We know about the power of affective lessons to involve the long-term memory (Tileston, 2005). We know that when students brainstorm about their favorite teachers and what made them effective, they are most likely to remember specific details from lessons based on affective issues—and to be able to recount those details far into the future (Mitchell & Weber, 1999).
7. *Concentrate on what you will enjoy about each lesson and each group of students*—not on what may go wrong or on the special challenges a group might present. If you concentrate on potential difficulties and pitfalls, you'll communicate nonverbally that you really dread the interaction with students—and your verbal message and non-verbal messages are likely to be in conflict. Students will, of course, believe the nonverbal message because they intuitively recognize its honesty. Concentrating on what you enjoy about each lesson and each group helps bring into being a caring community of learners—an environment in which learners, and teachers, feel safe in sharing positions on moral issues because all have been taught to respect each other's rights to share opinions. They have been taught to live an attitude captured by a phrase now seldom used: it is OK to disagree, but not OK to be disagreeable.
8. *The most comprehensive preparation for teaching about affective issues is learning to live fully*—to take the time to form deep relationships with others, to show compassion, to contribute to the good of all. With maturity comes the opportunity to love; to serve; to treasure moments with spouse, children, grandchildren, as well as with one's own parents; to hope; to witness one's dreams smashed; to see visions recreated; to appreciate the special opportunities of overhearing the comments of a survivor of the Lodz Ghetto about the power of the Lodz Ghetto exhibit. Reactions and solutions for life's dilemmas are individualistic and personal. Those reactions and perspectives come from one's world view and philosophy lived out in practice. Life's dilemmas continuously

stimulate us to forge personal philosophies—and whatever the origins of one's philosophy, being true to it can empower one to teach well. Living fully prepares teachers to teach the essence of a full life—and how life is enriched by taking stands on moral issues. That deep preparation gives a context for examining teaching styles that can serve as vehicles for instruction about the Holocaust and other affective issues.

THREE TEACHING STYLE MODELS THAT EMPHASIZE THE AFFECTIVE

Once the emotional and comfort factors are in readiness, the next most helpful preparation is to examine three specific teaching style formats that emphasize the affective. These three styles give practical choices for alternative ways you might organize your own affective lessons: (1) Existentialism, (2) Recon- structionism, and (3) Perennialism. For each style below two examples are given. The first example in each section is about a typical affective lesson teachers may be more accustomed to using. The second example for each section introduces deeper moral dilemmas and social justice issues associated with the Holocaust. Examples related to the Holocaust prepare readers for lesson ideas more fully developed in succeeding chapters of *Paths to Teaching the Holocaust.*

Existentialist Teaching Style

This approach is based on problem-solving for divergence with an affective emphasis. Problem-solving for divergence occurs whenever a teacher designs a lesson based on questions that encourage more than one right answer (Duck, 1994). For example, would you use a lesson about a lake in Cameroon that "exploded" because of escaping carbon dioxide and drowned or gassed several hundred people and cattle in nearby villages (Black, 2005; Brown, 2000)? If you decide to use such a lesson, you would apparently feel comfortable with affective issues. If you were to design your lesson around questions such as these, you would be emphasizing divergent thinking:

- How might you solve the problem of the "exploding" lake to prevent similar future disasters?
- What technologies might you consider using in your proposed solutions? Why? What are advantages and disadvantages of each?
- What role should government take in preventing such tragedies for the future?
- Would you recommend restricting development near the lake? Why or why not?
- How might such restrictions on development affect the culture and economics of the area?

Using this teaching style has several distinct advantages for teachers who are beginning to design affective lessons. This model allows teachers to bring up a moral dilemma and have students do their own thinking well in advance of having the teacher reveal his/her opinion. In fact, the teacher can encourage more and more rational responses about possible solutions—while asking probing questions that require students to support their positions and reveal details of their thought processes. At the same time the teacher can assure that many possibilities are investigated by injecting new factors and details into the discussion. After students have explored the dilemma thoroughly, the instructor can reveal his/her position, as well as factors considered in reaching a decision. The teacher could, however, delay sharing his/her personal opinion indefinitely—and thereby reinforce the point that students must learn to think for themselves. For this reason, the Existentialist style is often a comfortable model for most teachers who wish to begin using affective lessons. This model does have the drawback of emphasizing a relativist approach to morality. It reinforces the assumption that as long as a moral position can be supported, there may be many possible valid stands—even those which seem opposed to each other (Duck, 1994; Duck, 1999).

A sample Holocaust lesson using the Existentialist model might go something like this for the Nuremberg Laws of the 1930's. (In the Nuremberg Laws Nazis attempted to legitimize many discriminatory practices.) Place class members in small groups with different roles, such as student in a gymnasium, Jewish friend, clothing store owner, grandmother, etc. The key questions might be: What would you have done? When would you have stopped complying as new Nuremberg Laws were passed? Why would you have stopped complying at that point? Would you have tried to get others to stop complying? Why or why not? (U.S. Holocaust Memorial Museum fellows have field tested an excellent example of this strategy.)

Reconstructionist Teaching Style

This approach is also based on problem-solving for divergence with an affective emphasis, but with one crucial difference. The instructor, as part of the lesson's final stages, attempts to persuade students to adopt his/her position and seeks to enlist them in a specific social reform action. For example, a lesson on "Bias Crimes" from *Civic Mathematics: Fundamentals in the Context of Social Issues* (Vatter, 1996) asks students to learn about percentages and proportions by having them calculate the frequency of hate crimes in certain areas of the U.S. Class members are asked to express their opinions about the nature and frequency of hate crimes and to examine possible ways to reduce this problem. Near the end of the activity students are urged to write state legislators and members of Congress to request that they draft new hate crimes legislation.

This model is an approach to affective issues that requires the instructor to take an activitist position on social justice issues and make that activism clear to students. It has the advantage of not reinforcing a relativist approach to morality. The model does, however, go beyond typical boundaries for teaching about morality in U.S. schools—where the teacher models his/her own personal code of morality by being an exemplar—and moves to a position of encouraging direct social reform action by students (Duck, 1994).

A sample lesson for Holocaust and genocide issues might take this form. Have students analyze images related to genocide in Darfur and do research about the issue using documents, the internet, and experts on foreign policy. As part of the lesson's debriefing, encourage students to join groups attempting to get the U.S. government involved in ending the Darfur tragedy. Help students compare situations in Darfur with the Holocaust.

Perennialist Teaching Style

Perennialism is technically a model based on problem-solving for convergence with an affective emphasis. Problem-solving for convergence typically occurs when an instructor designs a lesson based on only one right answer per question. The words technically and typically have special importance here because in Perennialism there is an assumption that universal agreement already exists on all moral principles. There is, therefore, a belief that convergence will automatically be reached—but not necessarily during the time of discussion itself. Socratic seminars are currently the most prominent Perennialist technique (Duck, 1994).

For example, a Perennialist discussion based on Shel Silverstein's *The Giving Tree* might focus on the following questions:

- Is it possible to love too much? Why or why not?
- Is it possible to give too much? Why or why not?
- Are loving and giving the same? Why or why not?
- When was the boy happiest? Why?
- When was the tree happiest? Why?

The tree, you may recall from the Silverstein poem, sacrifices for the boy—even to the point of giving her trunk for a boat when the boy had reached manhood. Finally, in old age, the boy was happy just to be given an opportunity to sit quietly and rest on the tree's stump—and the tree was very pleased. In this example, the assumption is that everyone knows universal moral truth—and that understanding about moral truth comes from within one's self. All one has to do is to begin the Socratic dialectic—asking what appear to be divergent questions. Perennialists are convinced that, if the thought process continues long enough, everybody will reach agreement on moral truth and on the right thing to do. In this case, the belief is that all would agree on the exact nature of loving and giving, where they overlap and where they are separate—if the truth were pursued long enough.

This model has the advantage of allowing a teacher to bring up a moral dilemma and to assume that everyone, as they examine all facets of the dilemma, will ultimately agree on what is right. A lesson for the Holocaust based on this model might use Christopher Browning's *Ordinary men: Reserve Police Battalion 101 and the final solution in Poland* (Browning, 1996). Would you teach a Socratic dialogue based on the question: Why did these ordinary men from a reserve police battalion become part of the Nazi killing squads in Eastern Europe? This would give students an opportunity not only to examine the depths of human nature, but also to consider myriad social, cultural, and environmental factors running counter to the basic truths of morality already understood by members of the battalion. If you are ready to teach this lesson, you have apparently reached a level of full comfort in personalizing history through affective use of the subject matter.

If you are emotionally ready to deal with this intense level of affective instruction, you have apparently already mastered the eight points of advice given earlier in this chapter. This is also a dramatic indication that you have moved beyond the earlier stages of professional growth. The first stage—and all of us begin there—is the focus on self. It's the "how will I survive today's instructional challenges" stage. The major question here is: How will I have enough time to plan and enough energy to teach (Graves, 2001)? The next stages move away from self and focus on the needs of students. The major question then becomes: How will I meet students' learning style preferences and their need for cognitive and affective development (Tileston, 2005)?

READINESS ACHIEVED

This movement from concentrating mostly on self to concentrating mostly on students is where you want to be when you begin affective lessons. That stage of personal and professional development will allow you to see the Lodz Exhibit in new perspective and the "Daniel's Story" displays with new eyes. You'll be thinking less about your own comfort level in coming to terms with moral dilemmas—and more about how you can help students confront moral dilemmas rationally in a classroom and reach new levels of critical thinking and new commitments for turning knowledge about moral behavior into ideals that are lived out.

Through United States Holocaust Memorial Museum almost unlimited resource treasures are available for helping students discover their positions on moral dilemmas and developing the courage to live them out as ideals. Worlds of new perspectives await you. It isn't just the *Diary of Anne Frank* alone—no matter how important that document remains (Frank, 1995). It is also the poignancy of thousands of adolescents caught up in trying to live their ideals, as immortalized in Alexandra Zapruder's *Salvaged Pages*, too (Zapruder, 2002). Don't miss the light of what they can teach us.

REFERENCES

Alcott, A. B. (1836). *Conversations with children on the Gospels.* Boston: James Munroe & Co.

Berenbaum, M. (2006). *The world must know: The history of the Holocaust as told in the United States Holocaust Memorial Museum.* Washington, DC: United States Holocaust Memorial Museum.

Black, R. (2005, September 27). Action needed in deadly lakes. *BBC News World Edition.* Retrieved October 4, 2005, from http://news.bbc.co.uk/2/hi/science/nature/4285878.stm

Brown, D. (2000). Pipes will help volatile "killer lakes" vent. *Washington Post,* 31 January: A9.

Browning, C. R. (1996). *Ordinary men: Reserve Police Battalion 101 and the final solution in Poland.* New York: Harper Perennial.

Duck, L. (1994). *Teaching with charisma.* Burke, VA: Chatelaine Press. (Reprint of the Allyn & Bacon edition.)

Duck, L. (1996). *Understanding American education: Its past, practices, and promise.* Burke, VA: Chatelaine Press.
Duck, L. (1999). Moral education: Hard choices on the way to a new consensus. In F. Schultz (Ed.), *Annual editions: Education 99/00.* Guilford, CT: Dushkin/McGraw-Hill.
Duck, L. (2000). The ongoing professional journey. *Educational Leadership, 57*(8), 42–45.
Frank, A. (1995). *The diary of a young girl: The definitive edition.* New York: Doubleday.
Graves, D. (2001). *The energy to teach.* Portsmouth, NH: Heinemann.
Intrator, S. M., & Kunzman, R. (2007). Starting with the soul. In Fred Schultz (Ed.), *Annual editions: Education 07/08.* Dubuque, IA; McGraw-Hill.
Jersild, A. T. (1955). *When teachers face themselves.* New York: Teachers College Press.
Matas, C. (1993). *Daniel's story.* New York: Scholastic.
Mitchell, C., & Weber, S. (1999). *Reinventing ourselves as teachers: Beyond nostalgia.* London: Falmer Press.
Peabody, E. P. (1836). *Record of a school.* New York: Arno Press Reprints [1969].
Pettit, J. (1993). *A place to hide: True stories of Holocaust rescues.* New York: Scholastic.
Robinson, E. H., & Curry, J. R. (2007). Promoting altruism in the classroom. In F. Schultz (Ed.) *Annual editions: Education 07/08.* Dubuque, IA: McGraw-Hill.
Silverstein, S. (1964). *The giving tree.* New York: HarperCollins Publishing.
Stuart, S. A. (1999). *A treasury of poems: A collection of the world's most famous and familiar verse.* New York: Galahad Books.
Tileston, D. W. (2005). *Ten best teaching practices: How brain research, learning styles, and standards define teaching competencies.* Thousand Oaks, CA: Corwin Press.
Vatter, T. (1996). *Civic mathematics: Fundamentals in the context of social issues.* Englewood, CO: Teacher Ideas Press.
Zapruder, A. (2002). *Salvaged pages: Young writers' diaries of the Holocaust.* New Haven, CT: Yale University Press.

Lloyd Duck
College of Education and Human Development
George Mason University

HELEN BOND

TEACHING THE HOLOCAUST IN THE URBAN CLASSROOM

The Need to Know

INTRODUCTION

While all students need to learn about the Holocaust, students in urban schools are the least likely to have that opportunity due to challenges in the urban school environment. Urban classrooms are typically populated by culturally and linguistically diverse students. These students are often as underserved in their classrooms as they are in their communities. Since many urban schools are challenged with underachievement, poverty, and lack of resources, learning anything other than the core-tested curriculum becomes a luxury. The study of the Holocaust enables students to explore basic as well as complex moral and human rights issues. Students in urban schools particularly benefit from instruction that provides a window into their own challenged lives. Holocaust education can act as a bridge into the many historical, social, religious, political, and economic conditions that led to genocide. Urban students miss valuable content and learning opportunities that empower them to not only protect their own rights, but the rights of others. A new vision of urban schools developed by the Annenberg Institute for School Reform is discussed as a framework for implementing Holocaust education. This framework consists of five critical lenses that view the promise of urban schools as a democratizing agent in American society.

OVERVIEW OF HOLOCAUST EDUCATION

The Holocaust is a watershed event in human history. Approximately six million Jews were killed by Nazi Germany and their collaborators during World War II. Educators have a role and a responsibility to teach the moral and ethical lessons derived from one of the most documented histories available. These lessons span the range of content areas that include the historical, social, moral, cultural, political, and economic facets of our society. While there is no national curriculum for the teaching of the Holocaust in the United States, five states (California, Florida, Illinois, New Jersey, and New York) have established legislative mandates requiring the teaching of the Holocaust in public schools (United States Holocaust Memorial Museum, 2004). Florida was the first state to pass such a mandate in 1994. Other states have developed similar guidelines, standards, curriculum, and commissions that guide educators in developing lessons focused on the Holocaust.

T. Duboys (ed.), Paths to Teaching the Holocaust, 13–30.

With the aid of the National Council for Social Studies, 48 states along with the District of Columbia have developed social-studies standards that integrate the teaching of the Holocaust as part of the social studies curriculum for that state (United States Holocaust Memorial Museum, 2004).

One important mission of the United States Holocaust Memorial Museum as stated in its 2005-2006 annual report is to "teach millions of people each year about the dangers of unchecked hatred and antisemitism and the need to prevent genocide" (United States Holocaust Memorial Museum, 2006, p. 3). In 2004 approximately 125, 000 school students had the opportunity to visit the United States Holocaust Museum in Washington D.C. (United States Holocaust Memorial Museum, 2004). These are the lucky ones. Many students, especially those in urban schools often do not have the opportunity to learn about the Holocaust inside or outside the classroom. Challenges in urban schools can create obstacles for effective teaching and learning in general, but can really pose challenges with complex topics such as the Holocaust. However, with professional development along with a clear and guiding rationale, urban educators can begin the integration of Holocaust education into their curriculum. Urban schools educate approximately 25% of children in the United States, many of whom are minorities (Perkins, 2007). These students often experience water-downed curriculum that sometimes includes only items on standardized tests. Thus, they miss out on learning opportunities that might enable them to understand and recognize the consequences of inequality and oppression (Duncan, 2005). Urban students have a need and a right to learn about one of the most significant events in human history.

Rationale

Rationale statements for the study of the Holocaust provide a framework for curriculum, instruction, and assessment. Without clearly articulating the reasons why Holocaust education is important for a particular teaching context, educators may do more harm than good (Totten et al., 2001). The rationale for teaching the Holocaust in the urban classroom is embedded in larger rationales of why it is important for all students to learn about the Holocaust. There are lessons embedded in the Shoah (the modern Hebrew term for Holocaust) suitable for all developmental levels, grade levels, and students in rural, suburban, and urban contexts. As with any effective instruction, educators should keep in mind the development levels of students as they shape instruction. Age appropriate instruction for Holocaust education is discussed in greater detail below. While rationales for teaching the Holocaust may be developed specific to the context, all children should have the opportunity to learn how seemingly small prejudices can build momentum and grow. Equally important and what is sometimes forgotten is the role that antisemitism played in creating the context for genocide (Lindquist, 2006). This can lead to a greater understanding of the role of intolerance and its effect on human behavior (Short, 2000).

Equally important is a thorough grounding in the history of the Holocaust (Totten et al., 2001). Samantha Power (2002) in her award winning book refers to genocide as a problem from hell. While this description alludes to the enormousness of genocide, students should also understand that the orchestrated murder of six million Jews was not act from Hades, but perpetrated by one group of humans against another. It is also important to point out that during the Holocaust, other minority groups were targeted for annihilation, such as the Roma (Gypsies), the handicapped, communists, socialists, Jehovah's Witnesses, and homosexuals. Bauer (2001) suggests that the Holocaust should be demystified from an unfathomable event to one that is understood as a calculated progression of events. These events were situated in the context of World War II and were neither inevitable or happenstance. This demystification allows students to make critical connections to their own lives and as well as to the larger world. At the same time, students should also be exposed to the complexity of the Holocaust and the understanding that it may never be fully understood (Totten, et al., 2001).

DEVELOPING A RATIONALE FOR URBAN SCHOOLS

Context Specific

Are there special lessons in Holocaust education for urban youth? While there may not be special lessons for urban youth, there are certainly special conditions that must be taken in consideration when developing a rationale and instructional program to teach the Holocaust in urban schools. Developing a rationale for Holocaust education in urban classrooms means understanding the nature of the urban classroom, community, and urban student. Holocaust scholars emphasize how educators must organize the Holocaust curriculum, resources, and pedagogy in ways "that best assists students to understand both the past as well as the world in which they live today" (Totten et al., 2001, p. 2). In order to accomplish this, the context and needs of the students must be taken in consideration.

Gundare and Batelann (2003) found that Holocaust education differed depending upon the context in which it was taught. The author's argument is based upon a comparison of Holocaust education in Latvia with Holocaust education in the Netherlands, and the United States. The authors found distortions in the history in all three geographical areas. For example, American textbooks often failed to mention the antisemitic attitudes of automobile entrepreneur Henry Ford. Textbooks also failed to mention the fact that the American government knew of the Nazi death camps.

While Gundare and Batelann stress that the history of the Holocaust be accurate, the cultural, social, and political context will impact the rationale and the focus of Holocaust education. For example Holocaust education curriculum should address omissions and distortions as a part of Holocaust education in a particular context. Educator Cochran-Smith (2004) confirms the importance of context in shaping the program of education for K-12 students. Cochran-Smith recommends that educators must have a deep understanding of how the cultural identity and background of their students and their program of education have influenced their worldview and approach to learning. When educators have knowledge of their students learning styles and the communities in which they live, they become more effective in facilitating higher achievement among students.

Catholic Context

The Catholic Church is a case in point in how context influences the rationale and program for Holocaust education. In 2001 the U. S. Catholic Bishops required Catholic school educators to integrate Holocaust education in Catholic Schools across the United States (Laurita, 2003). Individual Catholic eductors had been integrating Holocaust education in Catholic schools prior to 2001. In 2003 educators congregated at the Sixth Holocaust Education Conference at Seton Hall University to develop Holocaust education curriculum and rationales specific for the Catholic school context (Laurita, 2003). Conference attendees determined that Catholic school educators needed professional development to understand the role of the Catholic Church in the Holocaust and the history of antisemitism within Christianity and the Catholic Church (Laurita, 2003). While it is important for all students to have an understanding of the role that antisemitism played in the Holocaust, it is particularly important to address these critical issues in a Catholic School context.

Urban Context

What are the contextual issues that should be considered in developing a rationale and instruction for Holocaust education in urban schools? Urban schools are defined as schools located within a central city or schools that generally serve high numbers of at-risk and minority students (Adams & Adams, 2003). Approximately 17.3 % of students in urban schools are categorized as limited English proficient versus 8. 2% of students in suburban schools (Jacob, 2007). Urban schools are often sites of concentrated poverty, with high numbers of students receiving free and reduced lunch. Approximately one-third of students living in poverty attend urban schools (Orfield & Lee, 2006).

Urban schools are also characterized by increasingly higher levels of segregation. African-American and Hispanic students attend urban schools where over half of the students in the school are African-American (52%) or Hispanic (55%), (Orfield & Lee, 2006). Hispanic students experience triple segregation through ethnicity, poverty and linguistic separation. The intense segregation of students in schools is also experienced by teachers. African-American teachers teach in schools that are predominantly African-American (Orfield & Lee, 2006). Complicating matters, urban teachers often do not have comparable levels of education, experience, and sometimes even teaching certification as their suburban and rural counterparts (Jacob, 2007).

Many urban schools are also plagued by low levels of academic achievement. Students with limited English proficiency tend to graduate at lower rates than students who are native speakers of English (Orfield & Lee, 2006). While African American students have made some gains, 2003 data reveal that African-American students complete high school with mathematics and reading skills equal to that of 8th grade white students (Education Trust, 2003).

Challenges and Possibilities

Challenges in urban schools should not inhibit educators from integrating Holocaust education into the curriculum. The challenges experienced by urban educators are not unlike challenges experienced by many educators in rural and suburban schools. The United States Holocaust Memorial Museum (2004) country report for the United States identified the following obstacles in Holocaust education in schools in the United States. The challenges include mandated teaching standards that focus more on facts than critical thinking, lack of funding for professional development and resources, time restrictions, inadequate teacher preparation, mandatory testing, and disagreement on instructional strategies and rationales for teaching the Holocaust.

Nevertheless, challenges of teaching the Holocaust in urban schools should be taken in careful consideration when developing a rationale and a course of study for Holocaust education. This includes a careful selection of materials, pedagogy, and other resources with respect to teaching the Holocaust. Textbooks often focus on facts and figures that do not contextualize Holocaust history or generate the moral lessons that first person accounts or primary sources can (Lindquist, 2006). Professional development in the history of Holocaust as well in curriculum and instruction must also be provided for urban educators who are often less experienced than their suburban or rural counterparts (Lindquist, 2006). Students in urban settings need to be exposed to a high quality and current curriculum, pedagogy, and materials (Duncan, 2005). The lack of current materials may be addressed by the use of instructional materials available on the Web sites of the United States Holocaust Memorial Museum and other Holocaust education related sites such as "Facing History and Ourselves" (Symer, 2001).

Promise of Urban Schools

The promise of urban schools can be found in the very meaning of what makes an urban school urban. Urban environments are diverse, environments where different cultures interface. Appreciating the promise of urban schools will help develop Holocaust education that incorporates the positive aspects of schools labelled urban. Cities are often home to a broad array of intellectual and cultural capital such as museums, art, ethnic restaurants, universities, businesses, technology innovation, and diversity. For examples school students in New York City approximately speak more than 120 different languages (Jacob, 2007). While this incredible linguistic diversity creates challenges for teachers and schools, it also creates opportunities. Schools can reach out to ethnic communities in ways that can integrate lessons about diversity and pluralism into the very fabric of the classroom. The Indianapolis Public Schools developed a parent liaison program to help parents make better use of services available for them and their children.

These services included helping parents become better advocates for their children (Howland, et al., 2006). This type of outreach provides a more receptive environment for Holocaust education.

The proximity of informal learning institutions such as museums and libraries in cities offer an array of learning resources and opportunities that extend learning outside the walls of the classroom. Museums serve as an excellent site for professional development for educators by provoking interest and inquiry in teachers that ultimately benefit students (Melber, 2007). Field trips that are effectively planned have many benefits and help urban children connect their learning to a world that may be alien to them (Confar, 1995). The United States Holocaust Memorial Museum is situated within Washington DC nearby several large urban school districts. The architectural design of the museum is such that Leon Wieseltier (1993) wrote that, "The building itself teaches" (p. 20). With careful planning and preparation schools in large cities can benefit from field trips to museums and other informal learning sites that may be geographically off limits to students in more isolated areas. As Tyack (1974) suggests it takes will and imagination of urban school systems and communities to effectively use the resources that are at their disposal.

RATIONALE FOR TEACHING THE HOLOCAUST IN THE URBAN CLASSROOM

The rationale for teaching the Holocaust in urban schools should be one that empowers students. Empowerment of students comes through understanding the complex history of the Shoah and making application to their own lives. Short (2000) described the value in the historical commemorating of the Holocaust. He reminds readers of Hitler's statement questioning whether anyone remembered the Armenians. Hitler was referring to the Armenian genocide that took place in 1915.

Shoemaker (2003) suggests connecting Holocaust memory to current events for non-Jewish students who may not have a communal context for Holocaust remembrance. Connecting Holocaust memory to the genocidal violence taking place in the Dafur region of Sudan is one to bridge historical relevance to current events. The United States Holocaust Museum is actively opposing the violence in Darfur which further creates a bridge from the past to the present.

Empowerment

A rationale for Holocaust study that empowers urban students should focus upon how respecting human rights and valuing pluralism can act as a safeguard against genocide. This is critical to urban students who are generally minorities and may have experienced human rights abuses in their schools and communities. Urban students need to understand their own agency as citizens in a democracy that has sometimes targeted them. Carter G. Woodson, originator of Black History week, rallied over half a century ago against the mis-education of the Negro (1933). Woodson argued that African-Americans in the 20th century were not receiving education that would help liberate them. Woodson developed Negro history week that eventually became Black history month to commemorate the contributions and sacrifices that African-Americans have made to America. Woodson argued that the inadequate education of African-Americans would result in African-Americans accepting second-class citizenship limiting their own agency to protect their human rights as well as the rights of others. Woodson wrote that "When you control a man's thinking you do not have to worry about his actions. You do not have to tell him not to stand here or go yonder. He will find his "proper place" and will stay in it" (p. 1).

It is also critical that urban students understand the ramifications of prejudice, stereotypes, and antisemitism as forces that undermine democracy and human rights that can escalate to genocide. While minorities have experienced prejudice and discrimination in ways that may enable them to see a commonality of experience with Jews, comparisons of pain should be avoided (Crowe, 2001). Du Bois in the 1930s wrote about how African-Americans and minorities in general saw commonality in the persecution of Jews with their own persecution in the United States. Du Bois (1936) writes, "No people in the world have the interest in the Jewish problem in Germany that the American Negroes have" (p. 1).

Urban students often experience the least rigorous curriculum. Oakes (1986) describes how tracking in urban schools reduces the opportunities for urban students to learn deeply and broadly. If only brief attention is given to Holocaust history, students may not fully grasp how the Nazis used the context of World War II to carry out genocide. Students must be taught Holocaust history contextualized within World War II (Lindquist, 2006). However care must be taken that the war and the Holocaust are not viewed as one in the same (Totten, et al., 2001).

Anti-racist Education

Holocaust education helps urban students understand the ramifications of racism and antisemitism. Ronnie Landau (1989) argued that teachers in schools in the United Kingdom should teach students about the Holocaust based upon the belief that if taught effectively it could "sensitise them to the dangers of indifference, intolerance, racism and the dehumanisation of others" (p. 20). Landau also supported the idea that Holocaust education could support the goals of anti-racist education by serving as "...the ideal educational formula for creating ... responsible citizens in a multi-cultural society" (p. 20). A study was carried out in a high school in Ontario, Canada that examined how Holocaust education could aid anti-racism efforts in schools. The researchers found that Holocaust education could decrease levels of racism if the teacher included the psychological and cognitive processes of stereotyping, prejudice, and scapegoating within the context of the lesson (Short, 2000).

The incidence of bullying in urban schools also underscores the need for students to understand the detrimental and long term effects of intolerance and the connection to genocide. The National School Boards Association's Council of Urban Boards of Education (CUBE) has called attention to bullying in urban schools in a survey on school climate (Perkins, 2007). Bully is defined as an indirect or direct form of aggression linked to school violence (Kalliotis, 2000).While bullying is a problem in rural and suburban schools as well, the CUBE report revealed that teachers and administrators in urban schools reported that a child was bullied every month in an urban school in America (Perkins, 2007). A study of five middle schools and three high schools in a largely African-American and Hispanic urban school district in Texas revealed that bullying and victimization were critical problems among low income minority youth (Peshkin et al., 2006). The study found that bullying was most prevalent among African-American males, but decreased as students got older.

Barbara Coloroso (2007) argues that genocide is a form of bullying to the extreme. Coloroso, a former Roman Catholic nun, author and internationally known expert on bullying, wrote that bullying occurs along a spectrum of violence that may begin in the school yard and end with extermination. In a study of several genocides, Coloroso found that young children can be socialized to small acts of violence in such a way that makes more extreme violence possible and bystander behavior likely. While Coloroso emphasized that actual genocide is far more extreme in scope, scale, and organization than school bullying, the seeds for contempt, intolerance, and dehumanization are sown early. Coloroso's work indicates a need for children in the elementary grades to begin learning about respect and tolerance early. The National School Boards Association (Peshkin et al, 2006) recommended that "Schools should teach students to identify, understand, prevent, oppose, and report bullying" (p. 16). Since the peak grade level for bullying was ninth grade in the Texas study, the need to address bullying should begin in the early grades.

FRAMEWORK FOR TEACHING THE HOLOCAUST IN THE URBAN CLASSROOM

Annenberg Institute for School Reform

The Annenberg Institute for School Reform at Brown University developed a new vision for improving urban schools titled *Promise of Urban Schools* (2000). This vision of urban schools can be used as a framework for implementing Holocaust education in urban settings. This requires a balanced view of urban students and school systems. The framework developed by the eight scholars referred to as the Annenberg Senior Fellows builds upon the positive aspects of urban schools, while keeping in mind the challenges (Annenberg Institute for School Reform, 2000). The goal of the group was to improve schooling urban education in the United States using a positive approach to reform of schooling instead of the more common deficit model. The deficit model of urban education characterizes urban schools and students as dysfunctional based upon their culture and background and is considered racist in nature (Weiner, 2006).

The Annenberg Senior Fellows approached the complexity of the urban school environment with the understanding that urban schools are not created in a vacuum (Annenberg Institute for School Reform, 2000). Instead they proposed that urban schools are characterized by failed bureaucracies, systemic inequality, and decreasing levels of public support. They concluded that a new vision of urban schools was in order. This new vision placed urban schools as critical to the education and uplift of urban communities. Urban schools are tasked with educating mostly poor and minority students, who will make up an increasingly larger share of the overall student body in the United States (Orfield & Lee, 2006). This makes urban schools a "laboratory for democracy" and central to realizing the promise equal opportunity (Annenberg Institute for School Reform, 2000, p. 4).

Five Critical Lenses

Building on the agenda of urban school reform, the Annenberg project social scientists developed five critical lenses to analyze, critique, and develop positive models of instruction for city schools. These lenses emphasize human agency, educational equity, high quality teaching, learning, and assessment within the urban context (Annenberg Institute for School Reform, 2000). The lens can be used as guide or framework that helps develop Holocaust education for urban schools.

Human agency. The Annenberg researchers view human agency as the ability to act (Annenberg Institute for School Reform, 2000). They believe that schools should prepare students to act as responsible citizens and participants in the democratic spirit of the nation. To act responsibly, students must have knowledge, confidence, and a sense of personal and collective identity in relationship to the broader society. To help develop student agency teachers can involve students in the development of the rationale (Totten et al., 2001). Asking students why the study of the Holocaust is important will help create a student centered classroom that is motivating to students and may help them to see how the study is relevant to their lives (Totten et al., 2001). Asking students what they know about the Holocaust, what they want to know, and what they have learned is one to approach to encouraging active participation in developing the rationale. The educator can use this information as a guide to a deeper and more thought provoking study of the Holocaust (Wieser, 2001). The information gained from this brainstorming activity can be used to highlight misconceptions about Jews or the Holocaust that might stymie learning. Involving students in the development of the rationale for the study of the Holocaust encourages them to become a responsible agent in their own learning and begins the journey of what Yehuda Bauer describes as the central problem for Holocaust educators and that is to "…anchor the Holocaust in the historical consciousness of the generation(s) that follow it" (p. 45).

Educational equity. The second critical lens highlighted by the Annenberg Senior Fellows is educational equity. Educational equity is deemed critical if urban schools are to have equal resources, funding, qualified teachers and administrators, and a strong curriculum (Annenberg Institute for School Reform, 2000). Equity is defined in close relationship to educational justice. Educational justice means that educators will hold high expectations that all children can achieve in school, despite race, ethnicity, language, religion, gender, or socioeconomic status. This notion is critical to urban schools as they primarily educate poor and minority children. The Annenberg Senior Fellows view educational justice as "a moral commitment to care for all children within an atmosphere of respect, dignity, and trust (p. 6). A survey of school climate conducted by the National School Boards Association found that students' trust of teachers and administrators had important implications for academic achievement and students' well being (Perkins, 2007). For the study of the Holocaust to be effective it must be taught within an atmosphere of respect if students are to gain the moral lessons (Wieser, 2001). For example, bullying in the urban classroom must be addressed if lessons of intolerance are to have any meaning at all.

Teaching, learning, and assessment. The remaining lenses developed by the Annenberg Senior Fellows have been combined due to their interrelatedness. They are high quality teaching, learning, and assessment within the urban context. The Annenberg Senior Fellows view good instruction by teachers as the staple of the urban classroom. Quality instruction cannot exist without continuous assessment. Effective assessment provides an understanding of what students know, but also what areas students need to improve in and directions to educators to help students in those areas. In some urban schools the focus on passing standardized tests has compromised the curriculum (Noguera, 2003). Confounding the problem are teachers who are inexperienced or lack the skills, materials, or appropriate dispositions to work effectively with minority children (Cochran-Smith, 2004; Gay, 1975). High quality instruction is needed in Holocaust education to combat misinformation and stereotypes (Wieser, 2001).

The Annenberg Senior Fellows defines good instruction as that which adheres to high quality content and performance standards (Annenberg Institute for School Reform, 2000). Educators teaching the Holocaust have numerous resources to draw from. The United States Holocaust Memorial Museum which focuses on teaching the history of the Holocaust has a wealth of teaching and learning materials available on their web site. These resources include guidelines for teaching the Holocaust and other materials that can be downloaded (Symer, 2001). "Facing History and Ourselves" is another education organization that focuses upon the lessons that can be learned from the Holocaust, such as tolerance (Symer, 2001). Web-based resources can be very helpful to educators in urban schools where teaching materials and textbooks may be outdated or not properly used (Duncan, 2005). Textbooks are often found to be seriously lacking in their treatment of the Holocaust (Lindquist, 2006). Even if urban educators have limited access to technology in their schools, access can usually be found in libraries and other places. However web-based resources must be evaluated as to their accuracy, relevancy, and credibility (Symer, 2001). Proper use of web-based resources can help with time and curriculum constraints often found in urban schools that inhibit proper exploration and teaching of the topic (Symer, 2001). Reflection and evaluation should also be used with web-based resources.

Professional Development

Professional development for teachers in urban settings is critical. Urban educators are often inexperienced and may lack the time, skills, and resources to teach the

Holocaust (Duncan, 2005). Professional development opportunities should focus upon understanding the history of the Holocaust education and how to teach the event. While there are a variety of professional development models, one urban public elementary school, PS165 in New York City, implemented teacher study groups as a way to encourage teachers to collaborate (Torres-Guzmán et al., 2006). Teachers found time and space, (which are both in short supply in urban schools) to share resources, ideas, and a sense of camaraderie that enabled them to become better teachers.

Professional development that occurs in the actual museum or informal learning site has also been found to be very effective for motivating teachers (Melber, 2007). Field trips to museums expose teachers and students to a range of primary sources, direct experiences, survivor stories and exhibitions that are considered critical to authentic and deep understanding of multifaceted topics like the Holocaust (Lindquist, 2006; Gay, 1975).

Experiential Learning Opportunities

Students in urban schools need a motivating curriculum to gain the most from Holocaust education. Experiential learning opportunities, such as field trips enhance students' understanding of the Holocaust and the ability to make relevant connections to the world (Clyde et al., 2005). Many American cities have access to Holocaust centers, memorials, speakers' bureaus of survivors.

One study found that principals of urban secondary schools reported that field trips and other learning opportunities outside the classroom had positive results in areas of student attendance, motivation, and achievement (Scales et al, 2006). However urban schools are sometimes stressed in ways that make it difficult to take field trips or museum excursions even if they are available or within traveling distance (Nespor, 2000). Many museums including the United States Holocaust Memorial Museum and other informal learning sites such as the Library of Congress have an increasingly amount of their resources and collections available online.

Relevance of Curriculum

The Annenberg Senior Fellows highlighted the importance of good teaching as making the curriculum relevant to the lives, interests, and backgrounds of urban students (Annenberg Institute for School Reform, 2000). This is critical for students whose rationale for learning the Holocaust is to understand how prejudice, stereotyping, racism, and antisemitism can act as a pathway to genocide (Coloroso, 2007). Using first person accounts are one way of helping students understand real individuals with real stories make up the unimaginably large number of six-million people who were lost in the Holocaust (Totten, 2001). It should be noted that first person accounts should be used to bring greater depth and meaning to the study of the Holocaust and not as means to just create interest (Friedlander, 1979). First person accounts include, but are not limited to eyewitness accounts, diaries, letters, interviews, audiovisual accounts, oral histories, memories, and autobiographies. First person accounts are best used in the context of the overall history of the Holocaust and may be used with younger children as well. Students need to be prepared to read some very emotional accounts of suffering, bravery, death, and courage. Afterwards they need to be debriefed (Totten, 2001). Friedlander (1979) and Totten (2001) discuss additional possibilities and limitations of integrating first person accounts into the study of the Holocaust. Integrating drama, art, and literature, writing, and music are also excellent ways to tap the full range of abilities and interest that urban students bring to bear on their learning (Wieser, 2001).

Holocaust Education in the Early Grades

The Annenberg Senior Fellows described high quality instruction as that which takes students on a journey (Annenberg Institute for School Reform, 2000). But when does that journey begin? In what grade level should the study of the Holocaust begin? Holocaust education has been typically taught at the middle grades and higher (Totten, et al., 2001). This is evident in the grade levels of students who visit the United States Holocaust Memorial Museum. Of the 125,000 students who visited the United States Holocaust Memorial Museum in 2004, over half (64%) were middle school students ranging from ages 11-14 (United States Holocaust Memorial Museum, 2004). Approximately 35% were high school students and less than 1% who went on field trips to the museum came from the elementary grades.

The state of New Jersey is one of the few that have developed a curriculum for Holocaust education that ranges from elementary through the secondary grades. The curriculum was developed by New Jersey Commission on Holocaust Education and focuses upon friendship, respect, and tolerance (New Jersey Commission on Holocaust Education, 2004). In a message to fellow teachers, the authors introduce the curriculum by stating that that they believe that elementary aged children should be introduced to the lessons of the Holocaust at a very early age because that is when children begin to learn prejudice, intolerance, and bullying (New Jersey Commission on Holocaust Education, 2004). The authors state that "Children cannot be too young to begin to learn about the harm done to all of us by these attitudes and the rewards of friendship, respect, and tolerance" (New Jersey Commission on Holocaust Education, 2004, p. iv).

The Berman Center for Research & Evaluation in Jewish Education (2006) issued a report that also supported introducing Holocaust education to elementary aged children with precautions. The report summarized best practices in Holocaust education and was to be used as a guide concerning future education activities and funding projects. One of the best practices outlined in the report was that children should learn about the harm of prejudice and bias at a young age, because that is when these attitudes are learned. The report also called for educators to exercise their best judgment in their choice of materials and teaching strategies when introducing something as traumatic as the Holocaust to elementary aged children (Berman Center for Research & Evaluation in Jewish Education, 2006).

Research supports that children learn prejudice and other forms of intolerance at a very young age (Aboud, 2005; Allport, 1954/1979). Allport (1954/1979) a researcher and psychologist investigated how children learned race in the 1950s and discovered that children could make racial distinctions as early as six years old. More contemporary researchers find preschool children able to express prejudice and carry out acts discrimination (Aboud, 2005). Paley (1996), a veteran kindergarten and nursery school teacher for over thirty-seven years in the University of Chicago Laboratory School noticed that children as early as kindergarten had developed a habit of systematically excluding children from their play groups and other activities. The context of the play did not matter. If it was a group of girls playing in the corner with their dolls, or a group of boys playing baseball on the playground, it was the same situation repeated from grades K-6. Groups of children were always excluding someone from their play groups. To combat the exclusion, Paley instituted one rule throughout the elementary school that required groups of students to include everyone that wanted to play with them. As the authors of the New Jersey Holocaust curriculum indicated, elementary aged children need foundational instruction to combat intolerance and other forms of aggressive behavior that appear early in their schooling (New Jersey Commission on Holocaust Education, 2004).

Students need instructional opportunities appropriate for their age or grade level (Wieser, 2001). According to the United States Holocaust Museum's country report for the United States (2004) the majority of Holocaust instruction occurs as part of history lessons or in English Language Arts classrooms. The report states that students in the secondary grades are able to grapple with the complexities of Holocaust history, while students in the elementary grades are able to empathize with individual survivor accounts that are not framed in a larger historical context. Even though younger children may not be able to grasp the full complexity of history, the foundation for further Holocaust education can be laid in the early grades.

The ability of younger students to empathize with first person accounts, such as Anne Frank can be used to introduce the Holocaust in the early grades. This was the case of the New Jersey curriculum that emphasized caring, respect, and tolerance (New Jersey Commission on Holocaust Education, 2004). These concepts can serve as a foundation for more explicit and detailed Holocaust education in later grades, such as introducing the history of the Holocaust. In this way historical knowledge and moral development can build upon one another.

The spiral curriculum or layer learning can help students develop moral reasoning by constructing their own learning. Kohlberg (1968) used Piaget's stages of development to develop a stage theory concept of moral development from childhood through adulthood. Kohlberg argued that children of all ages needed opportunities to be actively engaged in their own moral development to progress to higher stages of moral reasoning. Activities that help engage younger students in moral reasoning include cooperative activities, discussions about moral issues, and opportunities to consider different viewpoints. Engaging students at each grade level in these activities can help integrate cognitive knowledge with emotional reasoning.

Children's Literature as Bibliotherapy

Children's literature is one way to engage children's moral thinking around traumatic events like the Holocaust. Bibliotherapy is the term used to designate the use of books or other forms of literature to deal with traumatic or crisis events (Jones, 2006). Some educators suggest direct exposure to the Holocaust through children's literature while others suggest a more gradual approach that focuses upon core concepts like trust and respect (Baer, 2000; Lowry, 1990). Baer (2000) believes that young readers (elementary through middle school) can be exposed directly to the Holocaust through exemplary examples of children's literature, such as *Rose Blanche* by Roberto Innocenti (1985). Other authors, such as Lois Lowry (1990) suggest that an indirect approach is the most age appropriate when using children's literature to teach the Holocaust. Lowry expressed this sentiment when she was awarded the Newbery Medal for her novel *Number the Stars* (1989) that recounts how a Danish family helped rescue Jewish neighbors from Nazi-controlled Denmark. In her Newbery acceptance speech, Lowry describes her struggle of introducing traumatic literature to young children. Lowry states: "As a writer I find that I can cover only the small and the ordinary—the mittens on a shivering child—and hope that they evoke the larger events" (p. 416).

Exemplary examples of Holocaust literature for children must connect the past with the present as well highlight universal themes such as respect for human rights (Shawn, 2001). Shawn (2001) also outlines other criteria for selecting literature to teach the Holocaust, including concerns about age appropriateness. Laying the foundation for Holocaust education in the early grades can help support more direct study in the middle and high school grades. While it is important to not compare atrocities, students in urban schools may particularly connect stories of children during the Holocaust, such as Anne Frank with struggles of civil rights figures and slain youth such as Emmett Till and the slain children in the Birmingham church that fateful Sunday morning. The lessons of the Holocaust are especially applicably to the lives of urban students who experience discrimination, racism, and stereotyping on a daily basis. The skilled teacher must forge the connection.

CONCLUSION

Urban schools present both challenges and opportunities for teaching the Holocaust. Both challenges and opportunities need to be taken into consideration when integrating the Holocaust into the curriculum of urban schools. While the challenges of inner city schools are many, the promise of urban schools include the untapped talent of human potential that exist within them—the students. Urban schools educate primarily poor minority students who comprise some of the fastest growing demographic groups in the nation. It is important that urban students, who are primarily African-American and Hispanic understand their agency as citizens in a democracy, how to protect their rights as a citizen, as well as respecting the rights of others. As a part of their civic duty in a democracy, urban students need to know how small injustices can grow into big ones. Students who attend city schools need to know how prejudice, stereotyping, scapegoating, and antisemitism can undermine human rights and lead to genocide.

Urban students also have a right to know the full complex history of the Holocaust. Due to overemphasis on test preparation, tracking, and other factors, urban students are sometimes subjected to a less rigorous curriculum. This leaves an already vulnerable population, even more vulnerable. The foundation for Holocaust education can be built in the primary grades with increasingly complexity as students get older. The Annenberg Institute for School Reform developed a framework that outlined five critical lenses by which to focus on the positive aspects of urban schools. These lenses focus our attention on educational equity and effective teaching and learning as the backbone of urban school excellence. Using these lenses, one can develop effective Holocaust education that builds upon the challenges of urban schools and mobilizes the untapped strengths of urban students. Holocaust education has the potential to capture the imagination and address the promise of underserved youth to become ethical and responsible citizens.

REFERENCES/BIBLIOGRAPHY

Aboud, F. (2005). The development of prejudice in childhood and adolescence. In J. F. Dovidio, P. Glick, & L. A. Rudman (Eds.), *On the nature of prejudice: Fifty years after Allport*. Malden, MA: Blackwell.

Adams, K. L., & Adams, D. E. (2003). *Urban education: A reference handbook*. Santa Barbara, CA: ABC-CLIO.

Allport, G. (1954/1979) *The nature of prejudice*. Cambridge, MA: Perseus Books.

Antonio, A., Astin, H., & Cress, C. (2000). Community service in higher education: A look at the nation's faculty. *Review of Higher Education, 23*(4), 373–398.

Education Trust. (2003). *African-American achievement in America*. Washington DC: Author.

Annenberg Institute for School Reform. (2000). The promise of urban schools. Providence, Rhode Island: Author.

Anyon, J. (2006). Education policy and the needs of urban communities. *Journal of Curriculum & Pedagogy, 3*(1), 54–57.

Baer, E. R. (2000, September). A new algorithm in evil: Children's literature in a post-Holocaust world. *The Lion and the Unicorn, 24*(3), 378–401.

Baghban, M. (2007). Immigration in childhood: Using books to cope. *Social Studies, 98*(2), 71–76.

Baldwin, R. G. (1996). Faculty career stages and implications for professional development. In D. Finnegan, D. Webster, & Z. F. Gamson (Eds.), *Faculty and faculty issues in colleges and universities* (2nd ed.). Boston: Pearson Custom Publishing.

Bauer, Y. (1978). *The Holocaust in historical perspective*. Seattle: University of Washington.

Bauer, Y. (2001). *Rethinking the Holocaust*. New Haven and London: Yale University Press.

Berman Center for Research & Evaluation in Jewish Education. (2006). *Best practices in Holocaust education: Report to the San Francisco Jewish community*. New York: Author.

Brophy, J., & Alleman, J. (2002). Learning and teaching about cultural universals in primary-grade social studies. *Elementary School Journal, 103*(2), 99–115.

Brackman, H. (2000, March). Calamity almost beyond comprehension: Nazi anti-Semitism and the Holocaust in the thought of W. E. B. Du Bois. *American Jewish History, 88*(1). Retrieved September 30, 2007, from Expanded Academic ASAP via Gale: http://find.galegroup.com.ezproxy.umuc.edu/itx/start.do?prodId=EAIM

Cochran-Smith, M. (2004). Walking the road: Race, diversity, and social justice. New York: Teachers College Press.

Clyde, C. L., Walker, D. A., & Floyd, D. L. (2005). An experiential learning program for Holocaust education. *NASPA Journal, 42*(3), 326–341.

Collier, M. D. (2005). An ethic of caring: The fuel for high teacher efficacy. *Urban Review, 37*(4), 351–359.

Confar, P. (1995). Field trips worth the effort: Open your students' eyes and show them the world firsthand. *Learning, 23*(6), 34–36.

Crawford, P. A. (2005). Primarily peaceful: Nurturing peace in the primary grades. *Early Childhood Education Journal, 32*(5), 321–328.

Coloroso, B. (2007). Extraordinary evil: A short walk to genocide. New York: Nation Books.

Crowe, David, M. (2001). The Holocaust, historiography, and history. In: S. Totten & S. Feinberg (Eds.), *Teaching and studying the Holocaust.* Boston: Allyn & Bacon.

Du Bois, W. E. B. (1936, February, 22). Forum of fact and opinion. Pittsburgh Courier.

Duncan, G. A. (2005). Critical race ethnography in education: narrative, inequality and the problem of epistemology. *Race Ethnicity and Education, 8*(1), 93–114.

Education Trust. (2003). *African-American achievement in America.* Washington DC: Author.

Ellsworth, E. A. (2002). The U.S. Holocaust Museum as a scene of pedagogical address. *Symploke, 10*(1-2), 13–31.

Farkas, R. D. (2003). Effects of traditional versus learning-styles instructional methods on middle school students. *The Journal of Educational Research, 97*(1), 42–53.

Friedlander, H. (1979). Toward a methodology of teaching about the Holocaust. *Teachers College Record, 80*(5), 519–542.

Garrett A. D. (2005). Critical race ethnography in education: narrative, inequality and the problem of epistemology. *Race Ethnicity and Education, 8*(1), 93–114.

Gay, G. (1975). Organizing and designing a culturally pluralistic curriculum. *Educational Leadership, 33*(3), 176–183.

Gilbert, M. (1997). *Holocaust journey.* New York: Columbia University Press.

Gundare I., & Batelann, P. (2003). Learning about and from the Holocaust: The development and implementation of a complex instruction unit in Latvia. *Intercultural Education, 14*(2), 151–166.

Howland, A., Anderson, J. A., Smiley, D., & Abbott, D. J. (2006). School liaisons bridging the gap between home and school. *School Community Journal, 16*(2), 47–68.

Innocenti, R. (1985). *Rose Blanche.* Mankato, MN: Creative Education.

Jacob, B. A. (2007). The challenges of staffing urban schools with effective teachers. *Future of Children, 17*(1), 129–153.

Jones, J. L. (2006, Fall). A closer look at bibliotherapy. Young Adult Library Services (YALS), 24–27.

Kidd, K. B. (2005). "A" is for Auschwitz: Psychoanalysis, trauma theory, and the children's literature of atrocity. *Children's Literature, 33*, 120–149.

Kohlberg, L. (1968). Early education: A cognitive-developmental approach. *Child Development, 39,* 1013–1062.

Landau, R. (1992). *The Nazi Holocaust.* London, I. B. Taurus.

Laupa, M., Turiel, E., & Cowan, P. A. (1995). Obedience to authority in children and adults. In M. Killen & D. Hart (Eds.), *Morality in everyday life: Developmental perspectives.* Cambridge, UK: Cambridge University Press.

Laurita, P. (2003). U.S. Catholic secondary schools and Holocaust curricula: National Catholic Center for Holocaust Education, Proceedings of Teaching the Holocaust in Catholic Schools: Sixth Holocaust Education Conference, Sixth Holocaust Education Conference, Greensburg, PA.

Lindquist, D. H. (2006). Guidelines for teaching the Holocaust: Avoiding common pedagogical errors. *Social Studies, 97*(5), 215–221.

Lowry, L. (1990, July/Aug.). Newbery Medal Acceptance Speech. *The Horn Book Magazine*, 412–21.

Lowry, L. (1989). Number the stars. New York: Dell.

Lyle, S. (2000, January). Narrative understanding: developing a theoretical context for understanding how children make meaning in classroom settings. *Journal of Curriculum Studies, 32*(1), 45–64.

Lynch, P. (2007). Making Meaning Many Ways: An exploratory look at integrating the arts with classroom curriculum. *Art Education, 60*(4), 33–38.

Masko, A. L. (2005). Urban children's experiences and teacher pedagogical practices. *Curriculum & Teaching Dialogue, 7*(1/2), 175–194.

Melber, L. M. (2007). Museums and teacher professional development in science: Balancing educator needs with institutional mission. *Science Educator, 16*(1), 34–41.

Michael, R. (2005). A concise history of American antisemitism. Lanham, MD: Rowman & Littlefield.

Moore, J. R. (2006). Shattering stereotypes: A lesson plan for improving student attitudes and behavior toward minority groups. *Social Studies, 97*(1), 35–39.

Nansel, T. R., Overpeck, M., Pilla, R. S., Ruan, W. J., Simons-Morton, B., & Scheidt, P. (2001). Bullying behaviors among US youth: Prevalence and association with psychosocial adjustment. *JAMA, 285*, 2094–2100.

National Conference for Community and Justice (2000). *Taking America's pulse II: A survey of intergroup relations.* New York: Author.

Nespor, J. (2000). School field trips and the curriculum of public spaces. *Journal of Curriculum Studies, 32*(1), 25–43.

New Jersey Commission on Holocaust Education. (2004). *Caring makes a difference: A curriculum guide for grades K-4.* Trenton, New Jersey: Author.

Noguera, P. (2003). *City schools and the American dream: Reclaiming the promise of public education.* New York: Teachers College Press.

Oakes, J. (1986). Tracking, inequality, and the rhetoric of reform: why schools don't change. *Journal of Education, 168*(1), 60–79.

Orfield, G., & Lee, C. (2006). *Racial transformation and the changing nature of segregation.* Cambridge, MA: The Civil Rights Project at Harvard University.

Orfield G. & Lee, C. (2007). *Historic reversals, accelerating resegregation, and the need for new integration strategies.* Cambridge, MA: The Civil Rights Project at Harvard University.

Morison, S.E. (1936). *Harvard College in the seventeenth century.* Cambridge, MA: Harvard University Press.

Paley, V. G. (1992). *You Can't Say You Can't Play.* Cambridge, MA: Harvard University Press.

Perkins, B. K. (2007). *Where we teach: The CUBE survey of urban school climate.* Alexandria, VA: National School Boards Associations.

Peskin, M. F., Tortolero, S. R., & Markham, C. M., (2006). Bullying and victimization among black and Hispanic adolescents. *Adolescence, 41*(163), 467–484.

Power, S. (2002). *A problem from hell: America and the age of genocide.* New York: Basic Books.

Short, G. (1997). The role of Holocaust education in antiracist education: A view from the United Kingdom. *New Community, 23*, 75–88.

Short, G. (2000). Holocaust education in Ontario high schools: An antidote to racism? Cambridge *Journal of Education, 30*(2), 291–305.

Short, G. (2003). Lessons of the Holocaust: a response to the critics. *Educational Review, 55*(3).

Scales, P. C., Roehlkepartain, E. C., Neal, M. K., James C. B., & Peter L. (2006). Reducing academic achievement gaps: The role of community service and service-learning. *Journal of Experiential Education,29*(1), 38–60.

Shaw, L. A., & Wainryb, C. (July).When victims don't cry: Children's understandings of victimization, compliance, and subversion. *Child Development, 77*(4), 1050–1062.

Shawn, K. (2001). Choosing Holocaust literature for early adolescents. In: S. Totten & S. Feinberg (Eds.), *Teaching and studying the Holocaust.* Boston: Allyn & Bacon.

Shippen, M. E., Houchins, D. E., Puckett, D., & Ramsey, M. (2007). Preferred writing topics of urban and rural middle school students. *Journal of Instructional Psychology, 34*(1), 59–66.

Shoemaker, R. (2003). Teaching the Holocaust in America's schools: some considerations for teachers. *Intercultural Education, 14*(2),191–199.

Smetana, J. G. (2006). Social domain theory: Consistencies and variations in children's moral and social judgments. In M. Killen & J. G. Smetana (Eds.), *Handbook of moral development.* Mahwah, NJ: Erlbaum.

Smetana, J. G., Killen, M., & Turiel, E. (1991). Children's reasoning about interpersonal and moral conflicts. *Child Development, 62*, 629–644.

Symer, Derek, S. (2001). The internet and the study of the Holocaust. In: S. Totten & S. Feinberg (Eds.), *Teaching and studying the Holocaust* (pp. 233–238). Boston: Allyn & Bacon.

United States Holocaust Memorial Museum. (2000). *Annual report 2005-2006.* Washington, DC: Author.

United States Holocaust Memorial Museum. (2000). *Teaching about the Holocaust: A resource book for educators.* Washington, DC: Author.

Torres-Guzmán, M. E., Hunt, V. T. Ivonne M., Madrigal, R., Flecha, I., Lukas, S., et al. (2006). Teacher study groups: In search of teaching freedom. *New Educator, 2*(3), 207–226.

Totten S., Feinberg, S., & Fernekes, W. (2001). The significance of rationale statements in developing a sound education program. In: S. Totten & S. Feinberg (Eds.), *Teaching and studying the Holocaust.* Boston: Allyn & Bacon.

Totten, S. (2001). Incorporating first-person accounts into the study of the Holocaust. In: S. Totten & S. Feinberg (Eds.), *Teaching and studying the Holocaust.* Boston: Allyn & Bacon.

Tyack, D. B. (1974). *The one best system: A history of American urban education.* Cambridge, MA: Harvard University Press.

United States Holocaust Memorial Museum (2004). *Country report on Holocaust education in task force member countries: United States.* Washington, DC: Author.

United States Holocaust Memorial Museum (2006). *Annual Report 2005-2006.* Washington, DC: Author.

Weiner, L. (2006). Challenging deficit thinking. *Educational Leadership, 64*(1).

Wieser, P. (2001). Instructional issues and strategies in teaching the Holocaust. In: S. Totten & S. Feinberg (Eds.), *Teaching and studying the Holocaust.* Boston: Allyn & Bacon.

Wieseltier, L. (1993, May 3). After memory: Reflections on the Holocaust Memorial Museum. *New Republic*, 16–26.

Woodson, C. G. (1933). *The mis-education of the Negro.* Lawrenceville, NJ: Africa World Press.

Helen Bond
Howard University
Washington DC

JAN LABONTY

LOSS OF INNOCENCE

Holocaust Literature For Young Readers

Horrifying events in history exist as periods of denial and anger that parallel the stages of mourning. When adults share the darkest moments of the past with children and adolescents, it can signal a final step in the process of grieving, whether we are mourning one death or six million deaths. The Holocaust is an episode in history of unequaled human savagery. Even after six decades, adults are still questioning how such a thing could have happened, why it happened, and how we can assure ourselves that it will never happen again. Without prejudice and bigotry, the Nazi plan to annihilate the Jewish population in Europe would never have been possible. Their scheme was dependent on the seeds of hatred, or at the very least, indifference toward the Jewish people that were sown in childhood.

Unfortunately, children learn labels for groups of people years before they are able to make rational decisions based on factual information and personal experience. They can be taught to react negatively when they are confronted with the words 'Black', 'Mexican', 'American Indian', or, as was the case in Nazi Germany, 'Jew'. By presenting the events of the Holocaust through literature for young readers, we recognize that, those who are still being molded by life's experiences need to know it.

Presentation of the facts related to the attempted annihilation of the Jewish people is difficult; the numbers escape our comprehension. As Joseph Stalin, a man never noted for his sensitivity supposedly said, "A single death is a tragedy; a million deaths is a statistic."

Some psychologists refer to 'psychic numbing' or 'mental deadening' when referring to the inability of humans to grasp large-scale human tragedy. So we must approach the study of the Holocaust, not as the deaths of six million Jewish people, but as six million stories, each of a unique person with a heart and soul, entitled to hopes, dreams, and fears, whose death was not a casualty of war but whose death was a purpose of war.

THE VALUES OF LITERATURE

Sharing literature with children has numerous positive advantages: it transmits literary heritage from one generation to the next; it helps us understand and value our own cultural heritage and develop positive attitudes toward the cultural heritage of others, it provides opportunities for learning through vicarious experiences, it satisfies the need to know, and it entertains (Huck, Kiefer,

T. Duboys (ed.), Paths to Teaching the Holocaust, 31–49.

Hepler, & Hickman, 2004). By studying Holocaust literature young readers can be exposed to the complexities of moral issues that continue to confront society today and simultaneously develop literary skills and strategies that will serve them throughout their lives.

Where textbooks for young people dilute, censor, explain, protect, justify, and omit events in history, trade books allow the readers to reach their own conclusions. Skilled writers create literature for young readers on their social, emotional, and moral level to explain attitudes and practices that precipitated the Holocaust and the reactions of society to the events.

LITERATURE AND SOCIAL DEVELOPMENT

Literature can be a powerful tool in the process described by Maslow (1987) as the discovery of humanness. From birth, children are engaged in a continuous act of learning about themselves and their environment. As they grow, their environment expands from their own family to include their peers and eventually people and places they may come to understand but can never meet.

Much of Holocaust literature details the lives of families and follows characters from the secure world of friends and loved ones to the terror of war, concentration camps, and genocide. *The Dark Hour of Noon* (Szambelan-Strevinsky, 1982) begins with Trina enjoying a tranquil time with her father:

> Trina would always remember that spring and summer as the happiest times of her life. Trina and Tosh roamed the countryside together. Sometimes they would lie on their backs in the middle of a meadow, Tosh with a long stem of grass between his teeth. Trina with an even longer one (p. 47).

When Esther and her family are ordered to leave Vilna, Lithuania in *The Endless Steppe* (Hautzig, 1968) she takes one last look at what had always been home:

> I walked into my room and looked around. This was my room; my curtains were blowing in the breeze; my wallpaper continued to sprout its tiny rosebuds; my dolls were in their customary huddle on the divan (p. 13).

From a position of familiarity, along with the characters, we are transported to the unknown and frightening world of the Holocaust and experience it vicariously, from a safe distance. Jane Yolen uses time travel as a literary device to bring the Holocaust to modern readers, many of whom share some of the main character's skepticism regarding the need to remember. In *The Devil's Arithmetic* (Yolen, 1988), Hannah is reluctantly attending a Passover dinner when she opens the door for Elijah only to find that she has stepped into Nazi-occupied Poland:

> She certainly didn't believe that the prophet Elijah would come through the apartment door any more than she believed Darth Vader, or Robin Hood or . . . the Easter bunny would . . . Outside where there should have been a long, windowless hall with dark green numbered doors leading into other apartments, there was a greening field and a lowering sky. The moon hung

> ripely between two heavy gray clouds. A bird pelted the air with a strange, lilting song. And across the field, stepping in the furrow, marched a shadowy figure. He had a shapeless cap on his head, a hoe over his shoulder, and he was singing (p. 20).

Later the next day, Hannah is loaded into the cattle cars with the rest of her family:

> Someone shoved Hannah from behind so hard, she scraped her knee climbing up. She could feel the blood flowing down and the sharp gritty pain, but before she could bend over to look at it, someone else was behind her. Soon there were so many people crowded in, she couldn't move at all. It was worse than the worst subway jam she'd ever been in (p. 77).

Barbara Rogasky brings the reader to the experience of constant starvation in camps in *Smoke and Ashes* (1988):

> They would eat grass . . . steal crusts of bread from the bodies of dead inmates. Hunger formed the foundation of each moment of their lives in the camps (p. 91).

LITERATURE AND EMOTIONAL DEVELOPMENT

In order for literature to be appropriate for young readers, it must be consistent with their emotional development. Erikson (1993) describes psychosocial crises that individuals must successfully resolve as they mature. During the time of late childhood and adolescence, children practice skills of their culture, constantly measure themselves against their peers, search for identity, and while they are still attached to their parents, develop a growing need for separateness. Children can identify with characters in Holocaust literature who are experiencing these conflicts and struggles.

A desire to master the skills of a culture is described in *When Hitler Stole Pink Rabbit* (Kerr, 1972). Anna and her family have immigrated to Switzerland to avoid the growing control of the Nazis. Both Anna and her brother, Max, try to fit in with the children in the Swiss schools and Anna devotes considerable time trying to learn to yodel. Max quickly adopts the local custom of throwing things at the person one loves; he throws apples at a girl who has caught this eye.

The importance of identifying with peers provides the conflict in *Alan and Naomi* (Levoy, 1977). Alan, a young American boy, is forced by his parents to befriend a French refugee traumatized by the death of her father at the hands of the Gestapo. Alan resents this intrusion on his time since baseball and his friends are the most important things in his life:

> I won't do it. I have enough problems the way it is. . . The only thing I can do is play stickball! It's the only thing I'm good at! I got one friend on the block and he'll quit me! She's a girl and she's crazy! (p. 20).

Friedrich (Richter, 1961) is the haunting story of the friendship between Hans and his Jewish friend, Friedrich, from 1925 until Friedrich's death in 1942 and contains episodes that reflect the need of children to compare themselves. After Jewish children are forbidden to attend public schools, the new curriculum includes long hikes carrying briefcases and satchels filled with bricks. The author describes the columns of boys singing the anti-Jewish song "Do you see in the East?" The instructor, Herr Schuster, misuses competition when the class encounters a Jewish group on a similar hike:

> With the heavy bricks in our packs weighing us down, we used up our last breath. But we had barely left the district when we were ordered to continue double time . . . The handle of Franz Schulten's case had broken; he carried his case full of bricks on his shoulder. His jacket was soaked through with sweat. Karl Meisen, with his sprained ankle, had been left behind, crying. The rest of us could hardly walk straight. . . . In this condition we encountered another class. At first we didn't recognized anyone, but then we discovered Friedrich. It was his class from the Jewish school. Herr Schuster had also spied Friedrich. 'Boys!' he said crisply. 'Now we'll show them what German boys are made of. You're not going to let yourself be ridiculed by those inferior Jews, are you?' (p. 87).

The struggle for identity is exemplified in an early chapter of *Upon the Head of a Goat* (Siegal, 1981):

> Somewhere in my heart I had know that my Christian friends were different from me; that I lived in their worlds, not they in mine; that laws came from their world, not mine; that school closed for Christmas and Easter, not Hanukkah and Passover. I had accepted these rules without thinking much about them, just as I had accepted having to wash my face and brush my hair. Their code was part of my awareness, but I did not dwell on it (p. 14).

The frustration of the young when dealing with adults who shared a different view of the role of Jewish people is evident in this conversation between Judi and Mr. Sherman as they wait in the ghetto for transportation to Auschwitz in *Upon the Head of a Goat* (Siegal, 1981):

> 'If this is the way God chooses to use His people, I'd rather not be chosen,' said Judi defiantly. 'We are what we allow ourselves to be. The whole concept of Judaism is archaic!' (p. 206).

The natural gravitation away from one's parents is escalated in *The Dark Hour of Noon* (Szambelan-Strevinsky, 1982). Trina changes from a child whose life revolves around her parents to a member of the Gray Knights, a Polish resistance group. The naivete of her parents is obvious when Trina is given a doll for Christmas.

LITERATURE AND MORAL DEVELOPMENT

Kohlberg (1981) identified stages of moral development. Individuals and entire societies may graduate from a black/white interpretation of right and wrong, a deference to authority, a desire for law and order, to a perception that moral values reside in principles separate from those who hold and enforce them and learn to value the ideas of justice, respect, and equality.

In *The Borrowed House* (van Stockum, 1975) Janna is a member of the Hitler Youth group and initially accepts the dictates and absolute authority of the Nazis:

> 'It's a special meeting,' said Janna, noticing the frustrated expression on Frau Kipp's face. No one was allowed to interfere with the Hitler Youth meetings: not the church, or the school, parents, or employers (p. 4).

Armed with modern knowledge and a youthful disregard for the autonomy of someone in charge, Hanna tries to warn the local rabbi not to comply with the German order to transport to the camps in *The Devil's Arithmetic* (Yolen, 1988):

> 'The men down there,' she cried out desperately, 'They're not wedding guests. They're Nazis. Nazis! Do you understand? They kill people. They killed-kill-will kill Jews. Hundreds of them. Thousands of them. Six million of them!' 'My child, such a number,' he shook his head and smiled, but the corners of his mouth turned down instead of up. 'And as for running-where would we run to?' 'God is everywhere. There will always be Nazis among us.' 'No, my child, do not tremble before mere men. It is God before whom we should tremble. Only God' (p. 64).

Sadness caused by the death of President Roosevelt is described in *The Endless Steepe* (Hautzig,1968). Joyful news that Germany had surrendered was tempered by this loss of a man perceived as being responsible for saving the Europeans from Hitler. We see the need of people to live in a lawful and just society:

> We in the Polish community wept; we had lost our knight on a white horse, our hero who would save us. Who will take care of us now? Grandmother wailed. We had never counted on anyone so much as we had on President Roosevelt- and the United States Army—to save us from the Germans. 'Who is this Truman person?' we asked (p. 225).

Reading books on a level consistent with young readers' social, emotional, and moral level enriches the literary experience. Gifted writers can transport us through time and space and make us part of an event we never witnessed. We find ourselves drawn into plots as characters and places become real to us. Their conflict is our conflict. Their triumph is our triumph; their tragedy is ours. The people in the story are no longer statistics; they are real to us. We have an emotional investment in their lives.

THE ELEMENTS OF STORY GRAMMAR

Fiction, non-fiction, and poetry can recreate the Holocaust through the lives of a handful of central characters who are very much like their audience. Careful attention to the elements of story grammar: point of view, setting, characterization, plot, theme, and style, vitalize Holocaust literature.

POINT OF VIEW

When authors select the perspective through which a story will be told, they are making a critical decision. Much of Holocaust literature is told through first person accounts, creating conversations between the main character and the readers, establishing a sense of intimacy and trust. In *The Devil's Arithmetic*, Yolen (1988) describes the horrors of Auschwitz through the voice of a girl from New Jersey who has been transported back in time to Nazi-occupied Poland. Nolan (1994) writes *if I should die before I wake* in chapters that alternate between the brainwashed thoughts of Hilary, a contemporary neo-Nazi teenager in a coma, and Chana, a Jewish girl sent to Auschwitz whose life Hilary takes on:

> 'You ever hear of us? White Power, lady! We ever come crashing against your door in the middle of the night?' . . . My world spun forward, flinging me headlong into the midst of ghetto life. . . I followed her out toward the cemetery and worse yet, toward the large, foul-smelling garbage fields, crowded now with people dressed, partially dressed, or completely naked, down on their knees digging (p. 2, 25, & 86).

The Boy in the Striped Pajamas (Boyne, 2006) unfolds through the perspective of Bruno, a nine-year-old German boy whose father has been sent to Auschwitz as the commandant. Bruno's naïve interpretations of Germany, including a meeting with 'the Fury' and being sent to 'Out with', come to a climax when he meets a boy named Shmuel, a Jewish prisoner on the other side of the fence that separates a world of safety and privilege from a world of cruelty and death. The horrifying ending with both boys marching innocently to the crematorium represents the incomprehensible evil of a country that would deliberately kill children and serves as a stark metaphor for adults who followed a leader and a doctrine as though they themselves were children:

> Shmuel may well have opened his mouth to say something back, but Bruno never heard it because at that moment there was a loud gasp from all the marchers who had filled the room, as the door at the front was suddenly closed and a loud metallic sound rang through from the outside. . . And then the room went very dark and somehow, despite the chaos that followed, Bruno found that he was still holding Shmuel's hand in his own and nothing in the world would have persuaded him to let it go (p. 213).

Alfons Heck and Helen Waterford tell of their lives as young people in Germany during the war years, he as a member of the Hitler youth, she as a Jewish girl in *Parallel Journeys* (Ayer, Waterford, & Heck, 1995) Alfons writes:

> It was a terrific time to be young in Germany. If you were a healthy teenager, if you were a patriotic German, if you came from an Aryan family, a glorious future was yours. . . Soon, even our parents became afraid of us. Never in the history of the world has such power been wielded by teenagers (p. 1, 8).

Helen, sent to Auschwitz, writes of a different world:

> The streets resound with the futile screams of children dying of hunger. They whine, beg, sing, lament, and tremble in the cold, without underwear, without clothes, without shoes, covered only by rags and bags that are tied by strings to their meager skeletons (p. 99).

These two co-authors now visit schools, sharing their stories, both speaking as adults whose youth was stolen by a madman and a country that worshipped and empowered him.

SETTING

Setting in literature involves place, time, physical environment and sometimes weather. Talented writers use their tools to take readers back to the very different world of the Holocaust and include details that help us feel the tightening stranglehold of the Nazis, both geographic and social.

The inside of the boxcars is described by Esther in *The Endless Steppe* (Hautzig, 1968):

> The car stank of animals and . . . The heat and stink would become worse and worse . . . between the heat, the stench, and the lice, my body itched incessantly. My braids had become dirty and lifeless. The thought of a bath, a hair wash, and fresh clothes, became an obsession (p. 22 & 23).

The initial scene at Auschwitz is detailed in *My Enemy, My Brother* (Forman, 1960):

> There they were stripped of everything but their belts and shoes. A barber with a straight razor and a rough and unsteady hand came next; then immersion in a barrel of gasoline, delousing was followed by a naked run through a shower (p. 30).

Hannah describes the disgusting filth and smell of the garbage dumps in *The Devil's Arithmetic* (Yolen, 1988):

> Garbage slipped through her bare legs. She waded through a mixture of old rags, used bandages, the emptied-out waste of the slop buckets. The midden smell was overwhelming. Though she'd already gotten used to the pervasive

> camp smell, a mix of sweat and fear and sickness and the ever-present smoke that stained the sky, the smell of the midden was worse (p. 123).

Time is a difficult concept for children to master and their understanding of the past and of history is developmental. Marilyn Sachs uses the familiarity of attending school and the second person to give readers a sense of the time during WWII in *A Pocket Full of Seeds* (Sachs, 1973):

> After classes, in the study hall, nobody could concentrate on homework. There was no heat. Our clothes were cold and clammy. You sat in your chair over the table, and felt shivers radiating out in all directions from the back of your neck. And you were hungry (p. 6).

Crisp description of a time and place, when even the meakest creatures are secure, is given in *The Dark Hour of Noon* (Szambelan-Strevinsky, 1982):

> September 1, 1939, was a sparkling prelude to autumn, as orange and gold as only a late summer day in Poland can be. There was a sharp tang of smoke in the air, piles of jewel-toned leaves crackled in the gutters and delicate threads . . . spun by minute spiders, drifted in the breeze (p. 3).

Rogasky (1988) includes memoirs from survivors to reference the severe starvation in the camp in *Smoke and Ashes*:

> The food--watery saltless soup made with rotten vegetable and tainted meat, a few ounces of bread and 'tea'-- was not fit to eat, except by the already starving . . . hunger, above all was the greatest torment. . . A fortnight after my arrival, I already had the prescribed hunger, the chronic hunger unknown to free men, which makes one dream at night and settles in the limbs of one's body (p. 96).

Description of European life before the War provides a dramatic source of contrast. Late August in 1939 in Amsterdam is described in *The Survivor* (Forman, 1976):

> An old man and a boy stood on the high dunes overlooking the sea, which was dark as indigo and feathered white where the wind had kissed it. No boat was out. Below, the beach lay golden yellow in the late-afternoon light. A horseman trotting his mount splashed through the shallows. The hoof-marks were brief silver coins (p. 3).

The typical joy of sledding is described in the opening of *When Hitler Stole Pink Rabbit* (Kerr, 1972). In this scene the wintry cold that is a source of pleasure will become life-threatening during the war years:

> The powdery snow sprayed up all round her as the sledge struck it . . . The moonlight leapt all round her. At last she seemed to be flying through a mass of silver (p. 22).

Such scenes of peace and happiness provide a stark comparison for life during the Holocaust years. *Smoke and Ashes* (Rogasky, 1988) describes the bitter cold in the Warsaw ghetto:

> They even took away the warmest clothes. All sheepskin and furs, even fur-lined gloves, had to be turned in. . . Wrapped in rags, bundled in pieces of worn clothing too big for them or too small, paper stuffed into jackets and pants, they huddled in the streets. . . The most fearful sight is that of the freezing children, dumbly weeping in the street, with bare feet, bare knees, and torn clothing (p. 42-43).

CHARACTERIZATION

Characters are the heroes, heroines, villains, and entire supporting cast in literature. They are revealed four ways: through action, description, dialogue, and monologue. Characters must be believable for the time and situation and should behave in ways that are natural for their age, background, and education.

A focus on the lives of children and teenagers during the nightmare years emphasizes the innocence of the victims of unleashed hatred. Young readers can begin to grasp the magnitude of the Holocaust as they identify with the needs, feelings, and experiences of the people in the books. While the majority of the main Jewish characters in Holocaust literature are the ages of the readers of these books, so were the Hitler Youth, some of the most fanatical and hateful members of the Third Reich.

A law passed in 1936 required all German youth within the borders of the Reich to be members of the Hitler Youth; no other youth groups were allowed (Rogasky, 1988). Four characteristics of these groups were established; its members were trained in warfare, taught to obey without question, made to worship Hitler, and brainwashed to hate the Jews. Willing participants in violence against the Jews were frequently under fifteen:

> Of all the branches of the Nazi party, the Hitler Youth was by far the largest and by far the most fanatic. Its power increased each year. From our very first day in Jungvolk, we accepted it as a natural law that a leader's orders must be obeyed without question, even if they appeared foolish or harsh. It was the only way to avoid chaos. This chain of command started at the very bottom, with us children, and ended with Hitler (p. 8, 36 in *Parallel Journeys*, Ayers, et al., 1995).

Behind the Bedroom Wall (Williams, 1996) opens with three thirteen-year-old girls, all member of Jungmadel, a Nazi youth group for girls, watching a young boy torment the local butcher for being a 'Jew-lover'. Korinna longs, quite ironically, for the day when everyone would know the name of Adolph Hitler:

> Everyone would honor and love him as she did, and everyone would say what wonderful things he had done for Germany, the strongest and greatest power in the world (p. 18).

In the beginning of *When Hitler Stole Pink Rabbit*, (Kerr, 1972) Elsbeth is trying to explain what Hitler stands for:

> 'He wants everybody to vote for him in the elections and then he's going to stop the Jews,' said Elsbeth. 'Do you think he's going to stop Rachel Lowenstein? Nobody can stop Rachel Lowenstein,' said Anna (p. 8).

Shanghai Shadows (2006) by Lois Ruby chronicles the story of an Austrian Jewish family who leave for Singapore when the Nazis threaten their world. We meet the engaging main character, Ilse, and her street-wise Chinese accomplice, Liu, in the prologue:

> There's a lot to learn from a lying, cheating, knife-wielding pickpocket like Liu, and believe me, I soaked up all that he had to teach me. I was just his apprentice. I've bribed, stolen, cheated, sabotaged, sneaked, and lied. Liu's been a terrific teacher.

In *The Endless Steppe* (Hautzig, 1968), Esther, her parents and one set of grandparents are exiled to Siberia where they spend the war years because her father is a capitalist. The importance of being part of the group authenticates the character of Esther when she returns to school after an absence:

> The children gathered round me, even in Siberia there was nothing like a broken limb or a prolonged illness to make a momentary hero or heroine of the most ignored child. What had I been sick with? Typhus? Flu? Pneumonia? Scarlet fever? they asked cheerfully and were quite disappointed that it had been only bronchitis, although they did seem moderately pleased that I had survived (p. 121).

The Upstairs Room (Reiss, 1972) describes the lives of two Jewish sisters who are hidden by a Christian family in Holland during the war. Annie and Sini spend nearly three years in an attic to escape deportation to the camps. They lament what any young person would miss:

> If it weren't for this miserable war, I'd be at a party tonight. I would, too. I used to be popular. Did you know that? Boys were always asking me out. . . But look at me now. Here I am, twenty years old. And miserable. See what I'm wearing? See what my hair looks like? (p. 57).

In retaliation for the death of a favorite officer, Reinhard Heydrich, Nazis rounded up all the men and boys in Lidice, Czechoslovakia and had them shot. They sent most of the women and children to the Ravensbruk concentration camp, and destroyed the town. The story of Milada, in *Someone Named Eva* (Wolf, 2007), one of the few children who survives, represents a little known Nazi plot: the 'Germanization' of children who looked Aryan. Milada, a Jewish girl, is remaned 'Eva' and is sent to Berlin to be brainwashed and then and adopted by a German family. Milada keeps her grandmother's pin as a reminder of who she really is:

> Only part of me was at this place. The other part of me was back in Lidice, sitting under the huge tree in our backyard . . . This was where I would stay, I decided, in my memories of my home, until Mama and Papa came to rescue me (p. 50).

PLOT

Plot drives a story; it involves the conflict and the resolution and includes the goals, obstacles, and troubles in a story. Holocaust literature is filled with human drama, with tragedy and joy. Readers hold their breath as a boat carrying refugees is searched by the Nazis in *The Righteous Smuggler* (Spring, 2005). We feel the tension when the Gestapo methodically inspect the passports on a train carrying two Jewish brothers in *The Bag of Marbles* (Joffo, 1974). We huddle in a shelter during the bombing of the Warsaw ghetto in *The Man From the Other Side* (Orlev, 1989).

Each novel describes the chaos of a world at war and the hunt for the Jews with suspense and climaxes are literally of life and death. The plots of Holocaust literature are action packed and the conflict is introduced early in the story. In an opening chapter, Nazi soldiers detain Ellen, Kirsti, and Annamarie on their way home from school and signal the serious threat of occupation to the lives of Jewish citizens in *Number the Stars* (Lowry, 1989):

> They will remember your faces. Mrs. Rosen said, turning in the doorway to the hall. It is important to be one of the crowd, always. Be one of many. Be sure that they never have reason to remember your face (p. 8-9).

The invasion of the Nazis into Poland takes place immediately in *On the Other Side of the Gate* (Suhl, 1975). A German lieutenant announces that all weapons, ammunition, and radios must be surrendered within three days and that a curfew will be enacted. Mendel, the water-delivery man, doubts that the rules will change his life, but before the end of the first chapter, he is dead:

> 'What the German was saying did not apply to him,' Mendel thought. He had no weapons to give up and no radio and he made no deliveries after sundown. By eight o'clock he was usually getting ready for bed (p. 4).

The reader is drawn into the paralyzing fear of waiting for the Gestapo in *The Survivor* (Forman, 1976):

> People have been taken right from their homes, so about now, with dinner over and dusk coming on, you begin to feel that creeping fear, like a snake, winding up the canal coiling itself slowly around you. The streetcars are fewer and fewer. The sky goes red and then loses its color. It's nearly curfew time and the streets are deserted. There's not a sound. And you wait, until the big clock in the hall gives a wheeze and counts the hours. Eight o'clock, and time for the hunters to wipe the gravy from their chins and get into their trucks (p. 86).

Papa prepares his ten and twelve-year-old sons to leave the family and try to survive on their own in France as the Nazi noose tightens in *A Bag of Marbles* (Joffo, 1974):

> I know you can defend yourselves and that you aren't afraid, but there's one thing to bear in mind, when you're not the strongest, when you're two against ten, twenty, or a hundred, the bravest thing to do is to swallow your pride and run away (p. 33).

Behind the Bedroom Wall by Laura Williams (1996) is a fictionalized account of Korinna, a loyal member of the Jungmadel, a Nazi youth group, who has to confront her romanticized views of the Nazis when she finds out that her own parents are hiding Jewish people in their house. Her black and white view of the world must change as she gets to know Sophie and her mother and must choose where her loyalties lie when her own parents are turned in as traitors.

THEME

The theme of a book is the enduring message or central core of a story. It is what lingers with readers after a book is finished and justifies why the story had to be told. Several themes resonate in Holocaust literature. They are, it seems to me, the strength and resilience of the human spirit, the ability of ordinary people to become heroes and heroines in times of crisis, the security of family warmth and tenderness, the human need for memory, and the enduring power of hope.

The strength and resilience of the human spirit is evident in every story. Even in ghettos, concerts were held and school continued. Theatrical groups put on plays, noted authorities and scholars gave lectures, secret libraries sprang up. A survivor of Terezin, Susan Goldman Rubin, wrote *The Cat with the Yellow Star: Coming of Age in Terezin* (Rubin, & Weissberger, 2006). Her beautiful voice lands her the role of the cat in the opera 'Brundibar'. This illustrated chapter book with photos, copies of drawings, and ghetto documents give a glimpse into life in this concentration camp where artists, musicians, and scholars still gave voice to the need of humans for beauty and intellectual stimulation, regardless of their surroundings.

The misery of deportation to Siberia is momentarily set aside in *The Endless Steppe* (Hautzig, 1968) as Grandmother and Esther are the first in the family to venture into the village to trade:

> We coaxed our potential customers to note the beauty of the lace, the fact that there were sixteen, <u>sixteen</u> ribs in the umbrella . . . 'How much? Forty rubles. Forty rubles?' There was a roar of laughter. 'All right, thirty-eight rubles' . . . I caught Grandmother's eye; we smiled at each other; we were born traders and we were having a marvelous time (p. 69).

The perseverance to survive that cannot be extinguished is seen when David returns from Auschwitz to find a letter from his beloved grandfather in *The Survivor* (Forman, 1976):

> I am alone, David, and I will not be here long, but I want you to know that even now I do not despair of life. Life is a wonderful gift. Like the tropic sun, it can strike you blind, but it is magnificent. Never despair of it (p. 263-264).

Rogasky (1988) interviewed survivors of the camps to attempt to put words to the indomitable human spirit that wouldn't let go, even when surrounded by death:

> If there is any purpose to our survival, it is to give testimony. It is a debt we owe, not alone to the millions who were dragged to their deaths in crematoriums and gas chambers, but to all our fellow human beings who want to live in brotherhood – and who must find a way. . . Some of us had to live, to defy them all and one day to tell the truth (p. 127, 96, *Smoke and Ashes*).

A second theme addresses the capacity of ordinary people to be heroes and heroines during dangerous times. The decisions made by thousands of people, all risking their lives and the lives of their families transforms Holocaust literature from a litany of death, torture, and unspeakable suffering to a remembrance of the good of which we are capable. *Jacob's Resuce: A Holocaust Story* (Drucker & Halperin, 1993) is a story of a Polish family that hides two Jewish children during the war. The conflict surrounding this decision in the face of the military might of Germany and the constancy of death is crystallized in this conversation between Alex and Mela, his wife:

> 'No. We can't do it. Thousands of children are dying every day. What good would it do?' Alex had replied, 'We could save one life' (p. 25). When Alex later decides to hide Jacob's brother, his wife is alarmed: 'It's hard enough with one Jewish child!' Alex shrugged his shoulders, 'If they catch us with one, we might as well have two' (p. 47).

Milton Meltzer's book *Rescue: The Story of How Gentiles Saved Jews in the Holocaust* (Meltzer, 1988) is a collection of short stories about those who had courage. He quotes Elie Wiesel who wrote:

> In those times, there was a darkness everywhere. In heaven and on earth, all the gates of compassion seemed to have been closed. The killer killed and the Jews died . . . Only a few had the courage to care.

Hidden on the Mountain: Stories of Children Sheltered for the Nazis in Le Chambon by Deborah Durland DeSaix and Karen Gray Ruelle (2007) tells the stories of a place in southern France that became a refuge for Jews. The citizens of Le Chambon were Protestants, used to persecution, who refused to stand by and participate in the deportation of the Jewish people from France. From their remote region, nearly every member of the community participated, from pastors who relayed coded message, to members of the resistance, to families that hid Jewish people.

When Germany invaded Denmark in 1940 to 'protect' it from England, it was not expecting that its usual plan to identify, round-up, deport, and kill the Jews would meet with much resistance. But the Danes considered that all citizens in Denmark shared the same freedoms. *Darkness Over Denmark: The Danish Resistance and the Rescue of the Jews* (Levine, 2000) describes what the Danes did in the face of brutal consequences to save nearly 8000 Jewish people from death.

The understanding that humans could and should operate from higher principles is exemplified in an excerpt from a letter written by a member of a Danish Resistance the night before he was executed:

> . . . and I want you all to remember- that you must not dream yourselves back to the times before the war, but the dream for you all, young and old, must be to create an ideal of human decency, and not a narrow-minded and prejudiced one. That is the gift our country hungers for (*Number the Stars,* Lowry, 1989, p. 137).

A third predominant theme in these books is the security of warmth and tenderness between family and community members that overwhelms the reader. It is chronicled in nearly every chapter, on nearly every page. The author remembers his beloved father in *A Bag of Marbles* (Joffo, 1974):

> It was Papa with his wonderful stories – the king of the street – Papa, who went to the gas chambers (p. 4).

Esther describes her life in Vilna, before the Nazis invade in *The Endless Steppe* (Hautzig, 1968):

> It was a great, exuberant, busy, loving family, and heaven for an only child. Behind the windows looking out on our garden there were no strangers, no enemies, no hidden danger (p. 2).

Later, she recalls her father tending to her during transportation to Siberia:

> Father knew children; he knew they needed to know where they were. How else would they know where they were going? Even in a sealed cattle car they needed this information. Even? Particularly in a sealed cattle car (p. 26-27).

Anna's father uses humor to comfort her when she is terrified that the Nazis have put a price on her beloved Papa's head in *When Hitler Stole Pink Rabbit* (Kerr, 1972):

> 'Well, it's such a very small price,' explained Papa. 'A thousand Marks goes nowhere these days. I think I'm worth a lot more, don't you?' . . . 'No self-respecting kidnapper would touch it,' he shook his head sadly. 'I've a good mind to write to Hitler to complain!' (p. 91-92).

The love between his grandparents touches David in *The Survivor* (Forman, 1976):

> In fact, Vera's age was a secret known only to herself and possibly, to Moses, who if he did know, was not saying . . .She's got a song or two left in her yet . . . His eyes filled up with tears so that he could not find what he was looking for . . . David could scarcely imagine his grandmother other than how she was now, though it was said she had stirred great passions in her day and still kept a porcelain box on her vanity table full of love letters in six languages mailed from five continents. . . (p. 28).

The need for memory is a vital theme in Holocaust literature. Esther and her grandmother are remembering her grandfather's gardens in *The Endless Steppe* (Hautzig, 1968):

> Now my memory was to be honored, she seemed to say, it was to become an archive of her beloved past (p. 133).

Levine quotes Milan Kundera in *Darkness over Denmark* (Levine, 2000):

> The struggle of men against power is the struggle of memory against forgetting.

The dedications in Holocaust literature reiterate the importance of not forgetting those who perished:

> This is dedicated to the souls of those who did not survive (*Upon the Head of a Goat*, Siegal, 1981).
>
> This book is dedicated to the memory of the 1,200,000 Jewish children who perished at the hands of the Nazis (*My Hundred Children*, Kuchler-Silberman, 1976).
>
> In memory of my grandparents' (Rescue: The Story of How Gentiles Saved Jews in the Holocaust, Meltzer, 1988).
>
> To the memory of my Aunt Eleanor, who knew how to love children (*Jacob's Rescue: A Holocaust Story*, Drucker & Halperin, 1993).

The resilience of hope resonates in every piece of Holocaust literature. Rogasky (1988) quotes stories from survivors in *Smoke and Ashes*:

> Like most of the tortured and dying Jews they had left behind, they never believed the Nazis would win (p. 127). It seems odd, but everyone wanted to live. In this terrible world there was room for hopes and dreams. . . . There were other things I had to do, words I had to speak . . . in order to show the world what I had seen and lived through, on behalf of the millions who had seen it also—but who could no longer speak. Of their dead, burned bodies, I would be the voice (p. 96).

In *The Harmonica* (Johnston, 2004), the young boy who plays for the commandant each day is riddled with guilt until one of his fellow inmates thanks him for the memories of a better past and the hope for beauty that music represents:

> I despised myself for every note, every harmonica-breath until one day a whisper grazed my ear. Bless you. For what? I asked the dark. Schubert. I slipped that into my pocket. Each night, like the very stars, my notes had reached other prisoners (unpaginated).

One by one, the girls are ordered to go on the transports east, to certain death, by the Nazis in *The Cat with the Yellow Star: Coming of age in Terezin* (Rubin & Weissberger, 2006). When the author and only three girls are left they tear their blue-and-white Maagal flag into four pieces with each girl taking a piece and promising that after the war they would one day put the flag back together. Even though Ella loses her piece, she never gives up hope.

STYLE

Style concerns how words and sentences are put together; it involves the artistry of storytelling. A good book must have a style so engaging and compelling that the reader is barely aware of individual words but is carried along by the plot.

Stylistic devices used by authors enhance the value of Holocaust literature. Examples of foreshadowing can be found in books that open with description of pre-War Europe and allude to blood-red skies and smoke-filled winter air. The injection of humor, one of strongest weapons for tempering reality, provides momentary escape from the prevalence of dehumanization and death. In *The Survivor* (Forman, 1976) the news of a plot to murder Hitler spreads momentary joy in Amsterdam and kindles a wave of Hitler jokes:

> Supposedly, Adolph dies and goes to heaven and puts in a complaint to St. Peter when he sees Jesus there. 'What's that Jew doing here without a yellow star?' St. Peter replies, 'Leave him be. He's the boss's son' (p 172-173).

In *My Hundred Children* (Kuchler-Silberman, 1976), Lena makes her way back to Warsaw at the end of the war and through her evocative use of words, the reader travels with her:

> For three days I was on the road, wading through snow in some places and heavy mud in others . . . But somehow every obstacle acted as a stimulant to me to continue, to reach Warsaw, and to know. I had to know. I had to sweep away the veil of years that separated me from my past (p. 73).

In *Briar Rose* Jane Yolen (1992) borrows the familiarity of 'Sleeping Beauty' to tell the story, through flashbacks, of a grandmother who survived the gassing at Chelmo and softens the truth of her life for her granddaughters by telling it as a dark fairy tale. The use of symbolism is exceptional:

> Higher and higher the thorny bush grew until it covered the windows and it covered the doors. . . And no one cared about the sleeping folk inside. . . The prince came riding by with all his troops. He saw the hedge and he tried to see over it. Just then a peasant came by and saw him trying to see over and

> trying to see under. Better not, the peasant said. Whoever goes in doesn't come out (p. 58-59, 86-87).

Believing the lilting Yiddish voices of her family could only come alive through poetry, Jennifer Roy selects free verse to tell of her aunt, one of only twelve children from the the Lodz ghetto still alive at the end of the war in *Yellow Star* (Roy, 2006):

> I wish I could rip the star off (carefully, stitch by stitch, so as not to ruin my lovely coat) because yellow is meant to be a happy color, not the color of hate . . . 'Why do they hate us so much?' . . . 'They think we killed their God,' replies Dora. This makes little sense to me, because no one I know every killed anyone. Then I become worried . . .'God is dead?' I say. 'Not our God, their God,' Dora says, I'm still confused but I'm relieved. God is still alive (p. 7 & 90).

Picture books about the Holocaust are rare, since the topic of genocide is considered beyond the comprehension of younger readers. Tony Johnston, breaks from that notion with *The Harmonica* (2004), story of a young boy in a concentration camp who survives because the commandant likes to hear him play:

> He worked us, beat us for no reason, without mercy. Yet he recognized beauty. I could not imagine how that could be. . . Night after night I touched the harmonica to my lips. I thought of my father, who had given it to me. Of my mother, who once had danced. And of prisoners, without hope, who might hear the notes and be lifted, like flights of birds. I played for them with all my heart (unpaginated).

CONCLUSION

Studying Holocaust literature honors the lives of all the victims of the Nazis and forces people to accept that genocide of such magnitude occurred in a world that considered itself modern and civilized. Books representing nearly every literary genre also serve as exceptional examples of what quality writing should be. Holocaust literature meets the needs of young readers and provides an excellent means of studying the elements of story grammar.

Whether we attend to symbolism and metaphor or facts and figures, whether we are analyzing character development or conflict resolution, whether we are admiring style or theme, Holocaust literature lies at the core of all intellectual pursuits: the search for truth. Even with six million deaths, the Nazi plan, their final 'solution' to a problem they invented, failed. Every Jewish person who was murdered and every single individual who survived is a triumphant testimony that lives on through literature and poetry.

An ancient library in Thebes bore this inscription, "Healing place of the heart." Holocaust literature for young people can become a vehicle of healing for the reader as we move toward the final stage of grieving: acceptance. The poetry written by children in concentration camps serves as a final song of the sanctity of life and our hope for the future. This anonymous excerpt is from "On a Sunny Evening" (Spearman, 1965):

> The sun has made a veil of gold
> So lovely that my body aches.
> Above, the heavens shriek with blue
> Convinced I've smiled by some mistake.
> The world's abloom and seems to smile
> I want to fly but where, how high?
> If in a barbed wire, things can bloom
> Why couldn't I? I will not die.

REFERENCES

Erikson, E. (1993). *Childhood and society* (Rev. ed.). New York: W. W. Norton.

Huck, C. S, Kiefer, B. Z., Hepler, S., & Hickman, J. (2004). *Children's literature in the elementary school* (8th ed.). New York: McGraw Hill.

Kohlberg, L. (1981). *The meaning and measurement of moral development.* Worchester, MA: Clark University Heinz Wemer Institute.

Maslow, A. H. (1987). *Motivation and personality* (Rev. ed.). Reading, MA: Addison-Wesley.

CHILDREN'S BOOKS CITED:

Ayer, E., Waterford, H., & Heck, A. (1995). *Parallel journeys.* New York: Aladdin.

Boyne, J. (2006). *The boy in the striped pajamas.* New York: David Fickling Books.

DeSaix, D. D., & Ruelle, K. G. (2007). *Hidden on the mountain: Stories of children sheltered from the Nazis in LeChambon.* New York: Holiday House.

Drucker, M., & Halperin, M. (1993). *Jacob's rescue: A Holocaust story.* New York: Yearling.

Forman, J. (1960). *My enemy, my brother.* New York: Hawthorn.

Forman, J. (1976). *The survivor.* New York: Farrar, Straus, and Giroux.

Hautzig, E. (1968). *The endless steppe.* New York: Thomas Y. Crowell.

Johnston, T. C. (2004). *The harmonica.* Watertown, MA: Charlesbridge.

Joffo, J. (1974). In M. Sokolinsky (Trans.), *A bag of marbles.* Chicago: The University of Chicago Press.

Kerr, J. (1972). *When Hitler stole pink rabbit.* New York: Coward, McCann, and Geoghegan.

Kuchler-Silberman, L. (1976). *My hundred children.* New York: Laurel Leaf Books.

Levine, E. (2000). *Darkness over Denmark: The Danish resistance and the rescue of the Jews.* New York: Scholastic.

Levoy, M. (1977). *Alan and Naomi.* New York: Harper and Row.

Lowry, L. (1989). *Number the stars.* Boston: Houghton Mifflin.

Meltzer, M. (1988). *Rescue: The story of how Gentiles saved Jews in the Holocaust.* New York: Harper and Row.

Napoli, D. J. (1997). *Stones in water.* New York: Puffin.

Nolan, H. (1994). *If I should die before I wake.* New York: Harcourt Brace.

Orlev, U. (1989). *The man from the other side.* New York: Puffin.

Reiss, J. (1972). *The upstairs room.* New York: Thomas Y. Crowell.

Richter, H. P. (1961). *Friedrich.* New York: Holt, Rhinehart, and Winston.

Rogasky, B. (1988). *Smoke and ashes.* New York: Holiday House.

Roy, J. (2006). *Yellow star.* New York: Marshall Cavendish.

Ruby, L. (2006). *Shanghai shadows.* New York: Holiday House.
Rubin, S. G., & Weissberger, E. (2006). *The cat with the yellow star: Coming of age in Terezin.* New York: Holiday House.
Sachs, M. (1973). *A pocket full of seeds.* New York: Doubleday.
Segal, A. (1981). *Upon the head of a goat.* New York: Farrar, Straus, and Giroux.
Spearman, N. (1965). *I never saw another butterfly.* London: Neville Spearman.
Spring, D. (2005). *The righteous smuggler.* Toronto, Ontario: Second Story Press.
Suhl, Y. (1975). *On the other side of the gate.* New York: Franklin Watts.
Szambelan-Strevinsky, C. (1982). *Dark hour of noon.* New York: Farrar, Straus, and Giroux.
van Stockum, H. (1975). *The borrowed house.* New York: Farrar, Straus, and Giroux.
Williams, L. E. (1996). *Behind the bedroom wall.* Minneapolis, MN: Milkweed.
Wolf, J. M. (2007). *Someone named Eva.* New York: Clarion.
Yolen, J. (1992). *Briar Rose.* New York: Tor Books.
Yolen, J. (1988). *The devil's arithmetic.* New York: Viking Kestrel.

Jan LaBonty, Ph.D.
School of Education,
University of Montana

LEAH G. STAMBLER

CHARACTER AND CIVICS EDUCATION AS SCAFFOLDS FOR TEACHING ABOUT THE HOLOCAUST

INTRODUCTION

Some events in world History provide valuable lessons about moral choices. The Holocaust is a prime example of such an event. It is the responsibility of teacher education programs to prepare the K-12 classroom practitioner for his/her role in the curriculum reform movement that envisions Holocaust Education as a conduit to producing critically thinking citizens of high moral and civic character.

This task is well suited for university level courses that focus on how to use literature to teach literacy, character education, and civic engagement across the content areas of the secondary schools, grades 7 through 12. Holocaust case studies, such as the Kindertransport, are appropriate vehicles for teaching principles of character, moral, and civics education.

Using Holocaust literature in the secondary school classroom is important not only for enhancing those educational experiences which are designed to produce informed citizens, but also for honing the social studies' critical thinking skills of accessing, identifying, organizing, analysing, interpreting, and evaluating sources of information.

One and a half million Jewish children were murdered during the Holocaust. Thousands of other Jewish children survived the Holocaust because they were hidden in various parts of Nazi occupied Europe until the end of World War II (e.g. in Le Chambon, France), while others simultaneously were given sanctuary in countries not controlled by Nazi Germany (e.g. United Kingdom).

What can American adolescents learn about applying aspects of moral, character, and civics education while they analyse case studies about the experiences of Jewish children who were sent to safe locations through the Kindertransport? How can knowledge of character and civics education assist secondary level teachers with their classroom instruction about the story of the Kindertransport during the Holocaust?

WHY TEACH ABOUT THE HOLOCAUST?

Why Teach the Holocaust

George Santayana, the great philosopher, cautioned the world that "Those who cannot remember the past are condemned to repeat it." (Santayana, George,

T. Duboys (ed.), Paths to Teaching the Holocaust, 51–82.

1905). These words are significant when the subject of investigation into the past is the Holocaust.

The Task Force for International Cooperation on Holocaust Education, Remembrance, and Research, initiated by Swedish Prime Minister Göran Persson in 1998, seeks to gain political and social leaders' support behind the need for Holocaust education, remembrance, and research both nationally and internationally for a variety of reasons, as written in The Declaration of the Stockholm International Forum on the Holocaust. The Task Force, made up of twenty-four countries includes the United States. (Holocaust Task Force, 2000) Marc Grossman, then Under Secretary for Political Affairs in the U.S. State Department, commented about the Task Force's work: "Education has always been the best antidote to ignorance and hatred. Educating the next generation of Europeans, Americans, and others around the world on the lessons of the Holocaust is at the heart of the work of your Task Force." (Grossman, 2003) The deaths of Holocaust survivors in the contemporary period magnify the importance of governmental and non-governmental agencies providing education about the Holocaust for subsequent generations. (Weisskirchen, 2005)

Why the history of the Holocaust should be taught is stated clearly and succinctly in the United States Holocaust Memorial Museum (hereafter cited as USHMM) publication, *Teaching About the Holocaust, A Resource Book for Educators.* The Holocaust is "one of the most effective, and most extensively documented subjects for a pedagogical examination of basic moral issues…it yields critical lessons for an investigation of human behaviour through structured inquiry…it addresses one of the central tenets of education in the United States, which is to examine what it means to be a responsible citizen." (USHMM, 2001, p.1)

Margaret Lincoln, a media specialist in Michigan and 2002 Mandel Fellow at the USHMM, provided several answers as to why the Holocaust should be taught: it was a systematic persecution and annihilation of a target population (6 million Jews); contemporary high school students and their parents have limited to no knowledge about this massive event of genocide; and school age students must be alerted that vigilance is necessary in order to prevent a like event from occurring. (Lincoln, 2003) Lincoln inferred that the attributes of civic character and civics education are significant tools to arm citizens against future genocides.

The value of teaching about the Holocaust may be tied to the position that it was a unique event in history, and therefore merits study. Two authors, Avishai Motzkin and Gabriel Margalit, have defended the uniqueness of the Holocaust on the grounds that: the Nazis favoured death for all Jews; there is dignity in death for the individual; the Nazis wanted to deny the Jews that dignity; and, they combined humiliation of the target group prior to its industrial styled process of annihilation. According to the authors, the joining of humiliation of the Jewish victims with the application of German technological inventiveness to the act of killing made the Holocaust unique. (Margalit and Motzkin, 1996)

The uniqueness of the Holocaust and the universality of Holocaust education framed a comparative study of Holocaust education in the United States and Germany by Sybil Milton, who commented in her work that "The Holocaust raises the most complex and difficult questions about human behaviour."(Milton, 2007) Further, she indicated that the uniqueness of the Holocaust was that it was "systematic," "state organized," and exemplified "widening terror," and "brutality of the coercive institutions" that differentiated the Nazi government from other nations. This argument is similar to Margalit's and Motzkin's stance about Holocaust uniqueness. The Nazi program of genocide against the Jews was "incomprehensible," in "a class by itself as an example of evil, and should be remembered." (Blech, 1999)

> It was the only time in recorded history that a state tried to destroy an entire people, regardless of an individual's age, sex, location, profession, or belief. And it is the only instance in which the perpetrators conducted this genocide for no ostensible material, territorial, or political gain. (Lipstadt in Blech, 1999)

Milton also stressed that the Holocaust was universal in its lessons for comprehending cases of ethnic cleansing in the Balkans and Africa; and, for understanding that the legalization of discrimination in Nazi Germany came about as a result of decisions and choices made by "individuals, organizations, and governments." Milton pointed to the contextual reasons for why the Holocaust occurred. She supported continued Holocaust education because it contains many significant lessons that are universally applicable regarding discrimination, genocide, stereotyping, and other crimes against humanity.

CHARACTER AND CIVICS EDUCATION AS SCAFFOLDS FOR TEACHING THE HOLOCAUST

Contextual Framework for Change in American Education

We are living in a time of great ferment in American education. Since its release in 1983, the report on American schools entitled *"A Nation at Risk"* has set the tone for educational reform to create a world class educational system. (U.S. Government, 1983) This reform movement has been characterized by: school restructuring; the appearance of charter schools; support for the school voucher system; increased numbers of children involved with home schooling endeavours; implementation of authentic task performance and assessment in the teaching and learning processes; state departments of education testing teachers for licensure; creation of discipline based standards for teachers' performance and students' achievement; alignment of curriculum reform with standards for "best practices;" and, curriculum revision in most subject areas, especially those with affective objectives. Holocaust, character, and civics education represent this last area of reform.

Demographic projections about modifications in population dominance by ethnic Europeans, and the constitution of the American teaching pool (mostly female, white, and middle class) make it imperative for teacher education courses to be infused with the components of multicultural and global education. (NEA, 2006) Opportunities must be provided for the nation's future and current educators to become proficient in the teaching of the knowledge, skills, and dispositions which will prepare their students for the multiple challenges of the twenty-first century. Infusion of Holocaust education into the curricula of the nation's teacher preparation programs in colleges and universities will enhance their knowledge, skills, and dispositions, leading them to become culturally skilled educators.

Future actualization of the United Nations' motto "think globally, act locally" will depend on people's utilization of a global education content base to solve local and national socio-economic-political problems. Worldwide communication, transportation, and economic networks provide global interface for all of the earth's diverse populations in their nested local, national, and international political divisions. Human concerns about the fundamental issues of housing, nutrition, health, education, employment, justice, and peace are universal. Teaching the Holocaust, as a case in point of what can happen when there is a lack of concern for those fundamental issues, can contribute to the mindset that allows worldwide thinking that is global, and actions that are local. Global demographic shifts within and among countries (e.g. The European Union), as well as heightened worldwide ethnic awareness, are significant to the changing nature of the American population.

Responsibilities of Teacher Educators in a Time of Educational Ferment

Teacher Educators need to provide pre-service teaching candidates and teacher practitioners with learning conditions that will be conducive to their becoming culturally skilled educators. (Stambler, 1999) The major tasks necessary to achieve that level of cultural professionalism require the acquisition of attributes related to three domains of learning.

First, pre-service teaching candidates and practitioners need to expand their cognitive domain in order to gain extensive knowledge of the social and behavioural sciences about culture, race, ethnicity, and social class, as well as information about the ramifications of racism, discrimination, prejudice, injustice, and the implications of being culturally different in a predominantly other ethnic, religious, or linguistic milieu. Conceptual and factual knowledge of the Holocaust can contribute to the cognitive domain's role in preparing teachers to become culturally skilled. Infusing aspects of Holocaust education into teacher preparation courses, and using various literary genres, can serve to enhance the cognitive area of development. (e.g. studying the personal journals and diaries of children who were saved by the Kindertransports and survivors of the Holocaust as primary source documents of the period)

Second, the affective reflection domain calls for future and current educators to gain awareness and acknowledgment of their personal assumptions, values, and biases. They need to ascertain which of the affective aspects of their dispositions might interfere with the promotion of equitable treatment of students. Examination of Holocaust situations that demonstrated people's lack of or reflection of their values, beliefs, attitudes, and ethics would serve to expand the intra-personal intelligences of future and current teachers. (e.g. treatment of Jewish children in Nazi controlled schools; and the hiding of Jewish children by Pastor Andre Trocme in Le Chambon-sur-Lignon, during the Nazi occupation of France)

Third and last, the psychomotor or skills domain can support pre- and in-service teachers with perfecting their planning and implementing their chosen instructional strategies and techniques that contribute to the teaching of literacy across the content areas, and development of a non-discriminatory approach in the teaching/learning environment. Teachers ought to be familiar with strategies and techniques for use in their K-12 classrooms that necessitate the application of critical thinking skills during the teaching/learning process, encourage moral and good character skills, and model the processes of civic engagement. (e.g. the Socratic Seminar, variations of Cooperative Learning, the Center for Civic Education's *Project Citizen*)

OVERVIEW OF CHARACTER AND CIVICS EDUCATION IN AMERICAN SCHOOLS

Character and Civics Education in Early America to the 1940's

Schooling of society's youth has had the major goal of affecting students' values, habits, and behaviours. Dating from the time of Aristotle, society has believed that educating for good character should be a prime objective for schools to accomplish with the young. The history of American education chronicles a chequered record of societal and individual's support for character education being incorporated as a priority among the purposes of schooling.

Values education is at the heart of character education. It seeks to teach students what is right, and to have students want to do what is right. In the early years of the American Republic, Thomas Jefferson and John Adams believed that the continuation of the new nation depended upon democratic values. Education has been viewed as "the process that prepares young people for their social inheritance and advocates three dimensions of education--development of knowledge, training of mental abilities, and development of character." (Huitt, 2004 citing Walsh, 1990)

Educators in the early years of the nation believed that schools' focus on character education and the future of the Republic were entwined. Horace Mann, a leading advocate of the early nineteenth century Common School Movement, championed character and citizenship education as the public schools' most important purpose. Later on in the century and into the early twentieth century, Harvard University's Charles Eliot and the University of Chicago's John Dewey argued about the primacy of instruction for academics or moral character as the schools' focus. (Dewey, 1934 and James, 1930) The formation of the Character Education Movement in the 1920s and 1930s was a result of Dewey's writings and influence in that period. The events of the mid-1930s and 1940s, Depression and World War II, led to a de-emphasis in character education in the nation's schools. In its place "Life Adjustment" education, with its focus on well-roundedness, was established in many schools, under the leadership of the U.S. Office of Education. (Kliebard, 2004)

Character and Civics Education in the 1950's to the 1990's

Character education took a back seat to a focus on academics in the schools of the 1950s, most likely as a result of the public's and government's concern for the space race and the successful launching of Sputnik. The responsibility for the transmittal of social and personal values thereafter was minimized in the teacher education field, beginning in the 1960's. (Huitt, 2004) However, former National Education Association (NEA) President Robert Chase, writing in an *Education Week* advertisement paid for by the NEA, indicated that "teachers never stopped teaching values such as respect, self-discipline, and honesty" and that "teaching values is an essential mission of public schools." (Chase, November 1999) Character education, with its attendant focus on values, was defined by the NEA as seeking to effect opportunities for "families, schools, and related social institutions [to] support the positive character development of children and adults."(NEA, 2007)

There were intermittent efforts over the years to upgrade character education as a cardinal goal for the schools, as evidenced by Lawrence Kohlberg's work on Moral Development and Sidney Simon's "Values Clarification" program (Crain, 1985) and (Simon, 1972)

The purpose of Lawrence Kohlberg's efforts in directing his attention to the "Moral Dilemma Discussion Approach" was to facilitate students' reasoning and help them resolve moral conflicts. He studied the development of moral reasoning among children, adolescents, and adults by presenting them with ethical dilemmas embedded in hypothetical stories designed to allow Kohlberg to test how children conceived and reasoned about dilemmas that involved the conflict between human needs and the value of human life. (Alexander, 2007) However, his technique neglected the behavioural and emotional components of character education. Even though Kohlberg's methodology has been criticized, it would appear that the multiple real examples of ethical dilemmas (e.g. How to save children's lives in Nazi controlled countries during the Holocaust?) that occurred during the Holocaust would lend themselves to study and debate about human needs and the value of life, using his stages of moral reasoning to assess human actions.

Kohlberg's and Simon's respective contributions in the 1970's to the schools' curricula opened them to criticism about their weaknesses in fulfilling society's desire to move away from the personalism and the concern for self worth that dominated the 1960's. Kohlberg's reasoning about moral dilemmas and Simon's clarification of the individual's values did not compensate for the 1960's negative effects on moral norms, social commitment, marriage, parenting and the family, since "both expressed the individualist spirit of the age"…. "Each approach made contributions, but each had problems…" (Lickona, 1993)

The most popular aspect of the moral education revival of the 1970's was that teachers did not act in a judgmental manner, while students worked to clarify their moral values. Unfortunately, this led to instances in the classroom of students supporting anti-democratic values and teachers not contradicting the students' stances. Currently, schools focus on cross-cultural values that are universal in all societies; an example of "think globally, but act locally." The prickliest dilemma in the public square about values education frequently hinges on answers to the questions of whose values should be taught, and who should teach the values.

It was not until the 1990's that a new interest in "good" character education took hold in the nation's schools and among the public with the founding of two nonpartisan organizations: the Character Education Partnership (CEP), and CHARACTER COUNTS! (Josephson, autumn 2002) Sanford McDonnell, former chairman of the McDonnell-Douglas corporation founded CEP in 1992, and the Josephson Institute of Ethics organized CHARACTER COUNTS! in 1993.

Josephson and Lickona meet Character, Civics, and Holocaust Education

CHARACTER COUNTS! has become the most widely used program in the nation. (Case, 2001) The rationale for the founding of the program incorporated concern for the moral and civic attributes of future generations of American youth, and their ability to make ethical choices and decisions: "as stewards of our communities, nation and planet;" at critical times when "caring citizenry with good moral character" will look after society's well-being. (Josephson Institute, 1992) It was held, too, that "good moral character" does not automatically appear in people's psyche; and, that youths needed to engage in "effective character education….based on core ethical values rooted in democratic society," and which transcended individual's cultural, religious, and socio-economic differences in values. It was believed by supporters of CHARACTER COUNTS! that character traits should be nurtured by families and schools working "in concert" to provide effective character education among the nation's adult and young populations. The Josephson Institute envisioned subsets of the six pillars of character or values to function as enhancers of human interactions: 1. Trustworthiness [with honesty, integrity, reliability, loyalty]; 2. Respect [with civility, courtesy, and decency]; 3. Responsibility [with accountability, diligence, perseverance, continuous improvement, and self-restraint]; 4. Fairness [with process, impartiality, and equity; 5. Caring; and 6. Citizenship. (Josephson Institute, 2007) These six pillars of character easily could lend themselves to be used as criteria for evaluating the attitudes and actions of human interaction by perpetrators, victims, bystanders, rescuers, and liberators during the Holocaust.

CEP is considered to be "one of the nation's leaders in promoting effective character education in the public schools." (Case, 2001) The "Eleven Principles of Effective Character Education" serves as the bedrock document for public schools that plan to develop character education programs, and is used widely throughout the nation. A significant thinker, researcher, and professional training guide for educators within the CEP umbrella is the developmental psychologist, Thomas Lickona. (Center for the 4th & 5th Rs, 2007) His advocacy of a "12-Point Comprehensive Approach to Character Education" has achieved wide popularity in the field. (Case, 2001) Lickona's viewpoint depends upon every component in the schools' culture to promote the growth of students' character through awareness, attitude, and action. It supports the infusion of character education into the curriculum as a means of addressing moral dilemmas, and to help students "*develop a sense of what is noble and good and worth striving for in life*" by asking and seeking answers to fundamental questions pertaining to the human condition. (Center for the 4th & 5th Rs, 2007) The Eleven Principles of Effective Character Education, working in tandem with the 12-Point Comprehensive Approach to Character Education, could create a learning environment conducive to discussion and study of the Holocaust as a case of character and civics engagement gone astray.

Classroom teachers are vital participants in Lickona's model for the presence of character education in the schools. They are needed to conduct a variety of activities and represent multiple dispositions of a comprehensive nature to assist their students with what Lickona called "good" character education. These activities and dispositions would have to be implemented if schools wanted to "maximize their moral clout, make a lasting difference in students' character, and engage and develop all three parts of character (knowing, feeling, and behaviour)." (Lickona, 1993)

Schools, according to Lickona, are regarded as places for both the implicit and explicit teaching of morality; whose ethos is embedded in the institutions' rules, rewards. punishments, dress and honour codes, student government, emphasis on extra-curricula activities, and respect for students and teachers. Students are socialized into patterns of moral behaviour.

His vision holds schools accountable for spearheading a variety of responsibilities: (1) Act as caregiver, model, and mentor; (2) Create a moral community; (3) Practice moral discipline; (4) Create a democratic classroom environment: (5) Teach values through the curriculum, using the ethically rich content of academic subjects (such as literature, history, and science), as well as outstanding programs (such as Facing History and Ourselves and The Heartwood Ethics Curriculum for Children), as vehicles for teaching values and examining moral questions; (6) Use cooperative learning; (7) Develop the "conscience of craft": (8) Encourage moral reflection through reading, research, essay writing, journal keeping, discussion, and debate; (9) Teach conflict resolution; (10) Foster caring beyond the classroom; (11) Create a positive moral culture in the school, developing a school wide ethos: and, (12) Recruit parents and the community as partners in character education. It is noteworthy that number 5 on Lickona's list connects moral education with study of the Holocaust, as found in the Facing History and Ourselves program.

Each of Lickona's 12 Points is steeped not only in building students' characters; but, in providing a foundation for them to become engaged citizens in a democratic society, where they can recognize and make decisions or choices about governmental actions that lead to discriminatory, racist, unjust, and inhumane treatment of people considered to be outcasts in a particular society. Chaim Ginott, noted psychologist, has been quoted as saying that teachers must assist their students in becoming human, and that "Your efforts should never produce learned monsters, skilled psychopaths, educated Eichmans. Reading, writing and arithmetic are important only if they serve to make our children more humane." (Ginott, n.d.)

A Band-Aid Approach to Character and Civics Education in Schools

Contemporary society's concern with the apparent out of control behaviour of American youth led to a reawakening of interest in having schools systematically infuse their curricula with character and moral education as a school responsibility. Arguments about whose values would prescribe the contents of such curricula represented the diverse nature of the American population's beliefs and world views.

Values education was a significant part of American education until the 1950's, when it disappeared from the school curriculum, only to be revived in the 1960's and 1970's. Later on in the 1990's society refocused its concern for American youth's character development to that of young people's education for civic responsibility.

The publicized results of the 1998 NAEP tests validated a lack of proficiency in American students' knowledge base about civics and government. Consequently, there was a movement by state departments of education and legislatures to mandate the teaching of civics in the public schools' curricula. For example, the Connecticut State Department of Education set out requirements for K-12 teachers to instruct their students about character development and their civic responsibility as thinking American citizens. (Connecticut's Common Core of Learning, 1998) Thereafter, character and civics education programs and courses were included in varying degrees within the curricula of Connecticut's 169 districts. Students are required to know about moral, ethical, and legal conduct as they attempt to balance their individual rights with concerns for the common good of society. They need to learn that the foundations of democracy are supported by responsibility and integrity, and citizenship and a sense of community. There are similarities between these civic education traits and those character attributes found in the CEP's Eleven Principles and the six pillars of CHARACTER COUNTS!

Eight years later, the condition of civics education in the nation's schools was shown to be no better than it was in 1998. The release of the 2006 National Assessment of Educational Progress *Civics Report Card,* indicated "that the vast majority of our young people are either not taught civics and government at all, or they are taught too little, too late, and inadequately. The results confirm the fact that the past several decades of educational policy and practice have focused more and more on developing the worker at the expense of the citizen." (Center for Civic Education, 2007)

CIVICS, CHARACTER, AND HOLOCAUST EDUCATION HAVE NEED OF CRITICAL THINKING SKILLS

Education for Civic Responsibility and Critical Thinking Skills

Education for civic responsibility includes knowledge, skills, and dispositions that ought to be applied by the individual to his/her role as a citizen in society. Implementation of civic knowledge, skills, and dispositions during the study of the Holocaust allows students to reflect on personal and collective applications of the lessons that they learn. First, civic content refers to the ability to have core knowledge [e.g. past historical events and principles essential to constitutional democracy]. Second, necessary skills in civic education are made up of (1) intellectual skills for the understanding of historical issues; (2) participatory skills to work with diverse groups of people; (3) research skills to track the legislative process and its outcomes; and, (4) persuasive skills to write letters to citizens' government representatives. Finally, civic dispositions that encompass intra and interpersonal values, virtues, and behaviours complete the package that is known as civics education. (Stambler, 2007)

Attributes of intellectual civic skills are significant when studying the Holocaust because they encompass knowing how to identify, assess, interpret, describe, analyse, and explain matters of concern in civic life. Therefore, critical thinking, perspective taking, understanding and interpreting the media and various points of view, expressing the individual's informed opinions, active listening, and identifying public problems are vital to afford students the opportunities to use various genres of literature to look into individual lives and group experiences during the Holocaust (Stambler, 2007). Critical thinking skills are important ingredients in the mix that allows students to apply the lessons of the Holocaust to their civic lives.

Participatory civic skills also are valuable for learning about the Holocaust. This set of skills provides a basis for citizens to know how to cope in groups and organizational settings, interface with elected officials and community representatives, communicate perspectives and arguments, and plan strategically for civic change; thereby, enabling individuals .to compare their condition in a democratic form of government with that of non-representative governments under Nazi control during the Holocaust. Participatory civic skills include: (1) engaging in dialogue with those who hold different perspectives; (2) communicating through public speaking, letter writing, petitioning, canvassing, lobbying, protesting, (3) utilizing electoral processes, and (4) implementing strategic networks for public ends. (Stambler, 2007)

There are vital civic dispositions and character traits that connect to the various civic skills. These dispositions are critical in understanding the literature of the Holocaust: (1) acceptance and respect, (2) appreciation of differences among peoples and groups, (3) rejection of violence, (4) concern for the rights and welfare of other people, and (5) commitment to balancing personal liberties with social responsibility to others.

Students can learn several civics concepts and character traits in studying the Holocaust: "responsible citizenship; appreciation for democracy; silence and indifference can perpetuate problems; and History just doesn't happen. It occurs because individuals, organizations and government made choices." (Bartel, n.d.)

Why Teach Critical Thinking Skills?

An immediate goal of contemporary education focuses on teaching the nation's students to become effective thinkers in order to: become lifelong learners; keep up with a rapidly changing technical society, put into practice appropriate choices and decisions to support democratic government, and exist in a global environment where, as Thomas Friedman tells us, "the world is flat." (Friedman, 2007) Given these provocative conditions, American students must acquire the thinking skills that they need for making appropriate individual and collective decisions and choices about a variety of alternative actions, their education, careers, lives in general, and roles as citizens of the nation and the world. (Beyth-Marom, Novik, and Sloan, 1987)

Thinking skills are crucial underlying ingredients for students to manage these challenges and respond to the demands made on them by educators, employers, and various levels of government for them to behave as responsible learners, workers, and citizens. Consequently, effective secondary level schooling should include the essential element of decision-making skills in its interdisciplinary curricula. (Gregory and Clement, n.d.) This learning can enable students to apply their skills to studying the actions and motivations of perpetrators, victims, rescuers, and bystanders during the Holocaust, as well as applying those skills to understand past and contemporary genocides, especially in Armenia, Darfur and Rwanda.

A major problem facing the nation is that critical thinking ability among students has not been widespread in the recent past. (Beyth-Marom, Novik, and Sloan, 1987) There is dissonance in a situation where it is important for the nation's youth to be able to engage in higher order critical thinking, but lack the skills and attitudes to be effective thinkers. (Robinson, 1987) In addition, research has shown that "Critical thinking across the disciplines is a challenge for students because educators typically do not agree on what it means to think critically." (Hensley, 2002) However, it has been shown through a variety of research studies that the long held belief that the ability to think critically was a matter of nature was not accurate; and that, the ability to think critically was a matter of nurture; since, teaching and practicing the skills intrinsic to critical and creative thinking can increase students' capacities to engage in that higher order level of cognition. (Ristow, 1988. and Gough, 1991)

What Does the Research About Critical Thinking Tell Us?

General findings, from "a review of 56 documents" about whether or not academic achievement is enhanced by instructing students how to engage in thinking skills, indicated that "nearly all of the thinking skills programs and practices investigated were found to make a positive difference in the achievement levels of participating students." (Cotton, 1991) The research also showed gains in students' achievement when staff development programs were conducted, and when teachers were trained in the methods of how to teach critical thinking skills. Needless to say, the successful imparting of critical thinking skills' programs depended on other variables: the quality of teachers' competencies; the degree of administrative support for the teachers; the appropriate match of the students and the program used with them; and, the implementation of the program as it was intended by the developer. (Sternberg and Bhana, 1986)

There is a significant body of literature about teaching thinking skills that represents the controversial nature of how and what to teach students about thinking critically in order to achieve academic gains. The subjects of disagreement among researchers include the following questions: Should thinking skills be infused into the curriculum or taught apart from it? Should thinking skills techniques be delivered directly or by inference? How much time should be devoted to teaching thinking skills in the classroom to achieve improved results in students' performances? Are thirty-five minutes daily, four days a week, over the course of several months adequate to improve students' thinking achievement? Which components of positive classroom climate should be implemented to encourage students to feel free enough to participate in the risk taking activities that produce critical thinking individuals and groups? (Cotton, 1991)

The Essentials of Critical Thinking Skills

> Perhaps most importantly in today's information age, thinking skills are viewed as crucial for educated persons to cope with a rapidly changing world. Many educators believe that specific knowledge will not be as important to tomorrow's workers and citizens as the ability to learn and make sense of new information. (Gough, 1991)

Critical thinking may be understood as "the active intellectual process of conceptualizing, applying, analysing, synthesizing, and/or evaluating data collected during an individual's observation, experience, reflection, reasoning, or communication." (Paul and Elder. 2006) Reasoning is an important part of the critical thinking process, and as such has multiple functions: (1) all reasoning has a purpose; (2) it is an attempt to figure something out, to settle some question, solve some problem; (3) it is based on assumptions; (4) it is done from some point of view; (5) it is based on data, information, and evidence; (6) it is expressed through, and shaped by, concepts and ideas; (7) it contains inferences or interpretations by which we draw conclusions and give meaning to data; and (8) it leads somewhere or has implications and consequences. (Paul and Elder, 2006) All of these attributes of critical thinking are transferable to solving moral dilemmas of a civic nature, decision-making about issues of social injustice, and evaluating governmental action against individuals and groups, as exemplified by the events that occurred during the Holocaust. The essential value of critical thinking in the contemporary world is related to the educated individual's "ability to engage in careful, reflective thought" and that is obligatory "for responsible citizenship in a democratic society." (Cotton, 1991)

Civics Education Leads to Civic Engagement

Civic education's knowledge, skills, and dispositions clear the path for civic engagement by individuals and groups. Two components of civic engagement are "Working to make a difference in the civic life of our communities and developing the combination of knowledge, skills, values, and motivation to make that difference;" as well as "promoting the quality of life in a community through both political and non-political processes."(Ehrlich, 2000)

Specific democratic and educational values contribute to the underpinnings of civic engagement. There are three categories of citizens who practice civic engagement and combine educational values with those values of a democratic society. (Westheimer and Kahne, 2003) Integrity, respect, and hard work are the educational values that produce the personally responsible citizen who pays his/her taxes, obeys the laws of society, and helps those in need. The participatory citizen, active in civic affairs, has learned the educational values and skills that promote communication and group decision-making. Lastly, it is the justice-oriented citizen who seeks to address unfair root causes of situations, because of his/her ability to assess social, political, and economic structures while considering collective strategies for change. (Westheimer and Kahne, 2003) Learning about the Holocaust provides students with the opportunity to apply their civics and character education knowledge, skills, and dispositions, as well as their critical thinking skills, to specific cases and events that demonstrate the violation of good citizenship and character traits appropriate to maintaining a civil society.

> We must help students examine their thoughts and feelings......we must teach them to value their rights as citizens and take responsibility for their actions. To do so, they must know not only the triumphs of history but also the failures, the tragedies, and the humiliations. (Strom, n.d.)

OVERVIEW OF HOLOCAUST EDUCATION IN AMERICAN SCHOOLS

Increasing Adoption of Holocaust Education in the States

Supporters of character, moral, and civics education in the curricula have turned to Holocaust education as a means of analysing the principles of goodness of behaviour and implementation of moral decisions. This has enabled students to deal with issues connected with human suffering and pain, the use and abuse of power, prejudice, racism, and the disintegration of civilized values. (Lincoln, 2003 and 2006) Moral education is taught not only through study of the Holocaust, but through a number of other approaches: community service; civics education, sex and drug education, as well as through character and multicultural education.

In addition to the infusion of character and civics education into the instructional setting, there has been a visible trend for states to mandate the teaching of Holocaust and/or Genocide studies as part of the K-12 curricula. It appears that Holocaust/Genocide Education lies within the parameters of society's concerns for a revival in character, moral, and civics education in American schools, but inclusion of the former depends on connecting its moral and intellectual aims with the function of the latter.

Holocaust Education in the United States has a history of more than two decades of being in existence in the nation's schools, mostly as a result of mandated curriculum policies and laws passed by various states' legislatures. It is noteworthy that Holocaust Education "has accelerated dramatically" on the elementary and secondary school levels. (Ellison and Pisapia, 2006) Some authors believe that the opening of the United States Holocaust Memorial Museum (USHMM), financed with private funds, spurred interest in Holocaust Education as a means of teaching moral decision making, as well as "changing official American attitudes." (Milton, 2005)

An educational imperative for teaching Holocaust curricula in the nation's schools was visible in the 1990s. Robert Welker, a noted academic, indicated that there was a confluence of American educational ferment, revival of moral education, and increased public concerns about rates of teens' violence, pregnancy, and substance abuse. (Welker, 1996) He emphasized that state mandates for the incorporation of Holocaust or genocide studies in K-12 curricula were becoming a noticeable trend. The website *Beyond Our Walls: State Profiles on Holocaust Education* validates his observation. Twenty out of the nation's fifty states passed legislation between 1981 and 2005 in which they mandated the teaching of Holocaust curriculum in their states' public schools. (USHMM, State Profiles, n.d.)

Teaching About the Holocaust, A Resource Book for Teachers cautions those who would include the Holocaust in their curriculum plans to consider their rationale for choosing to teach this major historical event. (USHMM, 2001) Teachers are instructed to ask themselves several questions before they begin to plan their units and lessons: "Why should students learn this history? What are the most significant lessons students should learn from a study of the Holocaust? Why is a particular reading, image, document, or film an appropriate medium for conveying the lessons about the Holocaust that you wish to teach?" (USHMM, 2001, p. 1) The *Resource Book's* authors have synthesized educators' rationales for teaching it with these statements about the Holocaust: (1) It was a watershed event in human history; (2) It allows students the opportunity to learn about the consequences of prejudice, racism, and stereotyping, and to appreciate the value of pluralism and acceptance in a diverse society; (3) It demonstrates the implications of silence, apathy, and indifference toward the oppressed; (4) It exposes a government's use of high levels of technology and bureaucratic organization to execute destructive policies of social engineering and genocide; (5) It provides a context for students to consider the parameters of power, and think about how individuals, organizations and nations respond to impingement on people's civil rights or governmental use of genocide policies; and, (6) It exemplifies the variables that operated to destroy democratic values during the event known as the Holocaust, and teaches students that as citizens in a democratic nation they must be vigilant to protect its existence. (USHMM, 2001, p. 2) According to the *Resource Book,* students' interests are peaked in a study of the Holocaust because it speaks to their own concerns as adolescents about "fairness, justice, individual identity, peer pressure, conformity, indifference, and obedience." (USHM, 2001, p. 2)

The Examples of Holocaust Education in Florida and Connecticut

The State of Florida has been an active proponent since 1994 for the teaching of the Holocaust in the State's K-12 classrooms, when the Legislature passed the Holocaust Education Bill (SB660). (Florida Commissioner's Task Force on Holocaust Education, n.d.) The State does not limit the teaching of the Holocaust to particular grade levels, nor to particular subjects. Holocaust studies in Florida are found throughout the curricula, in a variety of appropriate areas. Six approaches to Holocaust education that are recommended in Florida to its school personnel comprise: (1) presentation of the event's history; (2) investigation of human behaviour; (3) study of prejudice; (4) recognition of pluralism as a model for American society; (5) recognition of the meaning of being a responsible and respectful person; and, (6) investigation of democratic values and institutions. Florida's Holocaust curriculum is an example of the application of the principles of character and civics education, which especially are discernible in recom-recommendations 2 through 6. It is noteworthy that the State of Florida's *Resource Manual on Holocaust Education for Grades 7-8* is subtitled "*A Study in Character Education.*" (Florida Commissioner's Task Force on Holocaust Education, n.d.)

Connecticut has another approach to the question of whether or how states should support the teaching of Holocaust education in the schools. It is one of ten states that chose to create resource materials for its teachers, instead of mandating the study of the Holocaust in the State's curricula. (Greene, 1997)

The Connecticut State Department of Education (CSDE), in line with the 1990's national trend of incorporating Holocaust education in the curricula, developed a Holocaust Resource Guide in 1997. This was one year prior to the publication of the Connecticut Common Core of Learning, which required the teaching of character and civics education in the State's schools. The condition of Holocaust education in Connecticut is an interesting one, since it is not mandated in the local educational agencies' curricula, only encouraged to be included in them. (USHMM, State Profiles, n.d.)

> Bill No. 126, Public Act 95-101, An Act Concerning Holocaust Education states that "The State Board of Education, within available appropriations and utilizing available resource materials, shall assist and encourage local and regional boards of education to include Holocaust education and awareness as part of the program of instruction offered pursuant to subsection (a) of this section."

The Connecticut Curriculum Framework for Social Studies, used as a curriculum guideline by Connecticut teachers, does not include the Holocaust as a requirement. (CSDE Social Studies Framework, May 1998) However, Content Standard 1 of the English/Language Arts for grades 9-12 explicitly mentions the Holocaust as an example of how students will apply collaborative skills to elaborate on concepts being addressed: "Students meet with their research team to share their findings on the causes of the Holocaust and to describe the process they went through to reach their conclusions." (CSDE Language Arts Framework, 2006)

Since the Connecticut State Board of Education's approval of the Act to encourage the teaching of the Holocaust in Connecticut in 1998, a new curriculum initiative was launched by the Connecticut branch of the Anti-Defamation League (ADL). This initiative was part of a pilot program to train classroom teachers in the State about how to use a unique Holocaust curriculum, *Echoes and Reflections,* which was created jointly by the ADL, Survivors of the Shoah Visual History Foundation, and Yad Vashem. (Dresner, 2006) Since its inception in Connecticut in 2006 and up until November 2007, the *Echoes and Reflections* curriculum has been used to train thirty teachers how to teach the Holocaust in each of six local educational districts: Danbury, Greenwich, Hartford, New Haven, New London, and Stamford; and has been endorsed by the Connecticut State Department of Education's Office of Multicultural Education and Gender Equity. (Colucci, November 12, 2007) *Echoes and Reflections* was recognized for its outstanding quality at the 12th Annual New England Conference on Multicultural Education, October 11, 2007, the curriculum received the New England Regional NAME Program Award for 2007. (ADL *Echoes, 2007)* In addition, the National Association for Multicultural Education (NAME) awarded *Echoes and Reflections* its National Media Award at the 17th Annual International NAME Conference in Baltimore on November 3, 2007. (ADL Press Release, October 30, 2007) The prospect for Holocaust education in Connecticut appears to be a positive one.

Research about Holocaust Education in the United States

Concern that there was no systematic investigation of the efficacy of Holocaust education in the school curriculum was the rationale for a major study about the condition of Illinois' Holocaust curriculum. (Ellison and Pisapia, 2006) The researchers reported that previous investigations about the condition of Holocaust curriculum in the schools focused on what should be taught about the event, instead of what the schools actually were teaching. An example of this observation included a description of where, what and how the Holocaust was taught: integrated into American history; incorporated into advanced placement courses; at the senior high school level; using various genres of Holocaust literature; units infused across the curriculum; and lasting two weeks in mandatory subjects. (Milton, 2005)

The absence of a national centralized educational system, and American education's consequent decentralized status has produced a problematic situation for researchers: "Within any given state, researchers are largely working blind and intuiting about the current state of Holocaust education." (Ellison and Piaspia,

2006) Conclusions about the condition of Holocaust education in Illinois, as reported by Ellison and Piaspia, need to be examined for their generalizability. Assessment of Holocaust education should reveal how well the various programs have: (1) conveyed a compelling and understandable narrative to the students; (2) afforded students the opportunities to look into individual lives and group experiences during the Holocaust; (3) presented appropriate geographical and historical contexts; and, (4) allowed students to reflect on personal and collective applications of the lessons that they learned during the study of the Holocaust. (Ellison and Piaspia, 2006) The application of critical thinking to study of survivors' personal stories and interviews pertaining to the Kindertransports could fulfil students' opportunities "to look into individual lives and group experiences during the Holocaust."

TEACHING THE HOLOCAUST WITH SENSITIVITY AND THOUGHTFULNESS

Guidelines for How to Teach the Holocaust

Three manuals or handbooks or resource books are compared in this section, as to their guidelines for how to teach the Holocaust. A definite pattern of leadership by the USHMM in creating the guidelines for how to teach the Holocaust exists among the various and assorted governmental and non-governmental agencies that publish information about the Holocaust and how to teach it. All publications that replicate the fourteen guidelines created by the USHMM cite the fact that they have been given permission to do so by the USHMM.

There are strong reasons included in the USHMM's publication, *Teaching About the Holocaust, A Resource Book for Educators*, as to why the Holocaust needs to be part of the curricula of the nation's schools. In addition, the *Resource Book* equips educators with advice about how to teach the Holocaust to their students, beginning in the seventh or eighth grades: (1) Define the term "Holocaust;" (2) Avoid comparisons of pain; (3) Avoid simple answers to complex history; (4) It was not necessarily inevitable; (5) Strive for precision of language; (6) Make careful distinctions about sources of information; (7) Avoid stereotypical descriptions; (8) Engage students' interest by striking a balance in the history; (9) Place the event in its historical European context; (10) Provide memoirs and first-person accounts to emphasize the human element of the historical statistics; (11) Approach horrific images and written content with sensitivity for students' individual differences and thresholds for violence; (12) Use balance in establishing whose perspective informs the study; (13) Select appropriate thought-provoking learning activities that support the rationale for which the Holocaust is being taught, and minimize the attempt to have students engage in simulations and role play; and, (14) Reinforce the lessons' objectives during their initiations and closures by dispelling misinformation and encouraging students to reflect on what they learned for their own purposes and as citizens in a democracy. (USHMM, 2001, pp. 3-8) Delving into the "memoirs and first-person accounts" of the children who were saved by the Kindertransports would "emphasize the human element of the historical statistics" for all grade levels of students.

> …..the events that led to the Holocaust raise profound and disturbing questions about the consequences of our actions and our beliefs, of how we as individuals make distinctions between right and wrong, good and evil. Those questions are universal even though the Holocaust is unique. (Strom, n.d., p.xviii)

The State of Florida's *Resource Manual on Holocaust Education, Grades 7-8, A Study in Character Education,* echoed the content in the beginning sections of the USHMM's *Resource Book,* particularly information about the definition of the term Holocaust, rationale for why the Holocaust should be studied, and suggestions for how to teach the units created by teachers in the various grade levels. (Commissioner's Task Force on Holocaust Education, n.d.) Several aspects of the Florida *Resource Manual* bear mentioning. Teachers are encouraged to use "best practice strategies to support engaged learners," and several graphic organizers are suggested: Venn diagrams and KWL charts. Both techniques can encourage students to utilize their critical thinking habits to investigate essential questions about the Holocaust. Also, the use of the term "best practice strategies" frequently is used by educators when focusing on Sheltered Instruction (SI) planning for English Language Learners (ELLs), whose first language is not English. It is very likely that the phrase was incorporated to meet the educational needs of ELL students, given the makeup of Florida's student population. In addition, the *Resource Manual* provides "Tips on Researching the World Wide Web," by providing an extensive set of questions that the students and teachers may utilize as guidelines for selecting valid, reliable, current, and authoritative information about the Holocaust. Eight links to selected sources of information on evaluating websites, as well as more than one hundred pages of various resources also are in the *Manual.*

The Task Force for International Cooperation on Holocaust Education, Remembrance, and Research developed a *Handbook for Teachers* with the cooperation of multiple institutions of renown: the Imperial War Museum in London, the Anne Frank House in Amsterdam, Yad Vashem in Jerusalem, the House of the Wannsee Conference in Berlin, the Auschwitz State museum, the French and Italian Centres for Contemporary Jewish Documentation, and the United States Holocaust Memorial Museum in Washington "in order to provide teachers and educators with clear and simple advice pertinent in various teaching and national contexts." (Task Force, 2004)

The Task Force writers noted that the contents of the *Handbook* should not be considered prescriptive, but rather respect the fact that the teaching and learning process must take into account the needs of individual students, according to their different personal requirements. Twenty-nine guidelines are included in the *Handbook,* of which fourteen are similar to or approximate the list of teaching caveats in the USHMM's *Resource Book.* Noteworthy unnumbered guidelines from the *Handbook* are: (1) Do not be afraid to approach the subject of the Holocaust; (2) Create a positive learning environment, with an active pedagogy and a student-centered approach; (3) Use a cross-curricular approach to enrich understandings; (4) Distinguish between history of the Holocaust and lessons from history; (5) Alert students that much of the evidence of the Holocaust was produced by the perpetrators; (6) Encourage students to critically analyze different interpretations of the Holocaust; (7) Take care not to define the Jewish people solely in terms of the Holocaust; (8) Take care to distinguish between past and present perpetrators in Europe and elsewhere; (9) Encourage students to study local, regional, national and global history and memory; and (10) Avoid legitimizing the denial of the past. (Task Force, n.d.)

Selected Guidelines for Teaching Holocaust Literature

Literature is taught primarily in English and Language Arts classes, across the grade levels of the nation's schools, from pre-school to university. However, for the past twenty years there has been a major movement to infuse the teaching of literacy skills [E.g. reading, writing, speaking, listening, viewing, and computing] across the content areas. Organizing teaching units to instruct students in a particular discipline through literature sources is not uncommon in the elementary and secondary grade levels. The rationale behind this approach relates to the thought-provoking quality of literature's numerous genres, and its ability to engage students' interest beyond that of textbooks. (USHMM, 2001, p. 14)

Holocaust literature edifies the reader with details about human nature, "models of dignity and heroism," and views of p capacity to commit evil acts that destroy other humans. According to the *Resource Book for Educators,* studying Holocaust literature can have a profound effect on students by: (1) deepening their respect for human decency and confronting the boundaries of Nazi evil; (2) recognizing heroic actions against the Nazis' control and authoritarianism in the ghettos and concentration camps; (3) exploring the concept of "spiritual resistance," "irrepressible human dignity and defiance" under inhuman circumstances; (4) recognizing the variety of roles that people had to assume as victims, oppressors, bystanders, and rescuers; (5) examining the moral choices or lack of choices that confronted young and old, victim and perpetrator; and (6) analysing the Nazis' manipulation of terminology to cover the evil intentions inherent in their actions. (USHM, 2001, pp. 14-15)

Holocaust and Human Behavior, a resource book published by the organization Facing History and Ourselves, uses various genres of literature to teach aspects of citizenship education across the disciplines. (Facing History Online Campus, n.d.) The readings and activities in the book assist students in their exploration of the consequences of discrimination, racism and anti-Semitism. The events leading to the rise of Nazism in Germany and the subsequent decline of democracy in that nation frame textual connections with Holocaust history "to the moral questions students must confront in their own lives—particularly those related to identity, violence, power, and conformity." (Facing History Online Campus, n.d.) The contents of *Holocaust and Human Behavior* consist of user friendly stories, poems, and autobiographies that assist students in relating what they read to their own identity formation, very much in line with the USHMM's suggestions for using literature to teach the Holocaust. Students' critical thinking skills are promoted by the text's inclusion of higher order questioning about the decisions that produced the Holocaust: "How does one acquire citizenship? Who belongs? Who does not? How do nations define their identity? What is the significance of those definitions?" (Facing History Online Campus, n.d.) The materials in the resource text conclude by moving the students from reflective questioning about right and wrong, as well as guilt and responsibility, to judging, and on to community, national, and global action.....a reversal of the United Nations' logo of think globally, but act locally. This process is aligned with the concept that instructing students in the use of critical thinking skills and civics education will lead them to civic engagement. (Stambler, 2007)

CASE IN POINT: HOW THE KINDERTRANSPORTS DEMONSTRATE CIVIC ENGAGEMENT AND ASPECTS OF CHARACTER AND MORAL COMMITMENT

Why Study the Kindertransports

Character and civics education serve as scaffolds for learning about the Holocaust when elementary, middle, and high school students engage in age appropriate study of questions about the Kindertransports: Who were the Kinder? Why were the Kindertransports put into operation? Who stepped forward to assist the Kinder? How were the Kinder housed, fed, educated, and socially integrated into a new society? How did the adult Kinder remember and assess their experiences? What emotional baggage did the Kindertransport survivors carry as adults? The nature of the Kindertransports and the people connected with them give cause to raise the question "What prompts some individuals and groups to help others in a time of crisis while others turn away? (Strom, 2003, p. 14)

One and a half million children were slaughtered by the Nazi killing machine during the Holocaust. Exhibits at the USHMM, the Simon Wiesenthal Museum of Tolerance, and Yad Vashem perpetuate the faces and biographies of those children in the eyes and minds of visitors to these sites. Another example of remembering children is fostered by the Kindertransport Association (KTA), formed by Eddy Behrendt in 1989, with the help of the Wiesenthal Center and the Anti-Defamation League (ADL). KTA's original purpose was to help needy children world wide, just as the Kindertransport Holocaust children had been helped by strangers. KTA's contemporary mission is to focus on educating and informing the general public about "an important part of Holocaust History," which is an example of caring and moral action. (KTA Mission,n.d.)

Historical Context of the Kindertransport

Adolf Hitler and his Nazi party came to power in Germany on January 30, 1933. Three months later, on April 25, 1933, the government limited the number of Jewish children who could attend high school. (Chamberlin and Skidmore, 2001, p. 8) Thereafter, a series of legislative acts (the Nuremberg Race Laws) was passed to remove Jews from their German national connections, restrict their marital, occupational, social, recreational and educational conditions, and control their general movement, (KTA, Complete, n.d.) The types of infringement on personal freedom that were inflicted on the Jews by the September 15, 1935 discriminatory laws consisted of orders that: Jews were declared to no longer be German citizens and were not allowed to display the German flag; women younger than the age of 45 could not work in Jewish homes; marriage or relationships between Jews and non-Jewish Germans was forbidden; and, Jews were defined by their biological heritage instead of their practicing religious or cultural identity. The months between July and December 1938 brought with them further personal incursions: newly born Jewish infants were to be named according to government approved lists; Jews were denied access to cultural events such as plays, movies, concerts, or exhibitions; and then, the Nazi government's expulsion of Jewish students from public school and university educational institutions. (Chamberlin and Skidmore, 2001, p. 8)

Ever increasing discrimination and brutality inflicted on Jews made their desire to leave Germany more cogent. However, the ability to emigrate was mitigated by the Nazi government's denial of such possibilities. On the not to be forgotten pogrom night of November 9-10, 1938, "German and Austrian Nazis burned and destroyed 267 synagogues, killed 100 people, smashed 7,500 Jewish stores (all that remained in the Reich), and incarcerated nearly 30,000 Jews in concentration camps." (KTA Brief History, n.d.) The German government organized this brutal attack on its own population, the German Jewish community. Several days later a law was issued in which the victims were penalized, in the amount of 1.25 million Reichsmarks, or six million U.S. dollars in contemporary monetary conversion, for the damages inflicted on them by their government. (Chamberlin and Skidmore, 2001, p. 8)

The desire to leave their homeland, because of discriminatory and dangerous governmental policies in Nazi Germany, escalated among Jewish families. The intensity was so great that when the opportunity presented itself for parents to save their children by shipping them out of Germany, they reluctantly and lovingly sent their offspring to safety outside of the Third Reich. This choice, that thousands of Jewish parents made when faced by the dilemma of how to secure their children's' safety, required exceptional inner strength because they did not know who would care for their children, whether or not they ever would see them again, because their own lives were not ensured. Students need to know that they may be presented with life or death dilemmas that will require them to use their critical thinking skills in order to make appropriate and moral choices for themselves, their family, and their community. This is one of the reasons why the story of the Kindertransport must be present across the disciplines and in civics and character education curricula.

Almost two weeks after what now is called "The Night of Broken Glass" or "KristallNacht," the British Parliament decided (November 21, 1938) to provide refuge in the United Kingdom for Jewish children from Germany, in order for them to escape Nazi persecution. This action was in response to lobbying by the British Jewish Refugee Committee. British Prime Minister Samuel Hoare was instrumental in convincing the government to save the children, "Here is a chance of taking the young generation of a great people, here is a chance of mitigating to some extent the terrible suffering of their parents and their friends." (KTA complete History, n.d.)

This rescue operation, only for Jewish children under the age of seventeen, later was labelled Kindertransport, and was organized by several German Jewish communities and non-German relief organizations. The coalition of various groups, under the name of the Movement for the Care of Children from Germany, was a unique event at the time, in that Quakers, Christians, and Jews united to save Jewish children. (KTA Complete History, n.d.) The immigration process normally would have been time consuming had the children applied for and been issued individual travel documents. The British Home Secretary authorized group lists to be filed for the applications. Strict bonding conditions were set on their entry into England to prevent the children from becoming financial risks or burdensome on the public treasury. The British intention for the relief movement was that the new comers would not be permanent residents.

Representatives of the renamed Refugee Children's Movement travelled to Germany to expedite the system for choosing, organizing, and transporting the children. On November 25, 1938 BBC radio announced nationally the need for foster homes for the refugee children, to which five hundred families responded. A cursory review of the volunteers' homes was conducted, and selections were made on the basis of sufficient cleanliness and respectability of the families for the children to be placed with them. Priority lists were drawn up in Germany by volunteers, who identified the children who were to travel, and informed parents of departure details and dates. The children considered to be in prime need for rescue were teens in concentration camps or subject to arrest, Jewish orphans, and Polish teens threatened with deportation by the Nazis. (Chamberlin and Skidmore, 2001, pp. 11-12)

Ten thousand Jewish children from Germany, Austria, Czechoslovakia, and Poland were brought to England between the Kindertransport's inception and when it ended at the start of World War II on September 1, 1939. The first group of 196 orphan children landed at the port of Harwich on December 2, 1938. (KTA Complete, n.d. and Cohn, n.d.) Some of the children were sent to London, where foster parent sponsors, who had posted bonds of 50 pounds Sterling, met and took them to their homes; while others were transported to various parts of the United Kingdom. Still other children lived in English hostels, orphanages, group homes, and on farms. Children over fourteen years of age who did not have foster care sponsors were placed in the agricultural and domestic service sectors, where they were trained to be part of the nation's labour force.(KTA Complete, n.d.) It is believed that twenty to twenty-five percent of the children eventually went on to settle in Canada and the United States. (KTA Brief, n.d.) One of the messages of the Kindertransport project is that ordinary people can make choices that make a difference for other humans. "History is made not just by leaders but by everyday people making everyday choices." (Annenberg Media, n.d.)

Sharing the Story of One of the Kinder

The story of how the Kindertransport children fared in their British environment is one of varied experiences. Most of the children were treated well, and were taken into the hearts of their sponsor foster parents and families. There are stories, too, of children who were abused in their new circumstances. Some of the older children enlisted in the armed forces of Great Britain and Australia. Most of the ten thousand Kindertransport children "never saw their parents again." (KTA Brief, n.d.)

Paul M. Cohn, writing about his childhood in Hamburg, recorded the multiple school moves that his parents negotiated on his behalf between his early years and the age of fifteen, when he was sent to England on May 21, 1939 with a Kindertransport. (Cohn, Paul M., n.d.) He wrote of his sadness in leaving his parents in Germany, the assumed good spirits displayed by them. He believed that his departure from Nazi Germany before his parents would make it easier for them to follow along after him. Paul was put to work on a chicken farm in England, awaiting his parents' emigration. The three family members corresponded for a while; but once World War II started, the monthly letters from Germany became shorter and less frequent, until they stopped by the end of 1941. He remained in England after the War, continued with his education, married an English Jewish woman, and eventually became a professor at University College in London. Paul, retired since 1989, indicated that the "unprejudiced manner in which my English colleagues have accepted me" was the key to his success in his adopted land. He wrote about his identity as one in which "I am conscious of my origins, I am not a genuine Englishman:-but I am also not German any more. I do not feel homesick. It is a yearning for something that no longer exists; something like a pain in a leg after it has been amputated." (Cohn, n.d.)

Selected Resources about the Kindertransport

There is a wide array of resource materials for young and adult readers about the history of the Kindertransport and the children who were rescued by people who took their responsibility as human beings seriously: memoirs; nonfiction accounts; government documents; poetry; films; Kindertransport survivors' oral testimonies; videos; DVDs; and theatrical productions.

The Kindertransport Association's website has an extensive list of resources in each of the genres. There are twenty-seven examples of memoirs, written between 1983 and 2005 by the adult Kinder, in which the survivors look back at their experiences after having left their parents, families, and homelands; embarking on an adventure into the unknown. (KTA Resources, n.d.) A well known TV and radio personality of years past, Dr. Ruth Westheimer, has her 1988 memoir *All in a Lifetime,* cited on the KTA resource list. The book recounts her travels from Frankfurt am Main, through a girls' refugee Swiss hostel, on to Israel, and finally to America where she became a broadcasting success as a well respected sex therapist.

Six of the memoirs are on linked web pages that can be accessed, read, and utilized with civics, character, and Holocaust education literacy tasks that focus on comprehension, vocabulary expansion, and critical thinking. Two of the most user friendly web sites in the memoirs category are *Irene Katzenstein Schmied's Memoirs* and *A Short Personal History of My Family During 30 Turbulent Months* by Hans Schneider. Another accessible web site link in the Nonfiction section tells the story of Walter Frank, who at the age of eleven was sent by his mother on a Kindertransport through Holland to England during the narrow escape window of opportunity between Kristallnacht (November 9-10, 1938) and the beginning of World War II (September 1, 1939. (Ahearn, 2006)

Two feature-length documentary films about the Kindertransport are worthy of inclusion for any age level of students working with a Holocaust curriculum. The first film, *My Knees Were Jumping*, was a 76 minutes IFC production that led the way in the film industry by uncovering the tale of the Kindertransport and the harrowing experiences of the children who were thrust into a strange land where they did not know the language and social mores of the people with whom they were living, nor feel the comforting reassurances of their parents as they met new life situations. The film, initiated by Melissa Hacker, daughter of Kindertransport survivor Ruth Morley, is narrated by famed actress Joanne Woodward. It includes testimony from the surviving Kinder, newsreel footage, old photos, and information that weave a look at the long lasting impact of the children's dislocation on their lives as adults. They share their guilt for having survived the Holocaust, as well as their fear of abandonment even as adults. It is available on loan through the Facing History Teacher Network, headquartered in Boston, Massachusetts. (Facing History and Ourselves, n.d.)

A very close childhood friend of the author expressed the same guilt about being saved and alive when she was a Jewish "hidden child" in Belgium during the Holocaust, a time when one and half million Jewish children went to their deaths. (Schnitzer, 1948-60) Life stories written and told by Holocaust survivors who were "hidden children" form a whole other body of literature that is worthy of students' investigation while educators teach civics and character education as scaffolds for learning the Holocaust. Many of the emotional perspectives about separation from their parents and families during the Holocaust, which were held by Kindertransport and "hidden children" survivors, were similar: sense of loss of identity, anxiety, fear of the unknown, abandonment, and despair. (Cohen, 2001)

The 117 minutes Warner Studio film *Into the Arms of Strangers* provides insight into the lives of the children who were saved by the Kindertransport. Inspiration for the film came from Deborah Oppenheimer, daughter of a Kindertransport survivor. The stories, told by the twelve child survivors, one parent, two rescuers, and one foster parent, are presented with a chronological contextual background narrated by the British actress, Judi Dench. The interviews with the film's participants reveal the emotional impact on the Kinder of leaving their homes and families during a period of desperate life threatening crises. Four parts of the survivors' lives are highlighted: their troublesome childhoods as Jewish children in Germany, distraught refugees departing from their homeland, selection by their foster families, and how they managed to integrate, survive, and grow in their new surroundings. The most difficult part of the journey for the children was their sense of loss and anxiety about their parents' safety and their inability to join them in England. It is a must see film for students because of its view of children's resiliency in the face of impending disaster. This film about Kindertransport survivors provides perspectives on the meanings of choice, responsibility, identity, memory, fitting in, and separation. The viewer becomes party to "the effects of intolerance, racism, and institutionalized violence on individuals." (Chamberlin and Skidmore, 2001, p. 6) Facing History and Ourselves produced a masterful forty pages study guide for teachers to use with their students. It contains multiple source materials, photographs, mini-biographies of the Kinder included in the film, and suggestions for thought provoking activities. This study guide may be downloaded from Facing History and Ourselves' website, Online Campus.

Another excellent source of information about the experiences of the Kinder who were saved from possible extermination by the Nazis is the book and companion CD, *The Children of Willesden Lane.* It was created by Facing History and Ourselves, and funded by the Milken Family Foundation. The teachers' study guide and curriculum for *The Children of Willesden Lane* contains a wide variety of literacy building and interdisciplinary critical thinking activities. It was created by Facing History and Ourselves, and is available for download on its Online Campus website. (Facing History, 2003) Once again, a daughter, Mona Golabek, of a Kindertransport survivor, Lisa Jura, initiated the project that became *The Children of Willesden Lane*; a piece that "explores such themes as identity, belonging, courage, and memory." (Strom, 2003, p. 6) *The Children of Willesden Lane* is the saga of Austrian born Lisa Jura who aspired to become a concert pianist, and whose future dreams were shattered by the German takeover of her homeland in 1938. *The Children of Willesden Lane* is a commendable piece of literature that implements the idea of character and civics education as scaffolds for teaching the Holocaust. Lisa Jura's parents were confronted by the dilemma of how to protect their three daughters from the onslaught of Nazi discrimination against Jews in Austria after Kristallnacht; when, they learned that there only was availability for one of their three children on the Kindertransport to Great Britain. They were faced with the wrenching choice of which daughter to send on the boat to freedom, and the decided that it would be their middle child, Lisa. Students reading this book learn that making choices can be a life or death situation. Their critical thinking skills must come into operation with their moral reasoning.

A powerful presentation of character and civic education issues, in the form of lesson plans, supplementary teaching video selections, and instructional activities related to the Kindertransports, is found on the Annenberg Media website, entitled "Teaching *The Children of Willesden Lane*, Resources to Help Teach the Book." A downloadable classroom video of a secondary level practitioner instructing her students with higher order critical thinking and inquiry strategies has special import for demonstrating that character and civics education serve as scaffolds for study of the Holocaust. The video is based on chapters nine through twelve of *The Children of Willesden Lane* and investigates the "Upstanders and Bystanders" who respectively either assist others in crisis at risk to themselves, or walk away from any involvement. The case study of the Kindertransport is a perfect venue for seeing both upstanders and bystanders at work. People who organized the Kindertransport and volunteered to serve as foster parents for the 10,000 refugee children were the upstanders; while the defeat of the Wagner-Rogers Bill in the U.S. Congress, which would have allowed 20,000 Jewish children to immigrate to America, was defeated by those who refused to be involved with a rescue effort. (Annenberg Media, n.d.)

RECOMMENDED METHODOLOGY TEXTS

Selected Texts for Teaching Literacy

Teaching Content Reading and Writing, by Martha Rapp Ruddell, is an excellent text that includes literacy techniques adaptable for instructing secondary level students about character and civics education as scaffolds for studying the Kindertransport and the Holocaust. (Ruddell, 2008) Chapters 4, 5, 7, and 8 especially are useful for teaching the critical thinking necessary for analysing the moral dilemmas and humane solutions related to the history of the Kindertransport: Comprehension Instruction in Content Areas; Vocabulary Learning in Content Areas; Reading Across the Curriculum; and, Writing Across The Curriculum.

A special manual for teaching literacy in the Social Studies content area provides support for the general strategies found in the Ruddell text. It is *Teaching Reading in Social Studies: A supplement to Teaching Reading in the Content Area Teacher's* Manual by Jane K. Doty, Gregory N. Cameron, and Mary Lee Barton. (2005) It is a McRel publication distributed by the Association for Supervision and Curriculum Development (ASCD) since 1998. The strategies are explained in a step-by-step manner, with blackline masters, and focus on teaching and improving Social Studies learning for comprehension and vocabulary development.

Selected Text for Teaching ELL Students

The changing nature of the demographics in the American classroom, with increasing numbers of students who are not fluent in spoken and written English, has placed an added responsibility on the teacher to provide appropriate instruction to students who are known as English Language Learners or ELL students. It is the obligation of teacher educators to prepare the classroom teachers with the knowledge, skills, and dispositions essential to successful second language acquisition for their ELL students. *Sheltered Content Instruction: Teaching English Language Learners with Diverse Abilities* by Jana Echevarria and Anne Graves, published by Allyn Bacon, is considered to be one of the prime texts for the teaching of "Sheltered Instruction."(SI) or what also is known as Specially Designed Academic Instruction in English(SDAIE) (2007) This text provides appropriate strategies for the successful implementation of SI in kindergarten through twelfth grade classrooms. The authors combine strategies for SI and adaptation for teaching students with special education needs. Instruction in the content areas is a prime focus for application of the strategies, since ELL students may struggle in their core courses. Case studies and vignettes are included in the text to illustrate teaching models for pre-service teachers.

Selected Texts for Teaching Methods and Strategies

The text, *Instruction: A Models Approach*, by Mary A. Gunter, Thomas H. Estes, and Susan L. Mintz is a significant source of information about the multiple models of teaching and strategies for instructing students in all grades and content areas. (2007). The authors provide step-by-step explanations, diagrams, how to differentiate instruction for each model of teaching, scenarios that demonstrate the use of the models, three case studies on the elementary, middle school, and high school levels, and sample lessons about how to teach the various disciplines with each of the families of teaching and their appropriate strategies. Chapters 4 through 15 include teaching techniques and strategies that are fundamental to advancing students' performance in history and social studies classrooms, especially for teaching critical thinking skills.

The instruction models included in the text are: Direct Instruction; Concept Attainment; Concept Development; Problem-Centered Inquiry, with WebQuest and Problem Based Learning; Synectics, Cause and effect; Socratic Seminar; Vocabulary Acquisition; Resolution of Conflict; Eggen and Kauchak's Integrative Model; and, three Cooperative Learning Models;

The authors also include a variety of supporting strategies in the text that may be used with the various Instructional Models. These strategies are Scaffolding, Information Recall, Non-linguistic Representations, Think/Pair/Share, Identifying Similarities and Differences, Summarizing, and Reciprocal Teaching.

REFERENCES

Ahearn, Lorraine. (2006, December 8). Winter People: Pebbles from the 'Kindertransport' in the Greensboro News-Record. *Walter Falk from the Kindertransport*. Retrieved November 5, 2007, from news-record.com/apps/pbcs.dll/article?AID=/20061208/NEWSREC010201/612080330/1015

Alexander, D. (2007, August 23). *Moral Development Theory*. Retrieved October 28, 2007, from ezinearticles.com/?Moral-Development-Theory&id=673564

Annenberg Media. (n.d.). Teaching The Children of Willesden Lane. *Teaching Resource for the Book*. Retrieved November 1, 2007, from learner.org/series/cowl/index.html

Annenberg Media. (n.d.). Teaching The Children of Willesden Lane. Chapters 9-12. *Upstanders and Bystanders*. Video. Retrieved November 10, 2007, from learner.org/series/cowl/ch9-12/index.html

Annenberg Media. (n.d.).Teaching The Children of Willesden Lane. Chapters 1-3. *Choices that make a difference*. Video. Retrieved November 10, 2007, from learner.org/series/cowl/ch1-3/choices.html

Anti-Defamation League. (2003). Guidelines for Teaching About The Holocaust Why Teach Holocaust History? Courtesy of the United States Holocaust Memorial Museum, Washington, D.C. Retrieved September 27, 2007, from adl.org/education/holocaust/holocaust_guidelines.asp

Anti-Defamation League. (2005-2007). Echoes and Reflections; A Multimedia Curriculum on the Holocaust. Retrieved November 12, 2007, from echoesandreflections.org/default.asp

Anti-Defamation League. (2007, October 30). Press Release. “Echoes and Reflections” Holocaust Curriculum Recognized by Peers with National Media Award. Retrieved November 12, 2007, from adl.org/PresRele/Education_01/5158_01.htm

Bartel, Judy. (2002). Guidelines for Teaching Holocaust. (power point). Retrieved September 20, 2007, from mandelproject.us/Bartel.ppt

Beyth-Marom, R., Novik, R., & Sloan, M. (1987). Enhancing Children’s Thinking Skills: An Instructional Model for Decision-Making Under Certainty. in *Instructional Science, 16*(3), 215–231.

Blech, R. B. (1999). *The complete idiot’s guide to Jewish history and culture*. New York: Alpha Books.

Boeree, G. C. (2003). General psychology. *Moral Development*. Retrieved October 12, 2007, from webspace.ship.edu/cgboer/genpsymoraldev.html

Brabham, E. G. (1997). Holocaust Education: Legislation, Practices, and Literature for Middle School Students. *Social Studies, 88*(3), 139. Retrieved November 5, 2007, from questia.com/PM.qst?a=o&d=95157961

Case, K. (2001). Can Public Schools Really Strengthen Moral Character? An annotated guide to select websites and articles. Center for Applied Christian Ethics. Wheaton College. Retrieved October 1, 2007, from wheaton.edu/CACE/resources/onlinearticles/Characterreadings.htm

Center for Civic Education. (2007). *Quotation by Thomas Jefferson on citizenship*. Retrieved October 15, 2007, from civiced.org/index.php?page=stds_preface

Center for the 4th & 5th Rs. (n.d.). A 12-Point Comprehensive Approach to Character Education. (Graphic organizer). Retrieved October 18, 2007, from cortland.edu/character/12pts.asp

Center for the 4th & 5th Rs. (n.d.). Center Staff. (Links to books, articles, organizations, and more.). Retrieved October 18, 2007, from cortland.edu/character/bios.htm

CEP Character Education Partnership, Lickona, T., Eric, S., & Catherine, L. (2005). *Eleven principles of effective character education*. Retrieved on September 29, 2007, from character.org/site/c.gwKUJhNYJrF/b.993263/k.D335/Eleven_Principles_of_Effective_Character_Education.htm

Chamberlin, S., & Gretchen, S. (2001). A study guide based on the Warner Home Video documentary film into the arms of strangers. Facing history and ourselves. Retrieved November 1, 2007, from facinghistory.org/campus/reslib.nsf/cmvideos/Into%20the%20Arms%20of%20Strangers:%20Stories%20of%20the%20Kindertransports?OpenDocument

Chase, R. (1999, November 24). Values in the Public Schools. Advertisement by the National Education Association in *Education Week*. Page number unknown.

Cohen, J. (n.d.). Women and the Holocaust. A Cyberspace of their own. Hidden children section: Personal reflections in hiding of Rosalind Goldenberg, hidden child in Belgium. Retrieved November 8, 2007, from theverylongview.com/WATH/

Cohn, P. M. (n.d.). The Kindertransports, childhood in Hamburg. Retrieved November 1, 2007, from 1.uni-hamburg.de/rz3a035//kindertransport.html

Colucci, D. (Project Director for ADL World of Difference, Connecticut Office). Telephone conversation with Leah G. Stambler at 3:30PM on November 12, 2007 re: Echoes and Reflections Program and its usage in Connecticut.

Connecticut State Department of Education. (1998). Connecticut common core of learning. (CCCL). *Aspects of Character* (pp. 26–28). Retrieved September 10, 2007 from sde.ct.gov/sde/cwp/view.asp?a=2618&q=320858

Connecticut State Department of Education. (May 1998). English Language Arts Curriculum Framework. Retrieved August 25, 2007, from sde.ct.gov/sde/cwp/view.asp?a=2618&q=320866

Connecticut State Department of Education. (May 1998). *Social studies curriculum framework*. Retrieved August 25, 2007, from sde.ct.gov/sde/lib/sde/PDF/Curriculum/Curriculum_Root_Web_Folder/frsocst.pdf

Cotton, K. (1991). Teaching thinking skills: Close-Up #11. Retrieved November 3, 2007 from, Northwest Regional Educational Laboratory’s School Improvement Research Series Web site: nwrel.org/scpd/sirs/6/cu11.html

Crain, W. C. (1985). Chapter seven: Kohlberg's stages of moral development. In *Theories of Development* (pp. 118–136). New Jersey: Prentice-Hall. Retrieved October 12, 2007, from faculty.plts.edu/gpence/html/kohlberg.htm

Dewey, J. (1909). *Moral principles in education.* Boston: Houghton Mifflin. Retrieved September 5, 2007, from questia.com/library/book/moral-principles-in-education-by-john-dewey.jsp

Dr. Doerr, K. (Updated: March, 2007). Holocaust Memoirs, Testimonies, Histories Select Bibliography (English). Concordia University, Montreal, Canada. Retrieved September 30, 2007, from theverylongview.com/WATH/biblio/biblio2.htm

Dresner, S. (2006, June 22). New ADL program aids teachers in Holocaust education. In the Jewish Ledger.

Echevarria, & Graves. (2007) *Sheltered content instruction: Teaching english language learners with diverse abilities* (3/E, p. 208). Allyn & Bacon.

Ehrlich, T. (Ed.) (2004, October 27) Service Learning for Civic Engagement. Retrieved October 11, 2007, from calstate.edu/csl/resource_center/documents/sl_for_ce.pdf

Ellison, J., & John, P. (2006, September 7). *The state of Holocaust education in Illinois.* Retrieved October 6, 2007 from, ideajournal.com/articles.php?id=41

Epstein, K. K. (2005, September 22). The Whitening of the American teaching force: A problem of recruitment or a problem of racism? In *Social Justice.* Retrieved October 15, 2007, from goliath.ecnext.com/coms2/gi_0199-5625615/The-whitening-of-the-American.html#abstract

Facing History and Ourselves. (.....). Resource Book. Holocaust and Human Behavior.

Facing History and Ourselves. (n.d.). My knees were jumping. Retrieved November 1, 2007, from facinghistory.org/campus/reslib.nsf/campus/reslib.nsf/scopeandsequenceidentity/1D53695511B9BD2A85257181006D2A04?opendocument

Florida Commission on the Holocaust. Commissioner's Task Force on Holocaust Education. (2004). State of Florida Resource Manual on Holocaust Education grades 4-6, A study in Character Education. Retrieved October 20, 2007, from teachinflorida.com/teachertoolkit/PDF_Files/HolocaustGrades46.PDF

Friedman, T. L. (2007, July). *The world is flat. A brief history of the twenty-first century.* Expanded edition. Picador. 672 pages.

Ginott, C. (2007.). Quotation and educational philosophy of the Holocaust museum of Houston, Texas. Retrieved October 15, 2007, from hmh.org/ed_teaching_guidelines.asp

Gough, D. (1991). *Thinking about thinking.* Alexandria, VA: National Association of Elementary School Principas. ED327 980).

Gregory, R. S., & Robert, T. C. (1995?). A framework for developing the decision-making skills of secondary school students. Retrieved on November 5, 2007, from faculty.fuqua.duke.edu/~clemen/bio/Beyond.pdf

Grossman, M., Under Secretary for Political Affairs. (2003, December 3) Keynote address to the Task Force for International Cooperation on Holocaust Education, Remembrance, and Research. Press release and report. Retrieved October 10, 2007, from state.gov/r/pa/prs/ps/2003/26713.htm and holocausttaskforce.org/meetings/archives/2003-12-03-02/report.pdf

Gunter, M. A., Thomas, H. E., Susan, L. M. (2007). Instruction: A Models Approach (5th ed.). Allyn & Bacon.

Hensley, S. (2002, March). What is critical thinking and how do we learn to do it? Retrieved October 17, 2007, from stanford.edu/group/i-rite/statements/2002/hensley.htm

Hildreth, R. (2004, April 15). John Dewey as a Critical Resource for the Theory and Pratice of Civic Engagement. Paper presented at the annual meeting of the The Midwest Political Science Association, Palmer House Hilton, Chicago, Illinois, 2004-04-15 Online <.PDF>. 2007-10-28. Conference Paper/Unpublished Manuscript Peer Reviewed. Retrieved September 22, 2007, from servicelearning.org/instant_info/fact_sheets/k-12_facts/char_ed/

Huitt, W. (2004). Moral and character development. In *Educational Psychology Interactive.* Retrieved October 28, 2007, from chiron.valdosta.edu/whuitt/col/morchr/morchr.html

James, H. (1930). Charles, W. E.: President of Harvard University, 1869-1909. Houghton Mifflin Company. Retrieved September 22, 2007, from questia.com/PM.qst?a=o&d=1107046

Jewish Virtual Library. (n.d.). The Nuremberg laws. Retrieved November 1, 2007, from jewishvirtuallibrary.org/jsource/Holocaust/nurlaws.html

Josephson Institute of Ethics. (2007). The six pillars of character. Retrieved October 26, 2007, from josephsoninstitute.org/MED/MED-2sixpillars.htm

Josephson Institute of Ethics. (1992, July). The Aspen declaration on character education. Retrieved on October 2, 2007, from charactercounts.org/aspen.htm

Josephson, M. (Autumn 2002). Character counts. Character education is back in our public schools. National Association of School Boards of Education. Retrieved October 3, 2007, from nasbe.org/Standard/11_Autumn2002/Character.pdf

Kindertransport Association. (n.d.). Brief history. Retrieved November 1, 2007, from kindertransport.org/history.html

Kindertransport Association. (n.d.). Complete history. The Nuremberg laws. Retrieved November 1, 2007, from kindertransport.org/history-more.html

Kindertransport Association. (n.d.). Mission and resources. Retrieved November 1, 2007, from kindertransport.org/resources.html#section_nonfiction

Kliebard, H. M. (2004, July 29). *The struggle for the American Curriculum, 1893-1958* (3rd ed.). London. Routledge.

Lickona, T. (1993, November). The Return of Character Education. *Educational Leadership, 51*(3), 6–11. Retrieved September 30, 2007, from hi-ho.ne.jp/taku77/refer/lickona.htm

Lincoln, M. (2003, September). The Holocaust Education project. A media specialist's success story in online resource use, staff collaboration, and community outreach. Retrieved from infotoday.com/MMSchools/sep03/lincoln.shtml

Lipstadt, D. (1999). Quotation in the complete idiot's guide to Jewish history and culture. Retrieved September 18, 2007, from aish.coholocaust/issues/The_Uniqueness_of_the_Holocaust.asp

Milton, S. (n.d.). Holocaust education in the United States and Germany. Unique or universal?

Motzkin, A., & Gabriel, M. (Winter 1996). The uniqueness of the Holocaust. In *Philosophy and public affairs*. Retrieved October 12, 2007, from codoh.com/reference/uniqofholo.html

National Education Association. (2006). National teacher day spotlights key issues facing profession NEA addresses top five teaching trends and outlines 'Portrait of American Teacher' Trend #4: The teaching corps in public schools does not reflect the diversity of the student population. Retrieved from nea.org/newsreleases/2006/nr060502.html

National Education Association. (2006). Teaching experience, character education, Ell, & Math. Retrieved November 3, 2007, from nea.org/teachexperience/wwcreports06.html

Paul, R., & Linda, E. (2006). The miniature guide to critical thinking concepts and tools (4th ed.). The Foundation for Critical Thinking.

Quigley, Charles N., Executive Director, Center for Civic Education. (2006). Response to the May 16, 2007, Release of the 2006 National Assessment of Educational Progress *Civics report card.* Retrieved October 10, 2007, from civiced.org/pdfs/CCE2007ResponseToNAEP.pdf

Ristow, R. S. (1988).The Teaching of Thinking Skills: Does It Improve Creativity? *Gifted Child Today, 11*(2), 44–46.

Robinson, I. S. (1987). A Program to incorporate high-order thinking skills into teaching and learning for grades K-3. Fort Lauderdale, FL. Nova University. (ED 284 689).

Ruddell, M. R. (2008). Teaching content reading and writing (5th ed.). John Wiley & Sons.

Santayana, G. (1905). Reason in common sense. In *The Life of Reason.* 1. Retrieved October 1, 2007, from chara.gsu.edu/~gudehus/Quotations/quotations_rst.html

Schmied, I. K. (n.d.). Memoirs. Retrieved November 6, 2007, from kindertransport.org/memoirs/memoir-schmied-menu.html

Schneider, H. A short personal history of my family during 30 turbulent months. Retrieved November 7, 2007, from math.wisc.edu/~hans/pers_hist.txt

Schnitzer, F. (1948–1960). Personal face to face conversations over twelve years time between Francine Schnitzer and author (nee Leah Green) regarding problems faced by Francine Schnitzer as a hidden child in Belgium during World War II.

Schugurensky, D. (ed.). (2007, April 24). History of education. *Selected moments of the 20th Century.* Retrieved September 18, 2007, from civiced.org/index.php?page=stds_preface

Scriven, M., & Richard, P. (2004). The Critical Thinking Community. Retrieved October 18, 2007, from criticalthinking.org/aboutCT/definingCT.shtml

Simon Wiesenthal Center. Museum of Tolerance. (2002–2006). Teachers' guide. Meeting twenty-first century challenges in education. (Quick Links to lesson plans for grades 3-12). Retrieved October 20, 2007, from teachers.museumoftolerance.com/

Simon, S., Leland, W. H., & Howard, K. (1972). Values clarification: A handbook of practical strategies for teachers and students. New York. Hart.

Simon, S. B., & Mary, B. B. (1974). What schools should be doing about values clarification. *NASSP Bulletin, 58*(379), 54–60. Retrieved October 12, 2007, from bul.sagepub.com/cgi/content/abstract/ 58/379/54

Stambler, L. G. (1999). Infusing Holocaust studies in pre-service and graduate level teacher education courses to assist educators in becoming culturally skilled. Paper delivered at the Eighth International Conference on Holocaust Studies, Hebrew University, Jerusalem, Israel. December 27, 1999 to January 2, 2000.

Stambler, L. G. (2000). Using character education and Holocaust studies to promote a culture of caring and peace in our schools. A poster/paper session at the WCSU Conference on Preventing Violence and Promoting a Culture of Caring and Peace in Our Schools, Danbury, CT June 22–23, 2000.

Stambler, L. G. (2003). Teaching character education and citizenship through Holocaust literature: 34th Northeast Regional Conference on the Social Studies, The Boston Park Plaza Hotel and Towers, Boston, March 11, 2003.

Stambler, L. G. (2007). Civic engagement through civic education. In *Democracy & Civic Education: Implications for Teacher Preparation and a National Agenda for Inquiry* (pp. 34–38). American Association for State Colleges and Universities (AASCU).

Stambler, L. G. (2007). Civics education as a stepping stone to civic engagement. Paper and power point presentation at the Annual National Meeting of the American Democracy Project-AASCU, June 6-9, 2007 in Philadelphia, Pennsylvania.

Sternberg, R. G., & Bhana, K. (1986). Synthesis of Research on the Effectiveness of Intellectual Skills Programs: Snake-Oil Remedies or Miracle Cures? *Educational Leadership*, *44*(2), 60–67.

Strom, M. S. (2003). A study guide for the children of Willesden Lane. Facing history and ourselves, with the Milken Foundation. Retrieved November 1, 2007, from facinghistory.org/campus/reslib. nsf/studyguides/Children+of+Willesden+Lane,+The?OpenDocument

The Task Force for International Cooperation on Holocaust Education, Remembrance, and Research. (200, January). Declaration of the Stockholm International Forum on the Holocaust. Retrieved October 10, 2007, from holocaustforum.gov.se/pdfandforms/deklarat..pdf

The Task Force for International Cooperation on Holocaust Education, Remembrance, and Research. (2004). Handbook for teachers & scholars guidelines for teaching about the Holocaust, documents of the Education Working Group. Ambassador Giorgio Franchetti Pardo, Task Force Chairman, Italy, Paul Salmons, Chair of the Task Force Education Working Group. Retrieved October 10, 2007, from holocausttaskforce.org/teachers/index.php?content=guidelines/menu.php

The Task Force for International Cooperation on Holocaust Education, Remembrance, and Research. (2004). *Guidelines for teaching about the Holocaust documents of the Education Working Group.* Retrieved October 20, 2007, from london.iwm.org.uk/upload/pdf/Holocaust_Ex_TeachHbook.pdf

U.S. Department of Education National Commission on Excellence in Education. (1983, April). An open letter to the American people. A Nation at risk: The imperative for educational reform. Retrieved from ed.gov/pubs/NatAtRisk/index.html

United States Holocaust Memorial Museum. (2001). Guidelines for teaching about the Holocaust. Retrieved September 27, 2007, from ushmm.org/education/foreducators/teachabo/part_2.pdf

United States Holocaust Memorial Museum. (2001). Teaching about the Holocaust: A resource guide for educators. Retrieved September 27, 2007, from ushmm.org

United States Holocaust Memorial Museum. Feinberg, S. (n.d.). Beyond our walls, state profiles on Holocaust Education (interactive map and state by state information). Retrieved August 22, 2007, from ushmm.org/education/foreducators/states/

Walsh, K. (1990). *The three dimensions of education.* Paper presented at the Annual Meeting of the Pennsylvania School Boards Association (Lewisburg, PA, July 19-21). Quoted in Huitt, W. (2004). Moral and character development. In *Educational psychology interactive*. Retrieved October 28, 2007, from chiron.valdosta.edu/whuitt/col/morchr/morchr.html

Weisskirchen, G., Moderator. (June 8–9, 2005). Introductory statement for panel on Holocaust education OSCE Conference on Anti-Semitism and on Other Forms of Intolerance. Cordoba, Spain. Retrieved from osce.org/documents/cio/2005/06/15358_en.pdf

Welker, R. P. (1996). Searching for the educational imperative in Holocaust Curricula. In L. M. Rochelle (Ed.), *New perspectives on the Holocaust*.

Westheimer, J., & Kahne, J. (2003) Educating the "Good Citizen" on slide 6 of ppt. *Service learning for civic engagement.* Retrieved from calstate.edu/csl/resource_center/documents/sl_for_ce.pdf

Wong, & Alan, S. L. (September 2000). Kohlberg's theory of moral development – explained & illustrated. Retrieved October 12, 2007, from vtaide.com/blessing/Kohlberg.htm

Leah G. Stambler
Education and Educational Psychology Department,
Western Connecticut State University

MARIAN J. MCKENNA

USING LITERATURE OF THE HOLOCAUST TO TEACH GLOBAL CITIZENSHIP

INTRODUCTION

In my tabletop fountain, I have a stone that is imprinted with the word, "Remember". And I do remember. I remember the horror of my father over WWII memories he couldn't discuss without tears or rage. I remember my mother's unspeakable and enduring grief over the loss of friends and their children. I remember every book, play, film, picture, and artifact that I have ever read, seen, or heard about the Holocaust and World War II. And so I remember. But what is it and why is it that we must "never forget"; that we must "always remember"? We must understand that some of the worst evil is perpetrated when good people do nothing to prevent it. The horror of the Holocaust is that it was a systematic, state-sanctioned murder of a cultural group of people. It was genocide, and for the most part, the whole world simply watched. We must teach the Holocaust, not to grind the unspeakable details of it into our students, but as a way to rise above ourselves, to teach our students and learn for ourselves how to respond in ways different from indifference and fear to events that are still happening. Although we know that genocide is taking place in parts of the world as I type this paragraph, it does not mean we can do nothing. Education is about hope for the future, for our children, and for our world. We are still evolving as human beings, as a species. We are not finished in our evolutionary development, and thus must continually strive for ways to be better people, neighbors, and global citizens.

There are no more powerful ways of teaching/learning than through modeling, personal experience, and the sharing of stories. This chapter combines these elements to develop a teaching/learning model for active global citizenship. The model combines the best we know of teaching practices, academic service learning, and quality literature toward the end that war, genocide, cruelty, and racism become untenable.

This chapter examines and discusses multiple titles from the body of Holocaust literature and builds a transformative teaching/learning model (McKenna, 2007) engaging teachers, students and community members in both personal response and academic service learning to build relevancy, and life altering experiences. The model developed in this chapter builds on the work of Louise Rosenblatt, John Dewey, and Ernest Boyer to embrace literature and learning as life, and life as reflection and action. Titles discussed in this chapter are largely

T. Duboys (ed.), Paths to Teaching the Holocaust, 83–98.

young adult literature, but for the purposes of the transformative model, discussion is directed to teachers and students of grades 4-12.

The following discourse provides a rationale and model for using literature of the Holocaust, connected with an academic service learning experience to not only teach students about the world and our history, but to transform them into engaged, informed, critically literate citizens, willing and able to take action for a better and more just world.

TEACHING/LEARNING MODEL FOR ACTIVE GLOBAL CITIZENSHIP

The model presented here is intended as a transformative teaching/learning model that combines the best in literature of the Holocaust, what we know about best practices in the classroom, and what research tells us about the efficacy of academic service learning to provide opportunities for our students to become dynamic readers and active players who connect text with their own lives and the lives of others near and far. "Transformative learning occurs when learners engage in a thorough process of critical reflection and rational discourse. Experiential learning is central to this process," (Mezirow, 1991 & 1995). Hence, academic service learning is a critical piece of this model. Teaching also transforms those of us who teach, making this teaching/learning model one that acknowledges teaching and learning as part of the same cycle of events. Thus we, as well as our students, the, next generation of leaders, must go outward into constructive activism.

Three levels of engagement will be discussed to develop this model. Although I am talking about stages, by no means do I propose these stages of involvement as linear or sequential. I present them in a linear fashion as a constraint of our language, but teachers adapting this model for their classrooms can find a beginning point at any stage of the model, depending on the age, and background knowledge of their students, as well as their own teaching/learning goals. The three levels of engagement proposed here are, the information stage, the integration stage, and the transformation stage. The model builds upon pedagogical theories and practices for supporting our students' development through three stages of engagement so they may learn from quality literature, active engagement, and thus become transformed so as to continue the practice of taking action for a better and more just world.

ACADEMIC SERVICE LEARNING AND QUALITY LITERATURE FOR CONSTRUCTIVE ACTIVISM: A TRANSFORMATIVE TEACHING/LEARNING MODEL

Recently, a student of mine asked if I really believed that we could support kids in being empathetic to others while learning in a homogenous classroom. I had to say yes, I do believe that we can create opportunities whereby our students learn to hold empathy in their hearts for those who are different from them, who have different opportunities, different experiences, and who raise different voices in shaping themselves and their world. As a teacher, I have to believe this is true or it would be difficult to go to work everyday. But I don't think we can achieve the ongoing goal of developing understanding, empathy, and the desire to engage in constructive activism by simply giving children powerful literature describing horrific events. Certainly some of my more sensitive students whether in elementary grades, or graduate classes, make this transformation without any input or guidance, but deep understanding and a personal empathetic response is rarely automatic. We have to take the learning and the experiences of these books to the next level. Where literature and service learning intersect is the heart of what I am promoting in this Transformative Teaching/Learning model. This is where literature and learning is life and life is action and reflection on that action. The following books and the corresponding service learning suggestions offered, demonstrate how the model of teaching using good, authentic literature coupled with quality academic service learning intersect at the core of our beings...the place where stories and personal experience become transformative agents for growth and the development of the human spirit. This model is grounded in the anticipation that teachers and teacher educators are themselves thoroughly engaged in cultural literature as well as understanding the unapologetically political nature of teaching.

USING THE MODEL WITH LITERATURE OF THE HOLOCAUST

The teaching/learning cycle, that is, the dynamic interplay between the teacher, student, community, and classroom, is such an organic and multidimensional entity that it is very difficult to discuss a model for it. There are many layers and variables at work in any classroom, so that attempts to script or control the variables is folly. Let me emphasize there is not a step-by-step "procedure" or "recipe" in following or adapting this model. Teachers can use this model from any beginning point depending on his or her students and educational goals. Therefore, the following discussion of the Transformative Teaching/Learning Model will necessarily be an oversimplification of a very complex process. As teachers who strive to translate this model into our own classrooms, each of us will move through it in a different way and create our own adaptations according to our teaching styles, our tolerance for not knowing all of the answers, our ability to let go of our students' learning and move outward into the larger community as learners and teachers with our students. Much will also depend on the courage and the support or lack thereof of those in administrative positions in our schools and schools and universities.

STAGE 1: INFORMATION

The best way to visualize this model is as a pyramid with the Information Stage being at the top and most narrow part of the model. This stage is aligned with the knowledge and comprehension stages of Bloom's taxonomy of thinking. Students get information from their teachers and textbooks. It is here that students engage in what Rosenblatt refers to as the efferent reading experience or reading for information (Rosenblatt, 1978). This is the beginning scaffolding from which students can and do build a deeper understanding of people and events, past and present, happening in places around the globe as well as in our backyards. The Information Stage of engagement is characterized by the teacher providing background knowledge such as introducing the book, the author, setting, context, rationale for the text, and establishing the purpose for the study about to begin. At this stage we see traditional interactions between teacher and students such as direct instruction, assignments, and discussion of the various literary elements. The focus is primarily on the efferent experience or laying the foundation for further investigation. Again, note that although the Information Stage of engagement is being discussed first, does not mean that it necessarily has to come first in the chronology of the classroom. For the sake of presentation, I am discussing the model from the simplest level of engagement, Information Stage, to the deepest and most personal level of engagement, the Transformation Stage.

The Information Stage can be described as the level where knowledge is acquired, comprehension is developed, and interest on the part of the students is heightened concerning the topic that is introduced. At this stage of engagement, the classroom is teacher-centered inasmuch as the teacher is providing information and sources for investigation. The classroom looks much like a traditional classroom where one might observe students asking questions for clarification and the teacher is engaged in lecture, read-alouds, and interrogative and guided discussion with students.

STAGE 2: INTEGRATION

The second stage of engagement, Integration, is what Rosenblatt (1976) referred to as the transactions between the reader and the text, such that the personal or aesthetic meaning of the text is created for and by the reader. Students are given the opportunity to read the literature that is central to the Transformative Teaching/Learning Model. They learn about heroes and horrors involved in the Holocaust and the events of the time. Younger students may learn of *Luba: The Angel of Bergen-Belsen* (Trysznynska-Frederick, as told to McCann, 2003), and of the children whose lives she was able to save. Middle or high school students may have the opportunity to read; *The Boy in the Striped Pajamas* (Boyne, 2006), for a completely different perspective on the Holocaust, and the endurance of friendships that will not be stopped. Reading of resistance within Nazi Germany, students can learn of three Mormon youths in *Brothers in Valor* (Tunnell, 2001) who risked their lives in resisting Hitler and telling the truth of what was happening. They learn about processes and experiences people have to go through when they flee their homes and become refugees as in *When Hitler Stole Pink Rabbit* (Kerr, 1971) and *Number the Stars* (Lowry,1989). They learn about very ordinary people and families just like theirs whose lives are eroded and ultimately destroyed by the horror that was the Holocaust by reading *The Devil's Arithmetic* (Yolen, 1988), *Malka* (Pressler, 2003), and the gentle, sad tale of *Hana's Suitcase* (Levine, 2002). However, it is evident in working with students at any grade level that simply being introduced to quality literature, no matter how powerful the actual story may be, does not directly translate into integrated or transformative learning. This is where a sensitive and highly qualified teacher must be at the center of the equation. Almost anyone can 'deliver' information. It takes a skilled, educated, and compassionate teacher to move students inward and onward for the learning to become truly meaningful and relevant and to provide opportunities for students to develop social empathy and take action that addresses specific community needs. Neither we nor our students can 'stand by' anymore when we witness injustices or imbalances in our communities and world.

The Integration Stage of engagement is characterized by a more constructivist classroom where the teacher serves as the facilitator of discussion and discovery among the students as they go deeper into the text and find the relevancy of it to their own lives and time. The focus here is on the experience of reading the book, enjoying the beauty of the language, and creating individual, personal meaning from the text. In keeping with the analogy of the pyramid, it is at this second stage of engagement that the understanding and experience gained becomes wider and deeper by applying the events and characters of the text to our own lives and situations. The Integration Stage brings in the depth of personal culture and the ability to see the lives of others with compassion and to learn to apply these lessons to our own lives. For example, after reading *If I Should Die Before I Wake* (Nolan, 1994), an eighth grader reported; "I think that it is important to read books about the Holocaust because they can tell you how to solve problems or how not to be a bully or something like that." This statement indicates that the student is moving into the Integration Stage of understanding the literature and is engaged in a transaction with the story. She has been able to personalize and make relevant the parallel stories and events in this book. Beyond information, this book is becoming integrated into the child's experiences of the world.

At the Integration Stage of engagement, an observer may see a classroom full of students reading the same or different books about a person, place, or an event of the Holocaust. This is the stage of Rosenblatt's transaction with the text where the students are reading high-quality literature for aesthetic purposes. It is here that the students are free to consider the connections of the literature under study to their own situations, inner lives, or imaginations. In this scenario, the teacher serves as a guide and participant in guided and reflective discussions in order to deepen students' understanding of the context, history, and authenticity of the story. Students may be participating in book clubs, pairing activities, double-entry journals, writing unsent letters, or creating frozen tableaus or reader's theatre scripts. Up to this stage of engagement, we are not seeing anything out of the normal range of activities in a classroom conducted by a highly skilled teacher, with the exception that literature of the Holocaust is at the heart of the curriculum.

STAGE 3: TRANSFORMATION

The final stage proposed for this model is that of Transformation. It is supported by John Dewey's theories of experiential learning and Louise

Rosenblatt's transactional theory. Theirs was a call for literary critics and teachers to be political activists, and they promoted the very powerful development of the movement for academic service learning at all levels of educational institutions. Neither Rosenblatt's theories nor the Transformative Teaching/Learning Model end with the personal and aesthetic event for the reader. As educators of any level, it is imperative that we move our students further and more comprehensively than ever before. The world is changing and schools and educational practices are changing with it. It is action that defines this level of engagement, where we are both transformed by our actions and our actions may transform our world and how we move through it. We have to develop the hope and belief that somehow we can lessen or eliminate racism, bullying, and the unthinkable genocides that are still occurring throughout the world.

Students and their teachers move from a level of knowing about something, someplace, or someone to understanding and being able to relate to that situation or person, to being willing and able to take positive action addressing a situation or an injustice. They begin to push the envelope of Morton's (1995) service-learning continuum from volunteerism to service learning for social justice, and begin to ask important questions about why things are the way they are; why is there bullying in our playgrounds; what can be done about the myriad of social and political injustices in our neighborhoods and in our world. The model defined in this chapter has as its goal the development of educated citizens as defined by Sumida and Meyer: "At the heart of teaching and learning, an educated citizen is viewed as one who can 'read the world,' think critically, question relationships of power, and become an agent of social change" (Sumida & Meyer, 2006, p. 444).

In the Transformation Stage of engagement students and their teachers go beyond the walls of the classroom, beyond personal and academic learning to the development of social empathy and awareness of social injustices being perpetrated in our neighborhoods as well as around the world. It is at this level of involvement that the classroom begins to look and sound different, as teachers and students become co-investigators asking questions such as; "What are we learning in our classrooms that we can take out into the community to address identified needs?" "What skills do we have and what skills can we develop to address some of the injustices of which we are now aware?" "How can we take our learning and our skills out into the community so that we may learn more deeply while addressing needs expressed by our community members?" In this classroom, students and their teachers are working together to identify a problem and possible solutions with their community partners and resources. Teachers, students, and interested community partners work as a group, individually, or in teams to develop a plan of action to address mutually identified needs. The students then take what they are learning or have learned and use that new knowledge and deeper understanding to participate in solving the problems of their community. They go out into the community and take positive action for the greater good of the community. They then bring these experiences back into the classroom so that their actions can be reflected upon in a structured environment whereby the learning is further deepened. Now the students have their own stories to tell. Here we are at the deepest and broadest stage of the pyramid. The walls between the classroom and community have become transparent. The action the students take drives the transformation as students, teachers, and community partners work together toward a common goal, using the skill of all participants. Action, as embodied in a service-learning project, transforms the partners by creating links for the learning to the community and the world. Learning is deepened through relevant action and the human spirit is expanded through connections and mutual support with all types of people and situations. The understanding that students gain as a result of having something to offer to their community or world affects their learning and the rest of their lives. These are the deeper understandings and behaviors that students, and their teachers will take with them into their futures, long after "lessons" have been forgotten. Beyond curricular goals lies a greater one: to nurture the imaginations and generosity of spirit of ourselves and our students.

THE FOUNDATION OF THE PYRAMID: ACADEMIC SERVICE LEARNING

As the culminating piece of the pyramid, academic service learning gives depth and breadth of learning and living as it takes us outside the realm of the classroom and demands that we interact with our neighborhoods, (however we define our neighborhoods), our own preconceived biases, and the learning in which we are engaged. The depth and width that is represented by the base of a pyramid is the result of the connections and richness that are added to the learning as a result of family, community, and cultural interchanges. It is a dynamic pedagogy that has been on the rise in the United States particularly in the last quarter of a century. To say that it has been on the rise connotes that it is a new pedagogy or theory, but this is not the case. Academic service learning has been embedded in the goals of public and higher education since the inception of these noble institutions. Therefore, the vehicle for personal as well as social transformation in the Transformative Teaching/Learning Model is the pedagogy of academic service learning, particularly as it extends from high quality cultural literature.

Service learning is primarily and foremost connected to the curriculum and curricular goals so that what is being learned in the classroom is taken out into the community to address local or global needs. This pedagogy can work for almost any age group or class size. A kindergarten or first-grade classroom might define its community as the playground connected to the school. A graduate class of students may want to develop service learning projects for an entire school district, while a team of teachers may want to adopt a school in a beleaguered community or another part of the world. Service learning opportunities can be taken to global levels by using mail services, extended field work, or advanced technologies. The learning can be in any area of literacy studies or other curricular connections, such as history, science, music, art, health and nutrition, or economics, to name a few. The curricular connections are limited only by your imagination and the needs of your community. The "service" aspect of the service learning will be dictated by the size of the community, the expressed needs of the community, and the expertise the students bring to that need. It is often most productive to work with existing community organizations, such as Big Sisters/Big Brothers, or local agencies already established such as food banks.

However the service learning projects are designed, the hallmarks of successful and meaningful service learning projects are the integration of the classroom curriculum and community needs, critical reflection where students bring their learning and experience back into the classroom discussion, involvement of student voice in the design of the service learning project, and an ever-growing awareness of the importance of civic responsibility and the meaning and purpose of true learning.

EXAMPLES OF USING THE TRANSFORMATIVE TEACHING/LEARNING MODEL WITH LITERATURE OF THE HOLOCAUST

In this section, quality works of literature about the Holocaust, each at a different age level, have been selected to serve as specific examples of how student engagement may evolve from the Information Stage to Integration, to Transformation. Even very young children can be encouraged in their ability to make decisions, negotiate with their peers, and select courses of action that have the most or least positive impacts on their community. Again, the notion of community is determined by the age and skill levels of the students so that the community for a kindergarten class could be some feature of the school itself, such as a garden, or the immediate neighborhood. The goal for students at any grade level and age is to live in such a way that recognizes, celebrates, and respects people and cultures from all over the world. Using quality literature as a starting point for both learning and living is powerfully expressed by the writer Anne Lamott: "Books help us understand who we are and how we are to behave. They show us what community and friendship mean; they show us how to live and die." (Lamott, 1994, p.15)

Luba Tryszynska, or the Angel of Bergen-Belsen, as she came to be known is one of the heroines of the Holocaust. She was able to keep 52 abandoned children alive during the winter of 1944-45, under conditions of starvation, disease, and the ravages of war. They were hidden in the barracks of the concentration camp of Bergen-Belsen. Luba's story (*The Angel of Bergen-Belsen,* Tryszynska, as told to McCann, 2003) exemplifies compassion, courage, and hunger. Therefore, the learning of this book can be based on the notion of hunger and who is hungry in our community? If the students are old enough, they can find the answer to this question. If not, the teacher can contact the local food bank or homeless shelter to see what they need in terms of support or help. These are just examples, of course. There may be any number of organizations or agencies that need help in feeding the hungry of the community. Although with young children, we don't want to teach the brutalities of the Holocaust or of WWII, we might focus simply on this book as a historical foundation, which highlights the trials of hunger, and how much difference one person's efforts can make in the lives of others. At the Integration Stage, students may want to be discussing what it feels like to be hungry, times when they themselves felt hungry, (be careful to protect children who may themselves be living in a shelter of some sort) and to be able to express the understanding that there are people who are hungry in our own community. In addition to history, health science, and perhaps music curriculum connections, this book lends itself to rich opportunities for oral and written communication skills to be enhanced and many of reading/language arts standards to be addressed. Even students at the primary level can progress to the Transformation Stage and begin to question why there is hunger in their community and think about what they might be able to do about it. Consider the ways these students can address and more deeply understand the notion of hunger in their communities. In one local school, our locale being in the west, students initiated a "Fill the Boot" drive. Parents donated old cowboy boots and the students collected change throughout the school in attempts to fill "their boots" and then donated that money to the local food bank. This falls more on the volunteerism end of Morton's (1995) continuum as it does not really involve the students in relationships with other people of their community. However, it does get young children thinking about the larger world and their role in it. An even richer experience that would move us further along Morton's continuum between volunteerism and service learning for social justice, would be for students to go to the local food bank or homeless shelter and help measure and weigh portions of food into storage bags to be used for cooking or donations. In this scenario, students move out of their classrooms, address cross-curricular standards, and reach out to the community to become aware of and transformed by engagement with the lives of their friends and neighbors. We must get our students, even at an early age, participating in activities that will help them develop critical thinking and questioning, while developing compassion and empathy for people near them and afar. We must teach our students that there is *never* 'nothing that we can do'. Students must be empowered and engaged. The Transformative Teaching/Learning Model proposes one avenue for doing this in our schools. There are many, many other works of non-fiction, fiction, poetry, and authentic documents of the Holocaust that are sensitive and done in such a way that they may be appropriate for younger children. Teachers and teacher educators are encouraged to seek these out and use them for all kinds of curriculum and service learning connections. See the end of this chapter for a brief bibliography of selected titles on the Holocaust.

USING THE TRANSFORMATION TEACHING/LEARNING MODEL IN THE UPPER ELEMENTARY GRADES

When Hitler Stole Pink Rabbit (Kerr 1971), is an autobiographical story of a young girl, Anna, who with her family must flee Berlin in 1933, just days before the National Socialist Party is voted into office. It is a very good selection to share with students in the 4th-6th grades, as 'everything is alright as long as Anna and her family are able to stay together'. This autobiography is a very touching story of family solidarity, but it also makes clear the sacrifices that had to be made by so many people who left their homes and searched for a new identity and nationality. Anna and her family must leave their very comfortable home, servants who were like family to them, and school friends. In the end, the family had to move three times, from Germany, to Switzerland, to France, and finally, to England. Every time they packed their things, there were fewer things to be packed. Most difficult however, was that Anna and her family had to learn a new language each time they entered a new country. Through the experiences of Anna and her family, students can learn what it is like to be a refugee. It was a very difficult time in the lives of this family despite the fact that they were together and their father was able to find work writing for various newspapers. At the Information Stage of engagement, the focus might be on the historical aspects of WWII and the displacement of so many people throughout Europe. Students' awareness and understanding of history and geography, as well as the many languages represented in Europe can be enhanced and deepened. Students may want to develop maps and chart the journey of Anna and her family. They may want to go further into research projects that look at the numbers of people who fled Germany, where they went, what resources they needed and what nations were willing to open their country to them.

At the Integration Stage of engagement, students' realization of the deprivations, hurts, confusion, and sacrifices of having to flee one's home becomes a personal experience with the text and the activities guided by a sensitive teacher. Students may want to write some unsent letters to Anna or her brother Max. They may want to write to the German children who were forbidden to play with Anna and Max even though they were all in Switzerland together. They may want to ask themselves how it feels when friends ignore us or turn their backs on us.

"Max shook his head. 'He didn't like us any more at the end,' he said. 'Not by the time his mother had finished with him.'

It was true, thought Anna. She wondered what the German boy was thinking now, what his mother had told him about her and Max, and what he would be like when he grew up." (Kerr, 1971, p.74) Ask students to write the German boy's story. How did he grow up? What kind of a person was he? What did his mother tell him about Max and Anna? Students can work on these parallel stories in teams to do the research and writing. Students can also engage in a book pairing activity where they compare this book with *Briar Rose* (Yolen, 1992), or *Number the Stars* (Lowry, 1989), or *Survivors: True Stories of Children in the Holocaust* (Zullo & Bovsun, 2004). By this time, some students may be on their way to developing a text set of books, stories, poems, and authentic sources about the Holocaust and World War II. These they could share with other students in other schools at their grade level. This step may take them into opportunities for the Transformation Stage of engagement. Students should be made aware of the fact that there continue to be refugees all over the world, for reasons just as insubstantial (racism, prejudice, and genocide…not that these phenomenon are insubstantial, but the artificial boundaries that we create between ourselves are in fact insubstantial as gossamer) as those that uprooted Anna and her family. Students at this age and into junior high school are particularly open to discussions of social justice and in taking part in activities that address them. At this age, students are very interested in issues of fairness and justice. In capitalizing on this growing awareness of students at this age, we may move them forward in understanding their roles in pursuing fairness and justice for their classmates, their neighbors, and children throughout the world who are still facing displacement and refugee camps. Therefore, the service learning opportunities that open up as a result of an integrative engagement with *When Hitler Stole Pink Rabbit* (Kerr, 1971) might be an understanding that there are refugees in the classroom, their neighborhoods, their larger communities, and certainly in distance parts of the world. Discussion and questions about these issues leads the way for transformative experiences. Students may want to know who are the current refugees in our neighborhoods, communities, and world. Why are people currently forced to leave their homes and seek sanctuary in other countries or places? What do they need? How can we take what we have learned in literature, history, and geography out of the classroom to support people who are refugees wherever they are? There may be students in the school who are struggling to learn another language and the ways of a new culture. Reciprocal transcultural and cross-language mentoring relationships can be fostered within the school culture. Perhaps there are younger students in the school community who are refugees and need language or cultural support or simply a friend they can depend on to help them. Other students and older students may want to participate with agencies already working to help refugees in the community or throughout the world to provide needed goods and services. Students may want to become politically involved and write to their congressional delegations to stop the genocides that they have discovered are unbelievably still occurring. Students become empowered, engaged citizens when they are involved in efforts to make a difference in the world, no matter how large or small that difference may be. Their learning is deepened; their lives are enriched, as are the lives of all of those they touch, including our own.

USING THE TRANSFORMATIVE TEACHING/LEARNING MODEL IN MIDDLE AND HIGH SCHOOL

When working with older and more mature students, the literature possibilities become greater, from non-fiction such as *Smoke and Ashes: The Story of the Holocaust,* Revised & Expanded, (2002, Rogasky) and *Auschwitz, A History* (Steinbacher, 2005), to Spiegelman' series of graphic novels, *Maus: A Survivor's Tale,* (1986), and *If I Should Die Before I Wake,* (Nolan, 1994), a story set in modern times that uses time travel as a device for building understanding of the reality of the Holocaust. Many high school students are certainly ready for adult literature such as *The Book Thief,* (Zusak, 2005). While not directly concerned with stories of people in death camps, it certainly shows the toll that is taken on community members and those who tried to protect thier Jewish neighbors.

For the purpose of discussing the Transformative Teaching/Learning Model, (McKenna, 2007), consider *Maus: A Survivor's Tale* by Art Spiegelman and winner of the Pulitzer Prize in 1992. The subtitle of this Book I is *My Father Bleeds History*. There is so much to this work that it is almost difficult to know how to approach it with a class of high school students. Certainly this work is an excellent and personal history of the slow stripping away of everything from the Jewish people in Poland. It is also the story of family and how to maintain a family amid terrible scars left from the experiences of the Holocaust. When using this book, it is recommended the students be allowed to simply experience the power of this work, the art, the story, and the weaving of the two stories together. Allow the students the aesthetic experience of this work; allow them to feel it and respond to it in personal ways. Allow the discussion and questions to come from the students and then from the teacher. In this case, a teacher can easily see how the three levels of engagement presented in this model can merge and appear to be seamless. Once students have read and had the opportunity to discuss the book in small groups, the teacher, depending on the teaching/learning goals of the class and/or the unit, may want to then give direct instruction on history, geography, science, art and/or music from the time period of this story. In the Integration stage of the model, students can pose questions to deliberate in their journals or discussion groups. This would be a good opportunity to compare other works of this time period, including their history textbooks and other sources, to determine different perspectives and the use of multiple texts to gain a deeper and closer approximation of the realities of such times as these.

There are numerous opportunities for students to move into the Transformation Stage using this text as a basis for understanding. An obvious connection is the use of oral histories to understand a person's life and experiences. There is an organization in our city called The Storykeepers. This group organizes volunteers to visit terminally ill people in local hospitals and listen to people's life stories. As the ill patients tell their stories, the volunteers jot notes down to share with the family and thus keep some of the people's stories alive for their loved ones. There is emerging medical research that points to a sense of peace being created in people just for having others listen to their stories. Some modification of the idea of taking oral histories could be a service, if it is connected to the curricular goals of the unit of study. Students might be partnered with willing and interested residents of a nursing home or assisted living facility to hear their stories and create works from them to either return to the families or create an historical piece for the school or local news. A local class of high school juniors, used oral history information to form a weather timeline that demonstrated changes in the local weather over the last 50 years. They published the timeline along with photos and drawings in the local paper as part of an expose on global climate change. We no longer have the ferocious winters of 50 years ago. Certainly taking oral histories is a very powerful way to develop interviewing techniques, writing skills, and an appreciation for history and the way we learn it. History is a story and we must learn to hear it with critical ears with an understanding of who is telling the story and from what perspective. This is especially true for our students today who are bombarded with media and text from many sources, many, many of them unreliable sources. The story of *Maus*

(Spiegelman, 1986), opens many avenues for developing transformative experiences for our students. An art class could recreate a scene from history, locally or globally, and learn how to paint it to the size of a mural for a building in the area that needs some brightening. Music students could study the music of the mid-1930's-40's and recreate a dance scene or vignette, and perform it for local residents. Psychology students could study to understand family reverberations from being the children of post traumatic stress survivors, and plan work with a local VFW hall to see what may be needed. Health classes could study nutrition and the physiology of hunger. Again work could be done around the notion of hunger and why there are men, women, and children in the richest nation on earth who are hungry. What is there to be done about this situation? Finally, many classes in the liberal arts, sociology, history, current events classes, may want to study the parallels of government between the mid-1930's in Germany to the United States now. Do students realize that libraries are closing due to lack of funding? What do local public libraries mean to a democratic society? Why are we in this country, not solving the problems of hunger, homelessness, health concerns, elderly care, and education? What steps are we taking, large and small, to address global climate change? The directions that academic service learning can take especially when prompted with quality literature, are boundless. Many of the best projects result when teachers, students and community members come together to discuss local needs, and allow the work itself to carry them to the fruition of a project. We should be encouraging social and political activism on the part of our students so that they may live fully in a participatory, democratic society.

THE RESPONSIBILITY OF EDUCATION

As students become involved in projects described above, their learning is deepened beyond academic interest to become a part of who they are. The learning is made relevant, and immediate. Their ability to be critically reflective of their own actions and those of others is greatly enhanced, and again, students realize that they can make a difference even through small efforts. We must never underestimate the power that feeling they are making a difference gives to our students. It is part of our responsibility as educators to nurture and develop a sense of civic responsibility in our students in all content areas. It is at the heart of the mission of public education.

Our world is rapidly changing through technology and globalization. But some things remain the same and we must continually work to make the world a better place. This demands that our students engage with their communities and education in such a way that they more deeply understand their role in society and begin to be transformed as they become more active and engaged participants. Concerns for my students and the world in which they are participating, led to the realization that many of our students need and deserve a very articulated model to support them in moving from where they may be numbed or overwhelmed with media, text messages, and bad news to an understanding of the connections and responsibilities inherent in a global society. They must be given the tools, dialogue, and experiences to 'read the world' and in so doing develop respect, understanding, and even an ethic of care for people and places all over the globe. Therefore, our tasks as teachers and citizens is to use everything at our disposal to bring some of the realities of life to our students, not to depress them or reveal global horrors to them, but to allow them to discover that these depredations are not tolerable or acceptable and that there are things we all can do to mitigate them. The literature presented in this chapter and indeed this edited text, are not just good books, nor are they simply the tools for educational tasks. These books provide our students and ourselves with experiences that become a part of us. These are the stories we feel in our hearts and are transformed by them as we move outward through the vehicle of service learning to give back to our homes, families, and the communities that house us.

CONCLUSION

None of us could continue to have the stamina to be teachers of any age or grade level if we did not somehow believe that we are making a difference in the lives of our students and our world. As our world becomes more global and more delicate, we are increasingly aware of our connections and responsibilities to one another. As teachers it is imperative for us to support out students in moving from feelings of paralysis and hopelessness to a place where they can take actions, no matter how large or small, to make the world a better place.

> What we need next is a new ethic—call it an 'ecological ethic of care', call it a 'moral ecology.' It's an ethic built on caring for people and caring for places, and on the intricate and beautiful ways that love for places and love for people nurture each other and sustain us all (Moore, 2004, p.65).

Once our students realize that they do have a very real ability to take action and have something to contribute to our global society, it will reverberate throughout all of their learning and quality of living.

Rosenblatt, in her work of finding the meaning of literature through a transaction between the reader and the text, encourages us to take that transaction out to enact the transformation of our society:

> ...we teachers of language and literature have a crucial role to play as educators and citizens. We phrase our goals as fostering the growth of the capacity for personally meaningful, self-critical literary experience. The educational process that achieves this aim most effectively will serve a broader purpose, the nurturing of men and women capable of building a fully democratic society. (quoted in Probst, 2005, p.12).

As teachers, we can not rest with the notion that our students are capable of building a fully democratic society; we must provide examples and models for them to learn from and build upon. Quality literature such as the books presented in this chapter and the hundreds of titles that are published every year provide portals through which we and our students can pass to develop deeper engagement with ourselves, our communities, and our world. The Transformative Teaching/ Learning Model (McKenna, 2007) uses quality literature and the pedagogy of academic service learning to achieve larger goals as educators. Above and beyond teaching the curriculum and addressing standards, it is our goal and responsibility to support the development of fully engaged citizens, capable and interested in choosing the life they lead and creating the world in which they live.

REFERENCES

Dewey, J. (1938). *Experience and education.* New York: Macmillan.

Lamott, A. (1994). *Bird by bird: Some instructions on writing and life.* New York: Random House.

McKenna, M. J. (2007). Transformative literature: A teaching/learning model for using global literature to positively impact our world. In N. L. Hadaway & M. J. McKenna (Eds.), *Breaking boundaries with global literature: Celebrating diversity in K-12 classrooms.* Newark, DE: International Reading Association.

Moore, K. D. (2004). *The Pine Island paradox.* Minneapolis, MN: Milkweed Editions.

Morton, K. (1995). The irony of service: Charity, project and social change in service-learning. *Michigan Journal of Community Service-Learning, 2,* 19–32.

Probst, R. E. (2005). In memory of Louise Rosenblatt. *Voices from the Middle, 12*(3), 9–12.

Rosenblatt, L. M. (1976). *Literature as exploration.* New York: Noble and Noble Publishers.

Sumida, A. Y., & Meyer, M. A. (2006). T4=Teaching to the fourth power: Transformative inquiry and the stirring of cultural waters. *Language Arts, 83*(5), 437–449.

LITERATURE OF THE HOLOCAUST: A SHORT LIST FORMATTED IN APA 5TH EDITION

Boyne, J. (2006). *The boy in the striped pajamas.* New York: Random House Children's Books. (MS/HS).

Jung, R. (2003). In B. Anthea (Trans.). *Dreaming in black and white.* New York: Phyllis Fogelman Books. (MS/HS).

Kerr, J. (1971). *When Hitler stole pink rabbit.* New York: The Putnam and Grosset Group. (UE/MS).

Levine, K. (2002). *Hana's suitcase.* Morton Grove, IL: Albert Whitman and Co. (ME).

Lowry, L. (1989). *Number the stars.* New York: Dell Publishing. (ME).

Nolan, H. (1994). *If I should die before I wake.* Orlando, FL: Harcourt Books (HS).

Pressler, M. (2003). In M. Brian (Trans.). *Malka.* New York: Philomel Books. (HS).

Rogasky, B. (2002). *Smoke and ashes: The story of the Holocaust.* (Rev. and expanded ed.). New York: Holiday House (HS).

Spiegleman, A. (1986). *Maus: A survivor's tale. Book I: My father bleeds history.* New York: Pantheon Books. (HS).

Styron, W. (1979). *Sophie's Choice.* New York: Random House Books. (HS/Adult).

Tunnell, M. O. (2001). *Brothers in valor: A story of resistance.* New York: Holiday House (HS).

Tryszynska-Frederick, L. (2003). *Luba: The angel of Bergen-Belsen.* As told to Michelle R. McCann. Ills. Ann Marshall. Berkeley, CA: Tricycle Press.

Yolen, J. (1988). *The Devil's Arithmetic.* New York: Puffin Books. (MS).

Yolen, J. (1992). *Briar Rose.* New York: Tom Doherty Associates, LLC. A Tor Book. (MS).

Zullo, A., & Bovsun, M. (2004). *Survivors: True stories of children in the Holocaust.* New York: Scholastic Books. (UE/MS).

Zusak, M. (2005). *The book thief.* New York: Alfred A. Knopf. (HS/Adult).

Marian J. Mckenna
The University of Montana

ELIZABETH SPALDING AND JESUS GARCIA

INFUSING HOLOCAUST EDUCATION INTO TEACHER EDUCATION THROUGH EXPERIENTIAL LEARNING

"We all grew up about two inches from Poland."

Rachel Stern, Participant, March of Remembrance and Hope

Preparing future educators to work effectively with culturally diverse students remains one of the most pressing issues facing teacher educators today. Understanding cultural diversity also means understanding issues of social justice that are frequently intertwined with race, ethnicity, culture, and socioeconomic status (Cochran-Smith, 2004). Many teacher education programs require one or more courses in understanding diversity or in multicultural education. The expectation is that course content will significantly influence future educators' beliefs about and actions toward people, especially young people, who differ along multiple dimensions. Unfortunately, research has been hard pressed to document significant changes in preservice teachers' beliefs, dispositions, or actions as a result of such coursework (McAllister & Irvine, 2000).

This chapter explores the potential of experiential learning for changing the way preservice teachers and other education professionals think about diversity and act upon their beliefs. In contrast to traditional learning which is "typically teacher-directed, content-driven, textbook-oriented, and classroom-based," experiential learning occurs when "students are placed in a situation where they think and interact, learn in and from a real-world environment" (Cornell University, 2007). The learning experience described here is the March of Remembrance and Hope (MRH), a nine-day, intensive experience in Poland visiting Holocaust sites. The authors analyzed the impact of this experience on the beliefs and actions of preservice teachers and other education professionals enrolled in the College of Education at a land grant university in the southeast United States.

EXPERIENTIAL EDUCATION: A NON-TRADITIONAL APPROACH TO TEACHING ABOUT DIVERSITY

In his review of the knowledge bases for diversity, G. Pritchy Smith (1998) emphasized the critical role of experiential knowledge for preservice teachers who "have lived insulated, monocultural lifestyles" (p. 91). According to Smith, a teacher education program that effectively prepares teachers to accept and respect diversity and to advocate for social justice should have a strong experiential

T. Duboys (ed.), Paths to Teaching the Holocaust, 99–115.

component. Upon graduation, preservice teachers should have developed friendships with a variety of people from backgrounds different from their own and experienced "a variety of cross-cultural events and activities that expanded their knowledge of and enhanced their sensitivity to other cultural groups" (p. 91). Smith also highlighted the value of international experiences. Merryfield (1995) has written extensively about the critical need for teacher education programs that provide opportunities to travel, study, or live in other parts of the world.

While not everyone can afford to live and work abroad for a semester, experiential learning, even of limited duration (e.g., Wiest, 1998), appears to be a promising approach in facilitating enduring change. For example, a review of the impact of outdoor adventure programs, such as Outward Bound, found that "the effects are long lasting and often increase over time" (Hattie, Marsh, Neill, & Richards, 1997). The authors defined "long lasting" as effects measured anywhere from one to twenty-four months following the experience. They stated, "These substantial follow-up effects are unlike most educational programs, where the typical follow-up effects are negative or at best zero and there is quick fading" (p. 57). This claim is corroborated by various critics of research in teacher education who note that changes in knowledge, attitudes, and beliefs are generally measured immediately following the end of the intervention, thus calling into question the long-term impact of programs and courses (e.g., McAllister & Irvine, 2000; Richardson, 1996; Wideen, Mayer-Smith & Moon, 1998).

Authentic experience may be a key factor in minimizing preservice teachers' resistance to diversity and guiding them into developing a commitment to multicultural education (Cochran-Smith, 2003; Nel, 1992). The advantages of cross-cultural immersion experiences for preservice teachers have been well documented (e.g., Fearance & Bell, 2004; Mahan & Rains, 1990; Mahan & Stachowski, 1990; Stachowski & Mahan, 1998). Willison (1989) has shown that culture-specific experiences help teachers develop attitudes and skills that are applicable in other cross-cultural contexts. In their research on and development of an instrument to measure teachers' beliefs about diversity, Pohan and Aguilar (2001) found that personal beliefs are positively influenced by direct cross-cultural experiences and recommended that teacher education programs provide such experiences both within and outside coursework. This chapter focuses on the March of Remembrance and Hope (MRH) , a cross-cultural experience intended to teach participants about the Holocaust and help them develop attitudes about and skills for addressing issues of diversity and social justice in their various professional contexts.

THE MARCH OF REMEMBRANCE AND HOPE: LEARNING ABOUT THE HOLOCAUST THROUGH EXPERIENCE

The March of Remembrance and Hope is an international educational leadership program that brings together college students of different religious and ethnic backgrounds to learn about prejudice through the study of the Holocaust in Poland and Israel (March of Remembrance and Hope, 2002). It is an outgrowth of the March of the Living, which, since 1988, has brought Jewish high school students from all over the world together each year to explore the death of Jews in Poland and the re-birth of Jews in Israel. Both initiatives are sponsored by the March of the Living International in Tel Aviv, Israel, an organization committed to keeping the memory of the Holocaust alive and to using the Holocaust as an example of one of many human tragedies attributed to ignorance, hatred, and violence. The MRH suggests a curriculum to be followed in preparation for the trip and asks that all participants return to their campuses and communities prepared to take action as a result of the immersion experience in Poland.

Participants from public and private, religious and secular institutions of higher education from across the country participated in the 1999 inaugural MRH, including Mr. Green (a pseudonym), then President of a state Board of Education. As a result, Mr. Green became a passionate supporter of Holocaust and human rights education and offered the financial support of the utility company of which he was CEO to students in the authors' College to participate in the 2001 MRH. This chapter reports on the experiences of thirteen College of Education students who participated in the MRH in May, 2001 and thirteen who participated in the MRH in May, 2003.[1]

Preparation for the MRH

The authors were members of a team of three leaders who recruited, selected, prepared students for, and participated in the MRH. The team publicized the opportunity to participate in the MRH throughout the College to both undergraduate and graduate students. Applications included essay questions designed to elicit applicants' motivation for wanting to participate. The leadership team reviewed the applications, selecting participants who seemed highly motivated to participate and who would commit to attending all preparatory seminars. In addition, the leadership team sought to compose groups that were diverse in gender, ethnicity, and field of specialization. Table One shows these characteristics for the 2001 and 2003 groups.

Participants engaged in five months of pre-trip preparation. During the spring semester, students registered for credit in an independent study course entitled *Exploring the Holocaust.* The seminar met for four hours on one Saturday per month for five months. The goal of the seminar was to prepare participants for the cross-cultural immersion experience in Poland. It was designed to enable students to examine the historical, sociological, psychological, and economic roots of the Holocaust. Students were encouraged to extrapolate knowledge of the Holocaust to historical and contemporary examples of social injustice throughout the world and in the United States, as well as to apply that knowledge to their work with individuals in a variety of settings. In accordance with Gallant and Hartman's

Table 1 Participants in MRH, May 2001 and 2003

Name*	Age	Gender	Ethnicity	Degree Program/ Specialization
2001 Participants				
Margaret**	*26*	*Female*	*African American*	*B. A., Elementary*
Rhonda	21	Female	White	B. A., Elementary
Kim	*26*	*Female*	*White*	*B. A. Elementary/Special Education*
Hank	21	Male	White	B. A. Middle School/Math & Social Studies
Sally	20	Female	White	B. A. Middle School/Math &English
Martin	27	Male	White	Secondary/English
Mike	*24*	*Male*	*White*	*B. A. Secondary English Education*
Cameron	*22*	*Male*	*White*	*M. A. Secondary English Education*
Carrie	26	Female	White	M. A. Secondary English Education
Meg	*27*	*Female*	*White*	*M. A. Secondary English Education*
Laura	22	Female	White	M. A. Secondary Social Studies Education
Dwayne	27	Male	White	M. A. Secondary Social Studies Education
Anna	*26*	*Female*	*White*	*M. A. Secondary Social Studies Education*
2003 Participants				
Alison	23	Female	White	Ed.S. Student/School Psychology
Barbara	26	Female	White	Ed.S. Student/School Psychology
Cyndi	21	Female	White	B. A. Middle School Language Arts & Social Studies
Silas	*23*	*Male*	*White*	*B. A. Secondary English Education*
Don	24	Male	White	M. A. Secondary Social Studies Education
Eva***	25	Female	African American	M. A. Secondary Business Education
Frank	26	Male	White	M. A. Secondary Social Studies Education
Ginny	25	Female	White	Ed.S. Student/School Psychology
Hal	26	Male	White	MS Student/Counseling Psychology
Penny	*27*	*Female*	*White*	*Ed.S.Student/School Psychology*
Irene	22	Female	White	B. A. Middle School Special Education/Math
Rachel	*28*	*Female*	*White*	*Ph.D. Student/ Counseling Psychology*
Jon	24	Male	White	Ed.S. Student/ Counseling Psychology

*All names are pseudonyms.
** The students whose names are italicized are described and/or quoted in this chapter.
*** Participated in preparation but ultimately did not participate in the MRH itself.

(2001) recommendations for effective Holocaust education, the specific course objectives were to:

- Heighten participants' *awareness* of the historical and current dialectical discussions concerning the Holocaust and other instances of social injustice present in multiple forms of media;
- aid participants in developing a *knowledge base* related to the Holocaust and social injustice and the impact of such issues on professional identity as a means of developing the skills necessary for becoming a reflective decision maker, creative problem solver, and a responsive educator;
- provide experiences for the *reflective application* of ideas, concepts, and information gained throughout the course and the cross-cultural experience in Poland to one's professional practice settings.

Student learning was supported through direct instruction, assigned readings, cooperative group work, guest speakers, videos, other print and electronic resources, journaling, self-directed projects, and, ultimately, the experience in Poland. Because students were from different disciplines within the COE, each student selected and critiqued articles from professional journals in her or his field, one that examined an issue related to the Holocaust and the other pertaining to another example of social injustice from the 20th century to the present.

The March of Remembrance and Hope in Poland

The experiences in 2001 and 2003 differed slightly but followed the same general itinerary. Approximately two hundred fifty North American college students, faculty, and MRH staff gathered for a two day orientation in Newark, New Jersey before departing for Krakow, Poland, where they were joined by an additional two hundred some college students from such diverse nations as the Peoples Republic of China, Mexico, Germany, and Rwanda. The packed itinerary included Krakow and environs (e.g., Plaszow concentration camp, Czestochowa), Auschwitz-Birkenau, Warsaw, Treblinka, Lublin, and Majdanek, perhaps the most horrific and best-preserved death camp site in Poland. MRH participants traveled on buses. Each bus had one guide trained by the MRH as well as a local Polish guide. A Holocaust survivor traveled on each bus, as did a Holocaust scholar. Each bus also had at least one clergy person, rabbi, or counselor. In 2003, a filmmaker, engaged by the local public television station to produce a documentary of the trip focusing on the participants in this study, accompanied the March and was assisted by a production team of student participants (Hutchings, 2004).

Research Design

In both 2001 and 2003, the leadership team systematically collected and analyzed data regarding the impact of the MRH on participants' thinking about diversity and social justice (Spalding, Savage & Garcia, 2003; 2007). Each year, data were gathered from participants (N=26) before, during, and after the trip to Poland.

Multiple data sources were used. Essays written for application to the program provided baseline information on each participant's motivations for wanting to join the MRH. Pre-trip questionnaires, administered at the first preparatory seminar, provided information about students' knowledge of the Holocaust, previous cross-cultural experiences, and expectations about the trip. Materials created by students for the independent study course were also used to determine the impact of the course on participants' thinking. The leadersip team took field notes before, during, and after the MRH.

Upon completion of the course and the MRH, most of the participants either graduated or left the area to complete internships. The leadership team continued to communicate informally by e-mail with some of the participants. In August, 2004, over a year after the completion of the MRH, the team sent email questionnaires to all participants whose whereabouts were known, regarding the quality of their preparation for and the subsequent impact of the MRH on their personal and professional lives. Responses were used to determine long-term effect of the experience.

The authors reviewed, discussed, and compared data from the various sources and ultimately compiled descriptive case studies of selected participants. Our selections were guided by Stake's (1998) advice: "The researcher examines various interests in the phenomenon, selecting a case of some typicality, but leaning toward those cases that seem to offer *opportunity to learn.* My choice would be to take that case from which we feel we can learn the most.... Often it is better to learn a lot from an atypical case than a little from a magnificently typical case" (p. 101). The students' whose cases are excerpted here each presented unique opportunities to learn.

IMPACT OF THE MARCH OF REMEMBRANCE AND HOPE

The MRH provided numerous opportunities for learning. The pre-trip preparation was designed to increase participants' awareness, knowledge base, and reflective application of ideas and concepts learned about the Holocaust. During the experience, learning occurred in at least three ways: 1) learning from personal interactions; 2) learning from place; and 3) learning from chance encounters. After the experience, participants continued to reflect and learn from the MRH, taking a variety of paths to fulfilling their commitment to be witnesses to the Holocaust.

Learning Before the Trip

Most of the participants had little prior knowledge of the Holocaust. Thus, it was essential not only to provide them with a knowledge base but also to offer numerous opportunities to personalize and apply that knowledge through reflection. For example, one assignment was to use Raul Hilberg's (2003) model of genocide (i.e., exclusion, expulsion, extermination) to examine other historical and contemporary examples of social injustice. Silas, a preservice secondary

English teacher who is described in more detail below, made connections between Hilberg's model and contemporary treatment of homosexuals, as well as the historical treatment of African Americans in the segregated South. He further observed the process at work in the local school system: "I saw in the high school [where] I observed last semester no open persecution of blacks or Latinos, but I did see signs of passive examples of Hilberg's three-stage model"

In an effort to demonstrate the struggle against social injustice in "our own backyard," a phrase frequently used by the course instructors, a local teacher, Dee Queen (a pseudonym), was invited to talk about her own exerience. A White, female, heterosexual English teacher in a nearby rural high school, Ms. Queen described her work with gay, lesbian, and bisexual teens who were fighting for the right to form a Gay Straight Alliance at their school. Ms. Queen took up their cause despite the personal and professional risk of doing so. She led the students in a successful suit against the district, which had denied them the right to assemble. Her influence on the participants' thinking was significant. For example, Rachel, a doctoral student in counseling psychology who is described in more detail below, recorded in her journal an encounter with "a gentleman from Louisiana" in a local bar. He was looking for an after-hours nightclub and she recommended one she knew. He asked her whether "they run off the homosexuals after 12 p.m." She responded, "I actually like homosexuals," and turned away. But afterward she replayed the incident over and over in her mind, thinking she should have done more. After hearing Dee Queen's story, Rachel realized that "a non-related minority may be more effective in seed planting. That's a good point and gave me more validation for speaking up for groups beyond my own."

Penny, a graduate student in school psychology, felt that her pre-trip course learning came to life during the MRH and enabled her to personalize the experience. Upon her return to the United States, she wrote,

> The most meaningful experience during this course was actually the experience that took place in Poland, in the concentration camps....As I walked through the camps I heard what I wrote in my journal, I heard the voices from the books that I read, and I heard the stories of survivors. I felt this experience in every sense of the word. All of my learning and my emotions aligned to make this experience my own. It cannot be unlearned, disregarded, or diminished. I can now see social injustice, I can feel it, and now I can do something about it

Learning During the Trip

Anna: Learning from Personal Interactions

Anna, a twenty-seven year old white female, held a B. A. degree in anthropology. At the time of the trip, she had completed most of the requirements, including student teaching, of a graduate-level certification program in secondary social studies. She wanted to participate in the March because

> I have learned that *ordinary* people commit atrocities.... I have learned that *ordinary* people stand by and allow it. And I have seen that a few extraordinary people find the strength to do neither. I want desperately to learn how to be the latter, and how to teach my students to want the same.

Anna explained that she "went into social studies because I wanted to combat social injustice, period...[S]ince then, I've found other reasons I want to be a teacher, but that's why I went into it." She expressed her commitment to infusing issues of social justice into the curriculum and described her ideas for combating prejudice against the Mexican migrant population in the community in which she student taught.

A self-described shy, introspective person whose serious demeanor was easily mistaken for melancholy, Anna was moved by a woman who approached her shortly after our group arrived in Poland:

> But through it all, I remember Judith, a woman who was so concerned about how tired I looked the night we arrived, and then casually told me she was a Holocaust survivor....[S]he told me she had come so she could go to Auschwitz to say good bye to her parents, yet she calmly told me that all I could or needed to do was 'be'.....

Anna expressed insights into her experiences in Poland that went beyond the appalling experience of viewing the evidence of genocide. For example, at Majdanek, one of the most moving sites we visited, Anna was shocked to see Polish couples strolling hand in hand and children bicycling through the former death camp:

> ...and that really blew my mind because that was like a screaming example of social injustice right there and I didn't understand how people could just erase it from memory...and then a fellow trip mate pointed out that we do the same things at [name of a local bar]...which was a former [slave market]—a place where they sold slaves, and we go there...and drink....

Overall, Anna felt that the trip had strengthened and expanded what she already knew and believed. She said that the March had made her more "energized" to address issues of social justice in the classroom, even at the level of "each little comment, like when one student calls another student 'gay.'"

Silas: Learning from Place

Silas, a White, male in his early twenties, had earned a B. A. in English and was anticipating entering a graduate-level teacher education program. Silas grew up in a small town in an isolated region of the state whose residents have deep roots in the community and a strong sense of place. After graduating as valedictorian of his high school class, he headed for the state's flagship institution. His first day on campus held a great surprise:

> [W] hen I first entered the University of XXX, I thought I was a well-rounded individual in the realm of racial understanding. I read Alex Haley's *Roots*. I

> listened to Martin Luther King, Jr.'s "I Have a Dream" speech. But when my black roommate walked into my dorm room for the very first time, I was on the phone with my parents (sitting in the hallway so Frank couldn't hear) asking to come home within minutes.

Silas engaged seriously in preparation for the trip, making many connections between his learning about the Holocaust and contemporary instances of social injustice. As a future English teacher, he decided to design a curricular unit around the topic "Children of the Holocaust" as his project for the MRH. He reflected on his own first reading of *Night* (Wiesel, 1982) as a high school student and felt he had missed the larger meaning of the book. Now several years older, he speculated

> What happens when we do not acknowledge social injustices that seem not to instantly affect us? More directly, *Night* is a cross-instructional book selection. English class can investigate the Holocaust through personal reflective writing, and social studies classes can investigate the implications of racism, persecutions, and pogroms....And beyond specific lessons, Elie teaches us to contemplate our own humanity, and students will understand how some suffered to bring this lesson to the world.

Silas expected the trip to Poland to deal him an "emotional blow," and it did. He wondered how he could even "look at everyone ...and tell them about it all," but trusted that he would eventually find the words to "describe the scratch marks on the walls [of the gas chamber] at Majdanek."

In mid-July, Silas reflected upon the ways in which the MRH had affected him. He stated that he had originally thought of the Holocaust in terms of facts, places, and statistics, but there were "no faces attached to the numbers." After meeting David, a Holocaust survivor, and hearing him tell his life story while standing on the steps of a building at Auschwitz, Silas realized: "At that moment I understood that it was important to fight for something greater than myself." Silas stated that he had changed his focus from "Adolf Hitler and how he killed millions of people" to Hannah, another survivor who had shared her family story while sitting under a tree at Treblinka. He wrote:

> I have seen too much now. I saw the scratch marks and was breathless. The pictures mean very little until you can place your own fingernails against the wall and see what hate can do to another person. When the high school teacher [a guest speaker] came to our[pre-trip preparation] class talking about homosexual persecution in the classroom, I felt sympathy for those students. But honestly, I would not have joined their cause. I would have been too worried about myself. But those gas stains. But those rooms of hair. But that endless track at Birkenau. How can I see that and not see the potential for a reoccurrence in my own society?

In retrospect the most significant moment of the MRH for him was walking out of Treblinka, holding hands with his group members and with the survivors who accompanied them there: "He [the survivor] said, 'Most people did not walk out of

Treblinka. We will defeat the Nazis and hatred by walking out together, as friends and human beings.'"

Margaret: Learning from Chance Encounters

Margaret, a twenty-seven year old African American female, was working toward a bachelor's degree in elementary education. Active in politics, service, and Christian ministry, Margaret explained why she wanted to participate in the March:

> ….[M]y people have had to survive many injustices that were placed upon them by their fellow man. I cannot, however, say that these injustices have had anything to do with my decision to apply to the MRH….My decision to apply to this program is in hope that I may gain a deeper understanding of the deliberate acts of genocide Jews encountered during World War II…. As an educator, it is my nature to instruct and to share my knowledge with others.

A native of Birmingham, Alabama, Margaret had grown up hearing her parents' stories of racism and discrimination, but she insisted that she herself had never encountered "blatant racism" or been affected by social injustice or stereotypes. For Margaret, one of the most powerful moments of the March occurred during a late-night meal at McDonald's:

> We were sitting in McDonalds…and some of these [Polish] kids, two kids really, just stared at me. And I mean it was like the stare like they had never seen anything like it—like me…before in their life. And at first it didn't bother me…but it was just something about these stares, and in thinking about it the next day…I started feeling really terrorized and really fearful. And it's because I felt like I had been discovered….And I began to think, if I was there during that time, I could very well have been in one of those cattle cars …and, walking through the ghettos I just felt really scared…thinking…how it must have been to be in hiding and then to have someone find me….

Margaret described herself as a "self-reflective" person who generally stayed to herself. She felt she grew personally as a result of the March by opening up to others around her and learning to hear and appreciate ideas different from her own. Overall, Margaret concluded that

> …[I]f I had not taken the trip, I probably would not give much attention to the Holocaust in my class. I would probably teach it—you know, give the basics, but there is so much more to it than just the basics. And you can say that for any number of events in history, especially those that involve social injustice….So, I think I will probably try to…personalize it more than just making it a textbook lesson.

Anna, Silas, and Margaret were by no means the only participants who were deeply affected by the MRH. Indeed, a distinctive feature of the experience was the variety of moments, planned and unplanned, which inspired participants' insights and empathy. For example, students on the trip complained bitterly and incessantly about the quality of the box lunches provided by the MRH. Finally, as he was walking out of Auschwitz and anticipating lunch, Jon realized, "How quickly I thought about my own hunger. But I felt that I must also eat as way to honor those who died. For it says to me to remain strong and healthy so that I may live to tell the story of what happened at Auschwitz. I have food in plenty. What right do I have to complain about how it tastes?"

Learning After the Trip: Professional and Personal Change

After the trip, most of the participants moved on to accept professional positions elsewhere. Although not every participant resonded to follow-up communications, those who did provided impressive evidence of the ways in which they have fulfilled their commitment to serve as "witnesses" both in their professional and personal lives.

All participants were obliged to complete a project demonstrating the learning from the MRH. Projects were designed in consultation with course instructors. Kim, a preservice elementary special education teacher, for example, spent countless hours filming and editing a video of the trip. The video was then professionally engineered and distributed to all the participants in a Holocaust symposium organized by our sponsor in spring 2002. Mike, a preservice secondary English teacher created a web site about his experience with the MRH that, as of this writing, has had over 9300 hits.

Now a high school English teacher, Silas explained how the MRH affected him and continues to influence his actions as a teacher: "I am more aware of simple forms of persecution now. I see that simple ridicule in the halls of high schools can actually cause great pain. It is only human nature to take advantage of weakness. Therefore, we need to protect the weak…so that they will not become victims." He also makes an effort to learn about difference. As an example, he described his experience with several Mormon students in his class. These students were uncomfortable with some of the topics being discussed, so Silas went to another teacher who was Mormon and asked her to teach him about Mormonism: "We (the Mormon students and I) are finally beginning to build a relationship…and that is because I took the initiative to understand them. We are scared of the unknown, and the only way to defeat fear is to learn about it."

Penny found it difficult to synthesize and integrate the experience into her personal and professional lives. After six months, she discussed her unsettled feelings with another student who had been on the trip and learned she had recently been tattooed as a way to process her experience. Penny did not want a tattoo; in fact, she indicated she did not even like tattoos. But, she decided she needed one as a permanent reminder of what she had seen and what she had learned. Her tattoo incorporates the Hebrew symbols signifying serenity, courage, and wisdom. Professionally, Penny has applied lessons learned from the Holocaust in working with students in the here-and-now. She has delved into the professional literature in school psychology and special education in an effort to learn more about the effects of labeling students in special education, using Hilberg's model as her guiding theory. She has presented her work in this area at a national conference and is currently evaluating the disciplinary data for students in her district of employment according to students' special education label and race, the results of which will be shared with principals in the district in the near future. "The difference between school psychologists who have not taken this trip and me is that I know what happens when we don't react to social injustice…I cannot change what took place during the Holocaust, but I can be involved with helping this group of students"

Immediately after the trip, Rachel felt "weathered and heavy-hearted." She felt she had "changed somehow on the inside" and a long-time friend noted, "This is a different Rachel." In July, she wrote in her journal:

> This weekend I met my family on Sanibel Island for a quick Fourth of July get together. As I was wading in the warm water I looked up on the beach and saw typical figures of bodies walking their dogs, laying out, lazily soaking up the sun-kissed environment. It seemed like out of nowhere I began to feel a sudden sense of compassion from looking at the physical forms in the distance. Beaches are one of those rare places where you see individuals without clothes camouflaging their forms…and this reminded me of endless naked lines heading to the gas chambers in Poland. My compassion was coming from somehow understanding in that moment how humiliating it must have been to be fully exposed in such manner. Who would have known the Florida beach would have brought that to mind?

Rachel described her progress in identifying how she could speak out against social injustice: "As a therapist, supervisor, and in daily living—personally I want to continue searching for language that can reach the supposed untouchables [people who refuse to listen to the messages they most need to hear]." She was incorporating her experiences into her therapy work. And to her "delight," her family and friends were "incredibly interested" in her "stories." A year later, Rachel reflected: "This trip changed my life. Any lofty goals I may have had regarding career or life in general…have all been touched by this experience. Now I feel like my purpose, beyond becoming a psychologist, is to educate people concerning the need for acceptance and kindness, toward themselves and others, as well as the tragic consequences of discrimination." She described other changes: "I've written letters and attended more marches/rallies. In my professional life, as a therapist, I've had a tendency to address any 'isms' that a client may belong to…and any discrimination they may be experiencing…and how they can channel that energy into something socially positive. Furthermore, I also will challenge clients on racist statements if it fits within their treatment paradigm" Rachel's rediscovery of her Jewish identify through her participation in the MRH became the topic of her dissertation, which she completed in 2007.

Cameron, a preservice secondary English teacher and at the time a recent convert to Islam, left the area after graduation and to teach in an Islamic school in a large Midwestern city. Several months after September 11, 2001, he wrote in an e-mail to the authors:

> With the simultaneous escalation of emotions throughout much of the Islamic world, teaching the Holocaust is not really a viable option for me right now. However, not specifically teaching the Holocaust doesn't mean not dealing with it in some way. I have purposefully battled that this year....I've been more than willing to discuss my experience in Poland. Many of these students have been programmed by others that all Jews are anti-Muslim. I have made a conscious effort to convey to them that like all groups of people, there are good, there are bad, and there are many in between.

After three years of teaching, Cameron entered a doctoral program in comparative education at a prestigious, private university in the Southeastern United States. He attributed his decision in part to the MRH, which opened his eyes to the importance of understanding others' perspectives.

Meg, a preservice English teacher, moved to a Western state shortly after the MRH. The curriculum of the private Christian school in which she taught did not include study of the Holocaust, but Meg found other ways to bear witness:

> ...[M]y students had a weekly assignment to do something to make the world a better place....I vowed never to give them homework on the weekends if they would do something to change the world every weekend. I have seen amazing things from my students in this respect—from volunteering to speaking up when they hear others being maligned for their beliefs or the color of their skin to giving money to worthy causes. My students are more tolerant, have a better worldview, and are more open to outsiders thanks to the time I spent in Poland.

One year after the MRH, Meg gave birth to a daughter and whom she named Talia, a name Meg had selected from the wall of the monument at the Umschlagplatz[2], the deportation station in Warsaw, so that "I will remember every day the things that I saw and learned as I call my daughter."

DISCUSSION

The March of Remembrance and Hope was a powerful learning experience that educated participants not only about the historical Holocaust but also about omnipresent and ongoing issues of social injustice in schools and communities.

It is particularly important that preservice teachers be educated about the Holocaust for several reasons. First, although Holocaust education is a relatively new development in American education, it is becoming more widespread as a number of states have made it a required part of the school curriculum (Ben-Bassat, 2000). Teachers use the history and literature of the Holocaust "to teach the effects of institutionalized intolerance and genocide and to prepare students to examine the role of uncontrolled racism in current conflicts" (Brabham, 1997, p. 139). Further, works such as *Anne Frank: The Diary of a Young Girl* (Frank, 1993) and Elie Wiesel's (1982) memoir *Night* are now almost canonical texts in middle school English language arts classes (Spector, 2007). These texts may be the first exposure to The Holocaust for both teachers and students.

Wegner (1998) has noted, as have others, that the quality of students' learning about the Holocaust is deeply dependent upon the quality of teachers' knowledge, attitudes, and skills (e.g., Brown & Davies, 1998; Reed & Lass, 1995).

MRH participants, like Margaret, Silas, Cameron, and Meg, brought little formal knowledge of the Holocaust to the MRH experience. If the status of these presrvice English teachers' knowledge is at all representative of that of the larger teaching population, then it seems at the very least that teachers who are required to or choose to teach about the Holocaust need in-depth knowledge of this difficult subject if they are to teach it well. Otherwise, a "Holocaust unit" can become the occasion for such well intentioned but educationally questionable activities as role-playing Nazi/Jew power relations or calculating how many bodies will fit in a railroad boxcar (Fallace, 2007). Or, as Spector (2007) found in her study of the teaching of Holocaust units in three secondary English classrooms: "The choice of using *Night* is obviously a mistake if teachers are not prepared to meet students on this [theological] issue and help them excavate the narratives that cause them to frame Jews in harmful ways. Teachers who hear defamatory statements and don't react to them have entered into a complicity of silence" (p. 49). When all Jews are represented as victims, all Holocaust victims represented as Jews, all Germans as Nazis, and all Nazis as satanic, it is all too easy for students to pity or blame the Jews, condemn the Nazis, while empathizing with neither group. Certainly, these are not the goals of Holocaust education. This study suggested that MRH participants gained both in-depth and nuanced knowledge of the Holocaust. Silas, for example, who actually planned to teach *Night*, returned not only with first-hand experience of Auschwitz-Birkenau but also with the disposition to stand up against social injustice in his daily life (his determination to build relationships with his Mormon students).

This study also confirmed that cross-cultural experiences can play a valuable role in sensitizing students to issues of diversity and social justice (Pohan & Aguilar, 2001). Chance encounters, such as Margaret's experience in MacDonald's and personal interactions, such as Anna's causal conversation with a Holocaust survivor, are made possible in cross-cultural settings. Effective learning occurred when, as in Penny's case, content knowledge of the Holocaust was connected to the physical experience of visiting important historical sites (e.g., Auschwitz-Birkenau) and to social interactions between preservice teachers, Holocaust survivors, and Jewish leaders. Many teachers and teacher educators hope that their efforts in classrooms will prompt their students to speak out against injustice, and the MRH seems to have been particularly effective in this regard, according to accounts from Silas, Meg, Cameron, Penny, Rachel, and others. As one participant put it a year after her trip, "My experience in the MRH has affected my life in numerous ways, including an increased sensitivity to crude remarks, an enhanced confidence in discussing and speaking out against incidences of social injustice, and heightened awareness of the actions and beliefs of others."

As Garmon (2004) has pointed out, "…[A]lthough multicultural teacher education courses and field experiences are certainly important tools for developing students' awareness of and sensitivity to diversity, these courses and experiences, by themselves may be insufficient to to counteract the power of students' preexisting attitudes and beliefs" (p. 211) While a cross-cultural immersion experience such as the MRH may not be feasible for many institutions or preservice teachers, its demonstrated impact makes it at least worth considering what features might be adaptable to other settings. First, teacher educators might consider providing cross-cultural experiences that do not necessarily take place in school settings. Indeed there is evidence that suggests that, without proper preparation and opportunity for guided reflection, cross-cultural experiences in schools can reinforce the very stereotypes teacher educators are attempting to combat. Sites of struggles against injustice may very well exist "in our own backyards," where citizens work to feed the homeless, obtain services for immigrants, or protect those who face discrimination. Second, personal interactions with those who have struggled against and/or survived injustice or persecution can be a powerful tool for change. Every community has its activists, who are often eager to share their stories, as well as survivors of the far-too-many historical and contemporary instances of persecution or genocide (e.g., refugees from Sudan or Rwanda, veterans of the Civil Rights movement, Native Americans, Americans of Armenian descent). Third, an important component of the MRH experience was the learning and reflection before and after the trip. The MRH participants described here took at sound knowledge base on the trip with them. Informal observation of participants from other institutions that did not provide such rigorous preparation suggested that academic knowledge was critical to processing the experience.

Without a generous and visionary sponsor who saw the value of extending this opportunity to future teachers, the trip would have been out of reach of the students described here, many of whom had little or no disposable income. Just as every community has its activists, so does every community have its benefactors who appreciate the long-term value of investing in tomorrow's teachers. Teacher educators can seek out such support in their own communities. But even without financial backing, all teacher educators can strive to provide authentic, participatory cross-cultural experiences in preparing preservice teachers to teach in an increasingly diverse society.

Rachel summarized her learning from the MRH with a metaphor that appears at the beginning of this chapter: "We all grew up about two inches from Poland." While Rachel did not elaborate on the meaning of this statement, it seems to the authors that Rachel saw in herself and her community the tremendous potential for evil *and* for good that exists in our own "back yard" whenever various "-isms" go unchallenged.

NOTES

[1] The MRH is a biennial event.

[2] The monument is a stone replica of a boxcar in which some 300,000 Jews were transported to Auschwitz. Its interior walls are engraved with names that memorialize the nameless victims.

REFERENCES/BIBLIOGRAPHY

Ben-Bassat, N. (2000). Holocaust awareness and education in the United States. *Religious Education 95,* 402–423.

Brabham, E. G. (1997). Holocaust education: Legislation, practices, and literature. *Social Studies, 88*(3), 139–142.

Brown, M., & Davies, I. (1998). The Holocaust and education for citizenship: The teaching of history, religion and human rights. *Educational Review, 50,* 75–83.

Cochran-Smith, M. (2004). Defining the outcomes of teacher education: What's social justice got to do with it? *Asia-Pacific Journal of Teacher Education, 32*(3), 193–212.

Cochran-Smith, M. (2003). Standing at the crossroads: Multicultural teacher education at the beginning of the 21st century. *Multicultural Perspectives, 5*(3), 3–11.

Cornell University College of Agriculture and Life Science. (2007). Experiential Learning Report: Executive Summary. Retrieved November 26, 2007, from http://www.cals.cornell.edu/cals/teaching/elr/index.cfm

Cowan, P., & Maitles, H. (2002). Developing positive values: A case study of Holocaust Memorial Day in the primary schools of one local authority in Scotland. *Educational Review, 54*(3), 219–229.

Fallace, T. (2007). Playing Holocaust: The origins of the *Gestapo* simulation game. *Teachers College Record, 109*(12). Retrieved November 26, 2007, from http://www.tcrecord.org ID number: 14489

Fearance, R. A., & Bell, S. (2004). A cross-cultural immersion in the U. S.: Changing preservice teacher attitudes toward Latino ESOL students. *Equity and Excellence in Education, 37,* 343–350.

Frank, A. (1993). *Anne Frank: The diary of a young girl.* New York: Bantam.

Gallant, M. J., & Hartman, H. (2001). Holocaust education for the new millennium: Assessing our progress. *Journal of Holocaust Education, 10*(2), 1–28.

Garmon, M. A. (2004). Changing preservice teachers' attitudes/beliefs about diversity: What are the critical factors? *Journal of Teacher Education, 55*(3), 201–213.

Hattie, J., Marsh, H. W., Neill, J. T., & Richards, G. E. (1997). Adventure education and Outward Bound: Out-of-class experiences that make a lasting difference. *Review of Educational Research, 61*(1), 43–87.

Hilberg, R. (2003). *The destruction of the European Jews* (Rev. ed.). New Haven, CT: Yale University Press.

Hutchings, A. (Producer). (2004). *Remembrance: A Journey of Hope.* [Film]. Available from Kentucky Educational Television, 600 Cooper Drive, Lexington, KY 40502.

Mahan, J. M., & Rains, F. V. (1990). Benefits of cultural immersion experiences. *Clearing House, 63,* 402–404.

Mahan, J. M., & Stachowski, L. L. (1990). New horizons: Student teaching abroad to enrich understanding of diversity. *Action in Teacher Education, 12*(3), 13–21.

March of Remembrance and Hope. Retrieved from http://www.remembranceandhope.com

McAllister, G., & Irvine, J. J. (2000). Cultural competency and multicultural teacher education. *Review of Educational Research, 70*(1), 3–25.

Merryfield, M. M. (1995). Institutionalizing cross-cultural experiences and international expertise in teacher education: The development and potential of a global education PDS network. *Journal of Teacher Education, 46*(1), 19–27.

Nel, J. (1992). Pre-service teacher resistance to diversity: Need to reconsider instructional methodologies. *Journal of Instructional Psychology, 19*(1), 23–27.

Pohan, C. A., & Aguilar, T. E. (2001). Measuring educators' beliefs about diversity in personal and professional contexts. *American Educational Research Journal, 38*(1), 159–182.

Reed, C. A., & Lass, H. (1995). Racism today - Echoes of the Holocaust. *Canadian Social Studies, 29,* 140–142.

Richardson, V. (1996). The role of attitudes and beliefs in learning to teach. In J. Sikula, T. J. Buttery, & E. Guyton (Eds.), *Handbook of research on teacher education* (2nd ed., pp. 102–119). New York: Macmillan.

Smith, G. P. (1998). *Common sense about uncommon knowledge: The knowledge bases for diversity.* Washington, DC: American Association of Colleges for Teacher Education.

Spalding, E., Savage, T., & Garcia, J. (2007). The March of Remembrance and Hope: Teaching about diversity and social justice through the Holocaust. *Teachers College Record, 109*(6), 1423–1456.

Spalding, E., Garcia, J., & Savage, T. (2003) The March of Remembrance and Hope: The effects of a Holocaust education experience on preservice teachers' thinking about diversity. *Multicultural Education, 11*(1), 35–40.

Spector, K. (2007). God on the gallows: Reading The Holocaust through narratives of redemption. *Research in the Teaching of English, 42*(1), 7–55.

Stachowski, L., & Mahan, J. (1998). Cross-cultural field placements: Student teachers learning from school and communities. *Theory into Practice, 37,* 155–162.

Stake, R. E. (1998). Case studies. In N. K. Denzin & Y. S. Lincoln (Eds.), *Strategies of qualitative inquiry* (pp. 86–109). Thousand Oaks, CA: SAGE Publications.

Stone, D. (2004). The historiography of genocide: Beyond 'uniqueness' and ethnic competition. *Rethinking History, 8*(1), 127–142.

Wegner, G. (1998). What lessons are there from the Holocaust for my generation today? Perspectives on civic virtue from middle school youth. *Journal of Curriculum and Supervision, 13,* 167–183.

Wideen, M., Mayer-Smith, J., & Moon, B. (1998). A critical analysis of the research on learning to teach: Making the case for an ecological perspective on inquiry. *Review of Educational Research, 68*(2), 130–178.

Wiesel, E. (1982). *Night.* New York: Bantam Books.

Wiest, L. R. (1998). Using immersion experiences to shake up preservice teachers' views about cultural differences. *Journal of Teacher Education, 49,* 358–365.

Willison, S. (1989). *Cultural immersion of student teachers on an American Indian reservation.* Unpublished doctoral dissertation, Indiana University.

Elizabeth Spalding
University of Nevada Las Vegas
Las Vegas, Nevada

Jesus Garcia
University of Nevada Las Vegas
Las Vegas, Nevada

DARYL PARKS & KAREN SPECTOR

TEACHERS, ADOLESCENTS, AND HOLOCAUST LITERATURE

Amy is a 10th grade English teacher in her third year. Teaching at Statistical High School in Majorityville, USA, Amy is enthusiastic about helping her Statistical students better understand the big, diverse world outside of their suburban environment. Passionate about powerful literature, she selects a text filled with the deep issues of life: *Night* by Elie Weisel (1982). Amy plans to provide students with some readings about the Nazi party's rise to power and their occupation of European countries, some photos of the horrors of Auschwitz, and a Weisel speech from recent years to show how far he has come. She knows that the book will provide numerous opportunities for her students to connect with the troubling issues at the heart of the human condition on the historical world stage: good and evil, faith and doubt, kindness and cruelty. Amy is optimistic that as students travel with Elie through *Night*, they will increase their sensitivity to Jewish people and, by extension, all other groups who have suffered discrimination or injustice. Maybe the students will become more tolerant of diversity. Maybe they will become less cruel to others in the halls. Or, maybe the major changes that Amy imagines won't be evident in next month's hallway behavior, but will appear as micro-changes: small adjustments in students' brought-along ways of thinking.

Numerous secondary teachers are incorporating Holocaust literatures into their classrooms, and they do so with the best of intentions. For example, Ellison and Pisapia (2006) surveyed teachers engaged in Holocaust-related instruction in Illinois. They found that while most Holocaust instruction took place in social studies classrooms, the literature classroom was the next most common location. Besides the course textbook, *The Diary of Anne Frank* (Goodrich & Hackett, 1956)[1] and *Night* (Weisel, 1982) were the most often used texts for teaching the Holocaust. Other literature also figured prominently as a means to deliver Holocaust content: *Survival in Auschwitz* (Levi, 1993), *All But My Life* (Klein, 1995), *Maus I* and *II* (Spiegelman, 1986, 1991), and *The Sunflower* (Wiesenthal, 1997). Of the respondents, 97% believed that Holocaust education "encouraged students not to discriminate and stereotype" (Ellison & Pisapia, 2006, p. 11).

Similarly, a study of Holocaust education near Cincinnati, Ohio, found that *Night* and some version of the *Diary* were the most widely used literary texts. Of teachers responding, 98% noted that "learning tolerance" and "valuing diversity" were benefits of Holocaust education (University of Cincinnati Evaluation Services Center, 2003). Finally, a national survey sponsored by the United States Holocaust Memorial Museum (USHMM; Donnelly, 2006) identified *Night* and the *Diary* as the most common classroom texts, with a majority of teachers (56%)

T. Duboys (ed.), Paths to Teaching the Holocaust, 117–142.

noting that the Holocaust was relevant because it conveyed lessons of tolerance through educating students about prejudice and stereotyping. Amy is in good company.

A number of factors have contributed to the use of Holocaust literature in secondary English classrooms: "the growing interest in minority history and the 'affective revolution' in the social studies" (Fallace, 2006, p. 97); states mandating Holocaust education and producing curriculum guides; the National Council of Teachers of English (NCTE) establishing a special committee for teaching about genocide and intolerance in 1993 (Danks & Rabinsky, 1999); the Holocaust entering American popular consciousness through movies like *Schindler's List* (Spielberg, 1993), "genre-bending, now-classic comix-books *Maus I & II*" (Schweber, 2006, p. 45) and the USHMM opening next to the mall in Washington, DC, in 1993 and becoming a popular tourist attraction.

The value of reading Holocaust literature like the *Diary* and *Night* often seems like common sense. As Milton Teichman (1976) argued, Holocaust literature is powerful in its ability to convey the realities of this history in ways that mere textbooks or cold statistics cannot:

> [T]he Holocaust cannot remain an abstraction to those who read the literature. It becomes infinitely more than historical facts, theories, speculations—important as these may be. It becomes the experience of individuals—victims, perpetrators, bystanders. (p. 615)

Teichman also noted that this literature is unique in that it allows students "opportunities for self-confrontation, self-understanding, and the enlargement of sensibility" (p. 613). This is consistent with much of the wisdom surrounding the teaching of this literature. Betty Carter, an assistant professor at Texas Women's University, polled her students each year to determine the most significant books they recalled reading as adolescents. In 1996, 60% of her students identified the *Diary* as having a strong impact on their lives (Rochman, 1998).

At the secondary level, stories of such power abound. Jeffrey Glanz (1999) drew inspiration from the tale of New York high school teacher Esther Meisel whose teaching of Holocaust literature to students encouraged them to "contribute to a more humane world" (p. 554). Specifically, Meisel (1982) told of teaching diverse high school students in New York City. In attempting to get the students to realize a number of goals, among them, "to see how racism and discrimination can lead to genocide," she taught *Night* within an integrated curricular unit. At the end of the unit, Meisel's students wrote letters to officials protesting the atrocities that were taking place with Cambodian and Vietnamese boat people, an issue of the day. Meisel (1982) noted, "The fact that any one of them is involved with today's moral issues is proof enough that the unit and the literature worked" (p. 44).

More than twenty years after Meisel's article appeared in *English Journal*, the idea that Holocaust literature promotes a more humane world still resonates with English teachers. Spector (2005) studied teachers and students engaged in teaching/studying Holocaust literature at two secondary schools in a large Midwestern metropolitan area: one school was composed primarily of middle-class

White students (Adams Junior High); the other school was composed primarily of working-class Black students (River Hill Academy, a high school). She found that all of the teacher-participants believed that increased tolerance and appreciation for diversity would accompany the study of Holocaust literature. For example, Ms. France, an English teacher at River Hill Academy explained:

> Teaching tolerance is an implicit part of the Holocaust, I think. My thought was for the reading to connect with kids' experiences and what they understand and know, and they know a lot about Civil Rights. I wanted them to realize that the things that have happened in their ethnic group have happened in other ethnic groups. Hoping they will see themselves in the humanity of other people, you know? (Spector, 2005, p. 121)

Down the Interstate highway at Adams Junior High, teacher Mrs. Parker also anticipated students would learn tolerance from the Holocaust literature unit:

> I want them to maybe stand up for themselves and also stand up for other people who are being persecuted for whatever reason. Um, I think that sometimes junior high can be the cruelest age. They are so mean to each other. And even if they learn nothing else than to say to someone, "Knock it off," or you know. (Spector, 2007, p. 19)

While Mrs. Parker did not seek to connect her students' awareness of racial oppression to the Holocaust literature as did Ms. France, she nonetheless believed that Holocaust literature could assist her students in learning to support those being persecuted. Teachers in these diverse settings held similar views regarding the Holocaust literature's power; they expected it to produce readily observable shifts in students' thinking and behavior.

To better understand what may be taking place in students' lives, Spector (2005) also analyzed their responses to the Holocaust units. While this analysis suggested student learning in a variety of categories, exactly which lessons students learned was unclear when she triangulated the data. More troubling was attempting to learn how students had "changed" through their Holocaust education experience. When Ms. France asked her 10th grade students about the changes they'd experienced through the reading and study of *Night*, Delaila's written response was a bit unexpected: "It didn't change me. I wouldn't want that for me, but [Jews] got to expect it, killing God" (Spector, 2007, p. 42).

Another student in Ms. France's class, Jessica, had a different way of explaining "change"—the students wanted to change the topic:

> I think that we spend too much time on the Holocaust. And I'm not the only one. Everybody do. Why don't we learn more about our own people? That's what's important to us. Some kids do make fun of it now, and I don't do that. That's cold. But some kids think it's a joke.

Ms. France's goal for students to "see themselves in the humanity of other people," was rejected by "everybody" in the class, according to Jessica.

Are Delaila and Jessica exceptions to the student "change" that we've assumed will happen when adolescents read Holocaust literature? Does the teaching of Holocaust literature really improve students' empathy for people of other cultures and increase their tolerance? The limited research on the topic suggests that such claims are complex at best, deceptive at worst.

Complexities of Teaching and Learning Holocaust Literature

Few studies have focused specifically on Holocaust literature units in English classrooms in the US: Wegner (1998), Schweber and Irwin (2003), Hernandez (2004), Spector (2005, 2007), Spector and Jones (2007), and Juzwik (in press).[2] These studies point toward the many challenges that Amy or other well-meaning teachers will face when teaching Holocaust literature.

Wegner (1998) studied 8th grade students' writings after they participated in an interdisciplinary course focused on the Holocaust, including the history of antisemitism, the *Diary,* and *Night*. Wegner collected brief essays from 200 students about the lessons they learned during the unit. Students said they learned not to allow the Holocaust to happen again, not to dehumanize others, and that we should develop greater tolerance and appreciation for human differences. They also related the Holocaust to past and present atrocities: slavery in the Americas and the prejudice encountered by the local Hmong community. Interestingly, no student mentioned contemporary antisemitism, an anticipated response given its regular discussion in the classroom. As others have noted, one lesson that students don't appear to glean from Holocaust education is that antisemitism abounds today and is deeply rooted in Christian theology (Dawidowicz, 1990; Lipstadt, 1995; Stotsky, 1999). Wegner reasoned that "despite the best intentions, the interdisciplinary context for Holocaust education may sow misconceptions, distortions, and even illusions in the minds of adolescents" (Wegner, 1998, p. 182).

Hernandez (2004) studied his middle school students' responses to engagement with Holocaust literature during a nine-week unit using "witness narratives"—first-person accounts of Holocaust experiences. Incorporating broad historical representation, non-fiction, media, and numerous opportunities for response, he hoped to understand the potential influence that the Holocaust unit might have on students' moral development and understanding of racism. His findings were mixed. At one point in the research, he became disappointed that students' journals didn't reflect the application of Holocaust knowledge to their everyday lives. He wrote:

> I had fully expected a prolonged encounter with Holocaust literature, which is filled with accounts of victims, perpetrators, and bystanders, to elicit more of a response from my students with regard to apathy and the need for social action in light of what goes on daily in our schools and our society as a whole. (p. 193)

By the end of the unit, Hernandez had come to believe that the students' abilities to define and understand racism had increased based on their brief responses in a pre-post writing sample. He also came to see students' responses as displaying an increased commitment to social action, at least in the words on the page. He attributed these shifts in written responses to "prolonged" exposure to witness narratives atop a strong historical grounding of the Holocaust. Yet, just as Wegner had found, students did not mention learning lessons related to antisemitism.

Schweber and Irwin (2003) studied an 8th grade classroom in a private, suburban, Christian high school. The teacher in this study used *The Hiding Place* (ten Boom, 1984) to encourage students' change: "I hope that the students become more sensitive to others, have more empathy and compassion for people with different beliefs" (p. 1700). Not only weren't these outcomes achieved, the uniquely Christian focus of the classroom caused teachers and students to frame texts and conversation with distortions and elisions. For example, the teacher and students regularly shifted when discussing Jews, presenting them as "ancient wanderers, as familiar neighbors or exotic others, and as the chosen people, specially loved but nonetheless superceded" by Christians (p. 1706).

These studies suggest that the use of Holocaust literature in secondary classrooms is complex in its relationship to students experiencing "change." That is not to say that the literature lacks power, but that the studies mentioned here do not widely support a cause and effect relationship between adolescents reading Holocaust literature and their reception of expected moral lessons. The studies do not support the 97% of the teacher-respondents in the Illinois study who believed that Holocaust education "encouraged students not to discriminate and stereotype" (Ellison & Pisapia, 2006, p.11).

What may hold potential for understanding student "change" in the teaching of Holocaust literature is to replace this simplistic cause/effect relationship for one of increased complexity through exploring the tense intersections of teacher identities, student identities, and the construction of texts.

Identities in the classroom We use the term "identities" to refer to the complex influences at work within a single person. Rather than the Western notion of a fixed, monolithic sense of self (Geertz, 1979), we forward scholarship that considers the diverse influences at work within a single individual across different social settings: the big "I" in human "I"dentity is actually composed of multiple 'i"dentities (Hermans & Kempen, 1993; Stryker 1968). For example, Amy is certainly healthy and whole, yet her "identity" is composed of extremely different parts, each connecting her to a differing community or culture in society (e.g. gender, race, religion, nationality). Each of these "identities" may be thought of as possessing a distinct "Discourse" within an individual, as Gee (2001) writes,

> A Discourse integrates ways of talking, listening, writing, reading, acting, interacting, believing, valuing, and feeling (and using various objects, symbols, images, tools, and technologies) in the service of enacting meaningful socially situated identities and activities. (p. 719)

For example, a boy growing to become a man in the US is likely to acquire a Discourse of masculinity that influences the ways in which he acts, thinks and values, ways that are prescribed by the society or culture in which he grows (Barker & Galasinski, 2001; Connell, 1995, 2001; Lesko, 2000). Similarly, a Jewish religious Discourse is likely to be acquired through the years of growing and interacting with others in a Jewish religious community. Over time, these perspectives become a nearly imperceptible part of the "self"; they become "normal" ways of seeing the world, living life, and making sense of things within specific situations. When engaging with other people (or texts) who share that aspect of your identity, such as an "Orthodox Jewish man" talking with or reading about other Orthodox Jewish men, the individual is not as likely to realize that he is operating with specific Discourses of gender or religion; however, when encountering people, situations, or texts that operate from and within different Discourses, he is more likely to feel tension, depending upon the extent of the difference. Awareness of these specific identities at work in individuals (Gee's "Discourses") is a useful way to understand both the tensions and the potential for change that exist in a Holocaust literature classroom.

Teacher identities Generic teachers don't exist; rather, they perform specific identities that shape and reshape their literature instruction (Beach, Thein, & Parks, 2008; Burroughs, 1999; Enciso, 1997; Fine, 1995). For example, a teacher like Amy at Statistical High will find that her White, middle-class, Christian, and female identities will influence her perspectives on and perceptions of literature due to race (Johnson, 2002; Lewis, Ketter, & Fabos, 2001; Singer & Smith, 2003), gender (Lafrance, 1991; Raftery, Harford, Valiulis, & Redmond, 2007), social class (Beach, Thein, & Parks, 2008; Hicks, 2002; Jones, 2006), and religion (Grant & Gomez, 2001; Schweber & Irwin, 2003; Spector, 2007). While much may be said about the influences of each of these identities, in this chapter we limit our conversation primarily to the influences of religious identity given its scant treatment in the literature.

Ellison and Pisapia (2006) found that the vast majority of teachers engaged in Holocaust education come from Christian backgrounds, findings that are congruent with the nation's overall demographics. The influences of such teachers are likely to affect the selection of texts within the body of Holocaust literature. As noted by Schweber and Irwin (2003), Mrs. Barrett, the Christian teacher at the private Christian school, selected the *The Hiding Place* by Corrie ten Boom (1984) for her 8th grade students. The story finds the author and her family hiding Dutch Jews during the Nazi occupation of The Netherlands. Eventually caught, Corrie and her sister were sent by the Nazis to the Ravensbruck Concentration Camp where they endured starvation and miserable conditions, yet they maintained their strong faith in God.

The teacher chose this text because "it teaches us many lessons about persecution of others and about persecution that we, as Christians, may someday face" (Schweber & Irwin, 2003, p. 1700). The researchers noted that "Mrs. Barrett saw the import of the Holocaust in its relevance to her identity as a Christian, and she hoped that learning about it would bolster her students' Christian identities" (p. 1701). She could have chosen to teach her students about the history of Christian antisemitism since one of her goals was to teach "lessons about persecution of others," but she focused instead on the persecution *of* Christians, rather than persecution *by* Christians, and she taught her students that "God can give [Christians] hope in any situation" (p. 1700). Mrs. Barrett's insistence upon finding hope attenuated "the reverberations of losing and being lost" which are part of the "difficult knowledge" of the Holocaust (Britzman, 1999, p. 304).

While less overt, teacher identity commitments in public school settings also have far-reaching effects on their use of Holocaust literatures. Few states mandate the teaching of Holocaust literature, so teachers include it in their curriculum with their own outcomes in mind. For example, teachers in Illinois reported that they used such literatures because they "feel it is important" (97%) or for other personal reasons (92%) (Ellison & Pisapia, 2006, p. 11). While teachers tend to avoid incendiary topics like race, class, politics, and religion in their classrooms (Black, 2003; Glazier & Seo, 2005; Haynes & Thomas, 2001; Morrison, 1992; Weiss & Fine, 2000, 2005), it is worth noting that teachers of Holocaust literature often expect their preferred moral lessons to simply emerge from the ashes of Auschwitz, lessons that are likely to be consistent with the teacher's own norms and values. For example, Mrs. Parker's hope that her students "stand up for other people who are being persecuted for whatever reason" or Ms. France's hope that "they will see themselves in the humanity of other people" both display the type of moral lessons that teachers expect to occur. While the goals are commendable across a spectrum of religious and secular identities, the teachers settled on these lessons through some degree of religious reflection (Spector, 2007), and it shouldn't be assumed that these lessons will align with students' understanding of Holocaust events.

Spector (2005) spoke with Ms. France, the English teacher at River Hill Academy, about her silence on the historical relationship between Christianity and antisemitism in her discussions of the Holocaust. Ms. France said,

> I kind of tread lightly with the religious things because while most of my students are Baptist in upbringing, I have had like a lot of weird stuff going on, and talking about Christian antisemitism would get people on all sides riled up. (p. 126)

What is clear is that the omission of the history of antisemitism was intentional on the teacher's part. Similarly, Mr. May, the social studies counterpart to Ms. France at River Hill Academy, was unwilling to teach about the history of Christian antisemitism, saying:

> We discussed it briefly in the 20th century, but that is more a, I think, from my point of view, is more a religious thing, and I didn't necessarily want to get into all that. I did point out that a lot of people blame Jews for, ah, ah, for the killing of Christ, and it just so happened *The Passion of the Christ* was out, and um, but I did point out that technically the Jews did send him to his death, but the Romans carried it out. Some Jews objected to that. So I kind of pointed out that it was a baseless criticism of Jews. (p. 127)

His desire to try to address the spurious deicide charge is laudable, but neglecting to place the slur within the context of millennia of persecution, forced conversions, expulsions, pogroms, property seizures, and mass murder had the effect of actually shining a spot light on Jewish culpability rather than Christian persecution of Jews. The tensions born from these religious considerations are noted by Holocaust scholars such as Lucy Dawidowicz (1990) who asked,

> How do teachers who may themselves be believing Christians explain this history to children from observant Christian homes? How will parents react when their children tell them what they have learned about Christian persecution of Jews? (p. 27)

The identities of these teachers, shifting though they were, delimited the kinds of topics they were willing to teach. For Mrs. Barrett, identification with Christianity circumscribed the material she covered in class. For Ms. France and Mr. May, the choice not to teach this foundational topic was spurred by fear of engaging in religious topics in public schools, though teachers may certainly do so if remaining neutral (Black, 2003). None of these teachers taught about the history of Christian antisemitism, and as a result their students (almost entirely Christian) were not exposed to material that may have enabled them to critically examine their religious heritage in relationship to the Holocaust literature. Teachers' identities matter.

Student identities Just as generic teachers don't exist, neither do generic students; rather, they possess specific identities that shape (and reshape) their transactions with literature (Rosenblatt, 1978). Much has been written in recent years regarding the ways in which gender (e.g. Dutro, 2002), social class (e.g. Hemphill, 1999; Hull & Rose, 1990), and race (e.g. Dressel, 2003; Johnson, 2002) influence students' meaning making. For example, Johnson (1994) noted that "non-Black" students reading texts outside of their cultural experience lacked the background knowledge needed to make meaning within the text, leading to less satisfactory reading experiences with the literature. Others have noted that in the absence of prerequisite cultural knowledge students frequently place their own cultural attitudes onto the texts in order to make sense of things, which leads to negative reactions to the literature when disconnections occur (Beach, 1997; Miller & Legge, 1999; Singer & Smith, 2003). The naive belief that students will actually understand the experiences of diverse characters in literature and come to change their attitudes during these short exchanges creates false expectations regarding the value of responding to literature (Lewis, 2000).

The reading of Holocaust literature evokes students' religious identities in distinctive ways. For example, Christian students in Spector's study (2007) overwhelmingly believed that supernatural forces intervening in human activity explained the experiences of Jews in the texts. The students' religious identities created frames or lenses for understanding the narratives, including 1) forces of light and forces of darkness intervene in human affairs; 2) there is a proper way to behave that people ignore at their peril; 3) God redeems or condemns Jews through what happened at the cross. These narrative frames were not mutually exclusive but were interconnected for most students. For example, the belief in supernatural forces of good and evil was often the basis for the other meanings that students constructed. These students' interactions with Holocaust literature evoked religious identities that shaped their responses.

The influence of these identities was overt when 10th grade students in Spector's study (2005) discussed Pastor Martin Niemoeller's poem, often referred to as "First they came for the communists" because of the opening line in some versions. Ms. France, the teacher at the working-class, Black school brought the poem to class to augment the students' reading of *Night*. Here, the often invisible worlds of students' identities surface vividly.

Mallory:	You want me to explain [the Pastor Niemoeller poem]?
Ms. France:	Please.
Mallory:	'Cause I'll preach it. If you don't speak up for another person, even though they different than you, even though they take away all the other people, you the only one left, and they'll be coming for you next.
Ms. France:	[nods affirmatively]
Roderick:	You got to speak up for people. You got to speak up for people because it could be you.
Erica[3]:	I just know I wouldn't speak up for no Jews. I wouldn't speak up
for	no Jews because I'm Muslim [said quietly].
Myron:	You cruel.
Ms. France:	[To Erica] Say that again. I didn't hear you.
Erica:	I don't know.
Ms. France:	No. You said you wouldn't stand up for the Jews.
Erica:	Yeah. No. Man. God, I don't know.
Myron:	Don't use God like that!
Class:	[Erupts in commotion. Some students are angry and others are laughing.] (Spector, 2005, pp. 117-118)

As displayed in this heated discussion, the complex identities of the students must be taken into account when considering the responses evoked by Holocaust literature. To hold the notion of generic, homogeneous "students" is to leave them ill-equipped to interpret, to respond, or to discuss the ideas of the text in authentic ways. Teachers must attempt to construct new ways for students to read and engage in these texts beyond those inherent in their "brought-along" identities, as we will discuss in later pages.

The constructed nature of texts Holocaust literature is constructed by authors in specific times and places for specific purposes. The unique influences at work in the lives of the authors, their imagined audiences, and the events to which they testify make them more than just another "multicultural novel" for Amy to use in her Statistical classroom. Research on their use in the classroom, in addition to conversations amongst Holocaust scholars, gets at this complexity.

The most common Holocaust texts used in secondary classrooms are the *Diary* and *Night*. Each represents a perspective within events that took the lives of six million Jewish men, women, and children in addition to millions of others in Eastern and Western Europe. As Parsons and Totten (1993) remind educators, first-person accounts, though useful, only provide a single glimpse of the total Holocaust. For example, Anne Frank did not bring her diary with her to Westerbork, Auschwitz, and Bergen-Belsen, so she couldn't record what happened to her once she was in the grip of the Nazi death machine; the main events represented in *Night* began in the Spring of 1944 when the demise of the 12-year Third Reich was about one year away.

These texts, like all texts, represent subjective experience and memory; they were constructed from the unique positions of the writers and were influenced by considerations of their imagined audiences. For example, Seidman (1996) argued that Wiesel's Yiddish memoir *Un di velt hot geshvign* (*And the World Remained Silent)* was full of Jewish rage and was constructed to resonate with its intended audience—fellow Jews. She also noted that *Night,* arguably a different version of *Un di velt hot geshvign*, was influenced by Francois Mauriac, the Catholic Nobel Laureate who encouraged Wiesel to write the memoir. This second memoir, according to Seidman, in the original French and in later translations, was better suited for gentile audiences that would likely shy away from reading it if the burden of guilt were placed too heavily upon them as part of the world that remained silent. Novick (1999) leveled a similar critique at *Night*. He suggested that the crucifixion imagery evoked by the three doomed men on the gallows, one of whom was an innocent young boy who was depicted as a "sad-eyed angel," would clearly resonate with a majority Christian reading public that preferred a redemptive story. Wiesel denounced such critiques of his work and maintains that *Night* is a testimony of actual events (Wyatt, 2006).

The *Diary* also exists in complication. According to *The Diary of Anne Frank: The Revised Critical Edition* edited by Barnouw and van der Stroom (2003), "version a" of her diary comes from her original diary entries as she represented her life in hiding; "version b" is her retelling and editing of her original diaries which she undertook after she learned via illegal radio that wartime diaries would be in demand at war's end; finally, "version c" is the text that Otto Frank published originally in Dutch in 1947, *Het Achterhuis* (*The Secret Annex*), which was subsequently published in English as *Anne Frank: Dairy of a Young Girl* (Frank, 1952). Each version of the *Diary* appears to have been adjusted in relationship to changing audiences.

The most persistent controversy surrounding the representation of the diary centers on the Goodrich and Hackett (1956) play. The play, having made its way into textbooks and classrooms, stretches credibility in representing Anne's experience. This version imposes a somewhat happy ending for Anne's horrific tale, made famous by the repetition of the line, "I still believe that people are really good at heart" (Goodrich & Hackett, 1956, p. 174). Such a line serves as a symbol of the ways in which a widely incorporated Holocaust text may push readers to accept particular trajectories of thought. Further, as Juzwik (in press) notes in her study of a teacher's oral Holocaust narrative texts, "... narrative construals of the Holocaust pose troubling problems for teachers just as they do for writers. While narratives can shape a painful past into coherent and meaningful order, they can also over-simplify, distort, and falsify that past" (preface, p. 2).

Conclusion of complexities Amy should certainly teach Holocaust literature to her students with the hope that they will experience some sort of change. Holocaust literature's power, however, is unwittingly undermined in the previously described ways: teachers holding unrealistic expectations regarding students' moral change, the unspoken influences of teachers' and students' identities, and in the rare consideration of the constructions of these texts.

In the following paragraphs we propose classroom practices that point toward improving Amy's teaching and students' learning of Holocaust literature. Specifically, we affirm the value of providing broad historical frames, constructing a "critical" classroom space, and identifying emerging practices and possibilities for students' "change" in their engagement with the literature.

Possibilities for Teaching Holocaust Literature

Providing social and historical context A common pre-reading activity for engaging adolescents in literature is to provide information about the author and the social and historical contexts in which the author is writing, even as Amy had planned. In the teaching of Holocaust literature such exposure is not only useful but critical if students are to move beyond a single author's voice as representative of the entire Holocaust. Scholars agree that literature-based study of the Holocaust must begin with a firm grounding in the history of the events (Brabham, 1997; Kessler, 1991; Totten, 2001; Totten & Feinberg, 2001; USHMM, 2007).

Merely providing a scripted historical backdrop for the texts is rarely enough to bring about the major changes in students that so many teachers seek. For example, all of the teachers in the previously cited studies of Holocaust literature units in English classrooms provided some social and historic context for their students with little resultant change. As noted by Spector and Jones (2007), providing such historical information does not necessarily mean that students will understand Jews, the Holocaust, or this literature in ways that supersede the students' brought-along identities at work in understanding the texts. The questions raised by this seeming contradiction are these: How much historical context is enough to influence students' reading in a meaningful way? How should it be provided?

Most teachers focus on expansive and universal representations of the Holocaust in their pre-reading activities with students (cf. University of Cincinnati, 2003). Instead, teachers should seek to understand the Holocaust knowledge students bring to the classroom. Addressing the gaps, teachers present historical information to support students in gaining a more robust understanding of actors and events. For example, if using the *Diary*, place the Jewish Frank family within the assimilationist milieu of prewar Germany and the Netherlands, provide information about the Frank family, the Jews of Holland, and antisemitism in prewar and wartime Germany (Bos, 2004; Kopf, 1997; USHMM, 2007). Teachers and students may benefit from exploring brief histories of antisemitism and the Holocaust in order to place the fate of Dutch Jewry within a wider context. The purpose of presenting the historical information is to accurately contextualize the particularity of Jewish suffering.

While Ms. France did not provide her students with the history of Christian antisemitism, she did provide them with other historical background to aid their understanding. For example, one successful strategy was taking students to a local Holocaust museum, a visit that influenced the brought-along beliefs of some who were previously uncertain of the Holocaust's reality. Following that visit (and the Holocaust unit), Ms. France asked each student to write a letter to a public official that addressed an issue of both civil rights and lessons from *Night*. Several students chose to write to the docent at the museum who had discussed the Holocaust evidence (in this case, a desecrated Torah scroll, taped and "live" survivor testimonies, and other artifacts). As collected by Spector (2004), one student wrote:

> When we started our unit on the Holocaust I really didn't understand or believe the facts of the holocaust. I was afraid to believe and come to grips with the horrible way in which the Jewish people were treated. When most people were asking questions about *Night*, I was in the back of the classroom in disbelief and misunderstanding.
>
> But now, with total help to you, I understand as well as respect the Holocaust and its survivors. You made us understand with facts, items, and stories. This experience helped me relate back to Elie Wiesel's book *Night* because in his book he explained his personal experience in the concentration camps and how the Nazi's were totally against the Jewish people and their customs. (Caroline)

Though uncommon, the shift described by this student hints at the power of providing meaningful Holocaust history to contextualize Holocaust literature, here allowing a student to "relate" back to *Night*. The teacher's provision of a historical context including first-hand artifacts and survivor testimonies was significant enough to allow the student to reconsider *Night* without the "brought-along" resistance that impeded her transactions with the text and the classroom activities around it.

Historical context alone is rarely enough to prevent students from continuing in distortions or elisions of Holocaust events. The most common obstacle for students exists in the power of the "narratives" that they bring or are constructed for them in their reading of the Holocaust literature (see Barton & Levstik, 2004). Bordwell and Thompson (1990) define narrative as "a chain of events in cause-effect relationship occurring in time and space" (p. 90). Narratives of historical events (e.g. the story of the American Revolutionary War) and national narratives (e.g. the story of freedom and progress) are used to assemble what may otherwise be seen as opposing or disconnected economic, geographical, political, and ideological elements into a comprehensible whole. To construct a historical narrative is always to compose it toward some purpose. For example, stories that end with liberation or over-emphasize rescue can reinforce lessons of humanity's triumph over evil instead of reflecting our capacity for depravity (Morris, 2001). In Schweber's (2004) study of secondary students reading Holocaust literature, the teachers' framing of the texts and their narratives influenced what students purported to learn. The importance of providing historical background is an unquestioned necessity: *what* background knowledge to use and how to supply it (print, film, objects) is key given its role in creating narratives that construct "frames" of influence for students' (and teachers') meaning-making in their engagement with Holocaust literature.

Lawrence Langer emphasizes that teachers of Holocaust literature must provide both context and support for their students. His experiences teaching the Holocaust to college students led him to conclude that "the average student of Holocaust literature is unequipped by his or her background to venture into those dark corners of the concealed self" (Langer, 1998, p. 189). This attempt to understand the "concealed self" is essential in the Holocaust literature classroom thus we encourage practices of "critical literacy" in these secondary classrooms.

Critical literacy instruction A critical literacy approach to teaching Holocaust literature is more than providing historical and authorial information, giving students a book, and creating quizzes, discussions, and a final exam: "A critical literacy approach attempts to make visible the sometimes invisible narratives that guide text choice, text authorship, and text consumption, all of which work together to open up or shut down particular avenues of meaning making" (Spector & Jones, 2007, p. 38). Put another way, critical literacy includes participation "in activities or practices in which we use language, oral and written, to reflect on given words and most importantly, on their familiar relational backdrops (Freire, 1970; Weiler, 1991)" (Haas-Dyson, 2001, p. 5). This means that the critical literacy classroom will seek to address the vectors of identity previously noted: the complex intersections of teachers, students, and texts. The goal of such a classroom is to foster opportunities that may increase social justice (Lewison, Flint & van Sluys, 2002).

The critical literacy teacher will often experience confusion, uncertainty, and hostility by regularly naming (and decentering) influences of religion, race, and gender (among others) in the classroom. Suzanne Miller (1993) considered the work of ten classroom teachers who were engaged in constructing critical literacy classrooms. She concluded that the potential benefits of such approaches are great, writing:

> Taken together, these empirical investigations provide evidence that in contexts open to multiple perspectives, students can learn to respond actively, and reflect critically on different ways of speaking and knowing. In their dialogic pedagogy, teachers initiated new roles, the motivating tasks, the social purposes for talking, and they provided assistance at points of need. In the presence of sociocultural differences, they pressed for explanation, for evidence, for understanding. Over time, their students became aware of the

multiple, sometimes conflicting languages (e.g., of classes, races, genders, families, ethnic communities) for understanding. (p. 259)

Looking at teacher and student identities The construction of such a classroom begins in the teacher's consideration and open conversation surrounding the influences of his or her own identity. Jacobs (2005) describes this as the "teacher as text" approach. In his college classroom, the African-American instructor encouraged his students to study him as a text whose construction of racism as a Black teacher was influencing his interpretation of race in texts and was constructing his narrative frames in the classroom. This approach was mirrored by Parks, the teacher of a high school literature class in a study at a Midwestern high school (Beach, Thein, & Parks, 2008). Here, the teacher engaging students with multicultural texts reflected upon and spoke often of his Whiteness, maleness, and working-class background (among other identity strands) that were at play in increasing, clouding, or preventing his understanding of events in texts and classroom practices, conversations that allowed his students to consider such influences in their own lives. For a teacher like Amy at Statistical High, her overt consideration of the ways in which a Christian background may limit, increase, or subtly frame her thoughts and actions serves as an honest way to model for students how identities influence both reading and classroom practices related to Holocaust literature.

Students should also be allowed opportunities to understand how their individual identities influence reading and response. When collecting data at Adams Junior High in 2004, Spector had students consider how cultural locations of race, class, gender, religion, politics, geography, and age created a nexus of brought-along identities that pulled them to consider and interpret the Holocaust in particular ways. As a point of entry into such activities, students thought that they would likely connect with Anne Frank given their similarities in age. Students also predicted that they would likely struggle to understand much of Elie Wiesel's perspective given the differences in their religious beliefs. At a minimum, such pre-reading activities allow students to notice that their brought-along identities may find them connecting or disconnecting with certain characters, ideas or "cultures" in texts. Such activities have the potential to become the foundation for semester-long conversations around the ways that meaning is constructed in reading and classroom practices.

Three specific activities in which Parks engaged opened up space for students to explore internal and external tensions between themselves and the text worlds about which they were reading: 1) providing competing versions of the same event; 2) attending to characters' contradictory allegiances; and 3) fostering conversations between students that allowed for the displays of their discursive identities and allegiances (Beach, Thein, & Parks, 2006). Though often momentary or situational (Thein, Beach, & Parks, 2007), these discursive adjustments established opportunities for some students to make major changes, for others to amend previous Discourses—add new components to previously held beliefs, and others to briefly interrupt their traditional Discourses before reclaiming their own (Beach,

Parks, Thein, & Lensmire, 2007; Lewis, 2004; Rogers, 2004). The goal for a teacher like Amy in such a classroom is not to envision immediate life changes—"they either get it or they don't"—but to focus upon the creation of opportunities in which students find that "my understanding of the world does not make sense in this situation" (Beach, Thein, & Parks 2008, p. 115). These instances become locations of what we refer to as "micro-changes" for students.

Competing versions of the same event Spector and Jones (2007) found that students' interactions with multiple versions of the *Diary* created tensions for students that led to micro-changes in their brought-along beliefs. Early in the semester, students read the play version of the *Diary* (Goodrich & Hackett, 1956) causing *all* of them to respond positively to the idea that Anne was likely "happy" in a concentration camp. Later, Spector showed them clips from the ABC miniseries *Anne Frank: The Whole Story* (Dornheim, 2001). The clips depicted events regarding the rest of Anne's reality: Westerbork, deportation to Auschwitz, slave labor, disease, deportation to Bergen-Belsen, and ultimately the death of Margot and word of Anne's death two months before liberation. A student discussion ensued:

Munen: After seeing the movie, Anne Frank's story didn't seem so hopeful anymore. After seeing her die [The scene doesn't show Anne's death; viewers learn of it through an explanatory epilogue at the end of the movie].
Spector: Yeah, but the play version also said that she died.
Munen: Yeah, but it was kind of mentioned as an afterthought, after an hour and a half of all happy things she had done. It made everything go out on a nice, positive tone.
[...]
Tom: She dies a lice infested, sickness-filled, horrible death. Quite an ending!
Stella: People stole her food, and she kicked that person to keep her away.
Nebula: As a story, the play ended better. You didn't have to see every horrible thing she went through. But it isn't a complete picture either.
Sam: The play gives you the better side of the Holocaust, whereas the movie gives you the worse side.
Tom: There is no *better* side. No one thinks the Holocaust is good.
Spector: But all of you, I mean, all of you, wrote that she could have been happy in the concentration camp!
Class: [Everyone starts talking at once.]
Spector: Here, let me read you some. [Reading from their papers] "Anne was always upbeat and optimistic. I think no matter where she was, she'd find a reason to be happy" [Leila], or "She looks at the bright side of

everything. She probably made jokes & sang songs. She just liked to run & jump" [Annabelle].

Annabelle: It seems kind of funny now, but at the same time it is still true. In the play it was that way, but then it changed in the movie.

In this exchange, Munen articulates newfound understanding of how authors framed his construction of meaning, specifically citing that Anne's death was mentioned "after an hour and a half of all happy things she had done." When he adds that "it *made*…" a particular response emerge for students ("nice, positive") he displays an awareness of the way his previous response was heavily influenced by the authors, leading to his change in understanding. Nebula retains her brought-along preference for a sanitized ("better") version of Anne's history, though she amends her preference by acknowledging that the "better" version will not tell the "complete" story.

Later in the semester, Spector provided students with brief clips from a variety of Holocaust-related films, among them scene 26 ("Liberation") from *Life is Beautiful* (Benigni, 1997)—a fictional story of a Jewish man who successfully hid his son in slave labor camp by telling him that everything endured was part of a contest, and the one who earned the most points for hiding and enduring in the camp would win. She prefaced the clip with a plot summary, and asked students to respond to portrayals in the clip and the roles of the filmmakers in students' responses.

As expected, students thought the ending of *Life is Beautiful* was "jubilant." Charlotte wrote, "Life is good because the little boy 'won' and everyone was happy because it was liberation. The heroes were the Americans." While students acknowledged that the ending was intended to be happy, they also began to problematize this "happiness binding" (Squire, 1963) given their earlier study of the history of the Holocaust. Soon, complications emerged in the discussions, as Geoffrey noted, "I think it is horrible that someone would make a comedy about the Holocaust." Others discussed the tensions between the ways fiction or non-fiction were able to represent historical events with accuracy. Eventually, Amanda noted, "I think it's okay to have a comedy about the Holocaust, as long as you really understand that it wasn't like that or funny and laughable." Spector's use of a film [got rid of "fictional"] clip allowed students to become more critical consumers of visual texts related to the Holocaust; they were invited to consider how fiction, non-fiction, and genre "worked" with the grave subject matter. It also allowed them an opportunity to apply their growing knowledge of the history of the Holocaust: "it wasn't like that." With those words, it also allowed Amanda to practice reconciling competing ideas regarding the stark realities of the Holocaust with the pleasure she found in a fictionalized film clip: a micro-change.

Perspective taking in text worlds Teachers must work to create opportunities for students to "enter" into the "text worlds" that they study (Beach & Meyers, 2001). During Spector's 2004 data-collection and teaching of Holocaust literature at Adams Junior High School, she asked students to adopt different perspectives within the text worlds when reading the *Diary*. For example, since her students' brought-along Discourses tended to frame the story in binary categories of good and bad people, Spector had them adopt new perspectives in the text: victim, rescuer, and perpetrator; she began with sympathetic characters. In these exercises, student responses reflected a variety of small shifts. One student described her perspective as a victim:

> I was very cold, either from the weather or from fear. I can't tell the difference. I am very scared. The Nazis have come and we're all walking through the streets. It's crowded. I don't know where we're going, but we were only able to take a few things. The Nazis are mean. They point guns and shoot. I heard gunshots and cries. There was an old man walking next to me, and he leaned against a pole and they shot him.

Such a response activity requires the adoption of a new perspective and provides a space for empathetic connection, though no increased empathy is certain.

In later writing activities, students assumed the role of rescuers—those who assisted Jews, often at considerable personal risk. In this instance, an 8th grade girl considered how the text-world character lived within discursive tensions as she was pulled by competing allegiances of family and faith. The student wrote:

> It's a scary world right now. At night I hear the sounds of enemy planes over head. I do not sleep for fear of being bombed. My mother used to say, "Now Miep, all you have to do is be faithful to your church, and the Lord will keep you safe." She always said these things and I didn't agree. If she were here now she would scold me. I don't go to church, and I'm helping Jews. I'm sure she's turned against my cause, but that's another thing I can't help thinking about.

Here, the student identifies with a text character whose actions and beliefs differ from those provided by her family within the envisioned text-world. As is common with Holocaust literature, the scenario evokes a religious Discourse for the student, one that she places at the forefront. The student brings the character's religious Discourse that was acquired in her home—"all you have to do is be faithful to your church"—into the context of the lived text-world of fear, violence, and death, which results in the character's discursive shift: "I don't go to church and I'm helping Jews." That is, assuming the role of this character caught between competing external forces (family and religion) and internal forces (a need to help others live) allows the student to consider needed ideological shifts that are demanded given the new circumstances. Such activities allow students to practice and consider discursive changes in their own lives.

Finally, students were asked to assume perspectives of perpetrators: the Gestapo. Students in the course tended to demonize Hitler and those whose actions served his ends. Framing perpetrators as supernaturally evil prevented students from understanding how human beings came to behave as murderers; they failed to understand how forces other than psychosis or demonic possession might inform a perpetrator's decision to kill innocents. In this response, Elmer (8th grader at

Adams Junior High) complicated the one-dimensional image that existed early in the course, writing:

> I lay awake every night wondering why I was chosen to be in the Gestapo. I always try to tell myself that it's for my family, so I can support them. This still tears me up, killing innocent Jews I mean.

This student has left behind the previously held notion of a Gestapo agent as a non-human entity functioning in puppet-like obedience to an evil demagogue; it is a micro-shift that points toward understanding how social and cultural influences shape individuals towards desired ends. This student's response suggests a realization that it is possible for an ordinary man to willingly engage in the execution of innocents due in large part to social and cultural factors (Browning, 1992). Trying on these different perspectives, though only artificially imagined, encourages students to adjust brought-along Discourses connected to the roles of individuals and their worlds.

Discussing differences around texts Allowing students to discuss differences evoked by their readings and identities is another way of fostering "change" through the critical teaching of Holocaust literature. Although reading is a highly personal event, Bruner (1986) suggests that it can awaken one "to dilemmas, to the hypothetical, to the range of possible worlds that a text can refer to" (p. 159). In discussion of such texts, students can engage a range of text-related situations that could not occur alone. Miller (1993) describes the discussion of literature in this way: "When the text becomes a 'more general medium of communication among readers' (Rosenblatt, 1978), such discussion can reveal values, assumptions, and life experiences based in cultures or subcultures, including questioning of dominant cultural 'truths'" (p. 250). The discussion of Holocaust literature can introduce a host of opportunities for students to make meaning of textual "worlds" in relation to their own cultural identifications, which may allow them to "derive a new critical awareness of the bases for their own and others' socio-cultural perspectives" (Miller, 1993, p. 250). The challenges of discussing differences in the classroom are familiar to all classroom teachers. Teun van Dijk, et al. (1997) acknowledges that members of differing cultural groups face challenges when engaging in discussion; the greatest level of "anxiety" during these intergroup communications occurs when social or group membership differences are directly raised. The benefit of finding ways to allow students to discuss cultural and discursive differences is a key component in students' understanding their own socio-cultural influences (Scollon, 2003; Sumara, 1996).

In his multicultural literature classroom of diverse students in an urban high school, Parks (Beach, Thein, & Parks, 2008) taught students to discuss competing ideas and perspectives without engaging in personal assaults. For example, he asked students to express reactions in writing, scanned student journals for key points of difference, then created anonymous sheets that contained students' divergent (sometimes competing) interpretations and analyses. The sheet would then become an object for other students' consideration and responses. The goal of these conversations was to consider how students' different identities were shaping their responses to the literature: Why might someone hold this interpretation or view? Why might someone reject this view in whole or in part? What type of person may have written this response? Why? Again, the goal is not to change a student, but "to help students develop perspective-taking as a habit of mind through which they acknowledge, respect, understand, and possibly still disagree with alternative perspectives" (Thein, Beach, & Parks, 2007, p. 58).

To support students in overcoming the awkwardness of these conversations, Parks provided students with specific strategies that would allow them to discuss competing perspectives. One strategy, "some people might say," encouraged students to preface their statements with that phrase in order to allow controversial ideas to be discussed without an individual student claiming allegiance to such a perspective (Beach, Thein, & Parks, 2008). Over the course of time, students utilized the rhetorical device less often as they became comfortable with an environment in which differences were understood as normal and the safety of the classroom seeking intellectual growth had been established.

Such safety is not always assured, however, especially when students are engaged in unsupervised group work. Spector collected data from students at Adams Junior High who read Wiesenthal's memoir *The Sunflower* (1998), a story about a dying Nazi soldier who asked Wiesenthal to forgive him for his part in herding Jewish villagers into a building and then setting it, and them, on fire. When Jews tried to escape the burning building, they were shot. In a small group discussion, students wrestled with the question that Simon Wiesenthal posed at the end of the book: "You, who have just read this sad and tragic episode in my life, can mentally change places with me and ask yourself the crucial question, 'What would I have done?'" (p. 98). The following is an excerpt from one small group discussion:

Nebula: Alright, so what was your first reason to forgive?

Frank: I think we should forgive people because it's like right.

Nebula: I said [reading from her paper], "You must have gone through what Simon experienced to be able to say if you would forgive the SS officer. I think you would kind of have to have gone through the experience to know whether or not you would forgive because that would determine it. If you weren't Simon you couldn't say, "Yes, I would forgive," or "No, I wouldn't forgive" because you weren't put in the situation personally.

Annabelle: You should forgive because that is the way of Christ.

Ted: [In a mock, preacher voice] "Forgive! Because the Bible tells you to, my children. Obey the Lord Jesus. It's the Christ-like thing to do. Hallelujah. Hey, let's gather and pray all my brothers!"

Annabelle: That is very interesting. I wonder what your home life is like.

Nebula: Annabelle forgives for the sole purpose of God wanting you to forgive, and I can say that an argument can be made to forgive if there is a genuine recognition of guilt.

As in other examples, this excerpt shows that students' brought-along religious identities create a trajectory for meaning making. Frank uses the modal "should" to convey that he is obliged to forgive the Nazi based on some discursive influence in his life. Nebula resists the lack of authenticity in attempting to assume the text-world perspective; she isn't able to answer the question. Annabelle's Christian identity asserts the power of forgiveness in any context, regardless of her ability to fully understand Simon's situation. While Annabelle's contribution is mocked by Ted, Nebula aligns herself with Annebelle (and her words) by amending her original position to allow for forgiveness if "genuine recognition of guilt" can be found. These tensions evoked by students' competing Discourses in relationship to the text and to one another allow for micro-changes to occur, as in Nebula's willingness to take on an amended perspective out of allegiance to a classmate, something that she was unwilling to let the text do on its own.

As students negotiate tensions like these, some will cling more tightly to the norms within specific Discourses that they've brought along, others will amend aspects of their previous Discourses to accommodate the new situations or evidence, and some will let go of the old ways of thinking in favor of new (Beach, Thein, & Parks, 2008). The goal for a teacher like Amy in creating large or small group encounters is not to expect that change looks a certain way, but to create possibilities for students to experience micro-changes that exist in the tensions in the text-world, the text-world/lived-world interaction, and the lived-world/lived-world display of identities brought about by classroom conversations around texts.

Application to "lived worlds" The power of Holocaust literature is seen clearly when students take the tensions that they experience in the text world and allow them to influence their lived world Discourses. In this response, Marie, an 8th grade girl reading *Night,* considered how the views that she brought into the classroom are inconsistent with those emerging in the text world. In this response, she told Hernandez (2004) how everyday death in the concentration camps led to the construction of a different morality. She said,

> Wiesel talks about how wrong it was to take things from those who were still living, but it was perfectly OK to take things from the dead. In our society, we consider stealing from the dead grave robbing. But in Auschwitz, it meant life. If someone died and had extra food in their pocket, or a better pair of shoes, or even a uniform, they certainly weren't going to use it, so you take it, or you take it and give it to someone who can use it. I'm not saying that it's ethical to steal from the dead, but if it means your life, I guess you have to. (p. 179)

In this situation, the student "amends" her previously held notion of a universal morality; that is, she keeps it intact, "I'm not saying that it's ethical to steal from the dead," but adds to it based on the new situation within the text-world: "but if it means your life, I guess you have to." Such amendments support students in understanding how values and norms embedded in specific Discourses may be situated and rooted within particular times, places, and allegiances.

In another instance with a tenth grade student at River Hill (Spector, 2007), Keniya, discussed how her reading of Night caused her to rethink her view of God. She explained this text-induced tension during an interview, "It just don't make sense. No sense at all. God is good. I know that. The Holocaust horror, hell on earth, is bad. How both are true? But they are. It's a paradox" (p. 43).

Keniya's thoughts were echoed by Sydney, an 8th grade student at the primarily White, middle-class school who responded to *Night* in her journal, writing:

> Why isn't God stopping the Nazis or, in our case, the terrorists? It makes me question my faith. As I read this book some questions came to mind. How did God let the Holocaust happen? This book is so disturbing, I think that I am going to be ill.

Students travel with text-world characters in their physical and discursive journeys. When Elie Weisel in *Night* cannot fathom how his brought-along view of God is consistent with the horrors he experiences, students accompany him. When the book is closed, students are left to reconcile their own religious identities with their text-world experiences. In the first case, Keniya fully articulates her previously held view—"God is good"—alongside the truth evoked by *Night*—"the Holocaust horror, hell on earth, is bad"—leading to a hybrid or amended religious Discourse in which paradoxical thinking about God is required: a micro-change. In the second, Sydney reconsiders her previously held view related to God's ongoing involvement in the affairs of humanity. The tension for her appears as she considers the Holocaust and contemporary events of US horrors—"the terrorists." Ultimately, she struggles to entertain these seeming contradictions, able to express them as a "question" in relationship to her faith; micro-changes have taken place in these students' thinking, meaning-making, and perhaps in their lives.

CONCLUSION

In this chapter we have explored complications and possibilities related to teaching Holocaust literature with adolescents in the US. We have challenged the cause and effect assumptions of teachers regarding the literature's ability to "change" students in particular ways; we have identified numerous tensions that arise when reading the "literature of atrocity" (Langer, 1975, p. xii) in secondary schools, including the power of teachers' and students' identities, and the complex constructions of the texts themselves. We then explored opportunities that exist for reconfiguring classroom practices in ways likely to improve teaching and learning Holocaust literature, including deep, targeted teaching of Holocaust history that will support students in exploring their brought-along Discourses; the construction of a critical classroom that openly considers the influences of identities in teachers and students; and a variety of emerging practices that encourage us to reconceptualize student change. Specifically, we encourage opportunities for students to try on new perspectives, to examine the social and cultural forces that influence characters in text worlds, and to discuss their ideas with other students in ways that allow for competing views to coexist. The goal in these practices is to encourage generative tensions that may lead to changes in students; occasionally these changes are large, but more often they appear as a series of "micro-changes" which foster flexibility in thinking. These types of changes are likely to produce effects in students long after the teacher and researcher are gone.

We encourage Amy to bring Holocaust literature to Statistical students. As she does, we hope she realizes the tensions at work within the classroom: Holocaust meaning emerges from the intersections of unique teachers, unique texts, unique readers, and the Discourses embedded in each of them. Is the work complicated? Yes. Essential? Yes. As Elie Wiesel, cited in Landau's *The Nazi Holocaust* (1994) noted, "The Holocaust defies literature...We think we are describing an event, we transmit only its reflection...Still, the story had to be told. In spite of all the risks, all possible misunderstandings. It needed to be told for the sake of our children" (p. 3).

NOTES

[1] Because of the many versions of Anne Frank's diary, we will refer to it simply as "the *Diary*" unless we are indicating a particular version. The Goodrich and Hackett version is the stage play that opened on Broadway in 1956.

[2] We are not considering the evaluation studies of published curricula like *Facing History and Ourselves* (Strom & Parsons, 1983).

[3]Two students in Spector's (2005) study chose the pseudonym "Erica." The Erica of this interchange was the only Muslim student of the 126 participants.

REFERENCES

Barker, C., & Galinski, D. (2001). *Cultural studies and discourse analysis.* Thousand Oaks, CA: Sage.

Barnouw, D., & van der Stroom, G. (Eds.). (2003). In A. J. Pomerans, B. M. Mooyaart-Doubleday, & S. Massotty (Trans.), *The diary of Anne Frank: The revised critical edition.* Prepared by the Netherlands Institute for War Documentation. New York: Doubleday.

Barton, K. C., & Levstik, L. (2004). *Teaching history for the common good.* Mahwah, NJ: Erlbaum.

Beach, R. (1997). Students' resistance to engagement with multicultural literature. In T. Rogers & A. O. Soter (Eds.), *Reading across cultures: Teaching literature in a diverse society* (pp. 69–94). New York: Teachers College Press.

Beach, R., & Myers, J. (2001). *Inquiry-based English instruction: Engaging students in literature and life*. New York: Teachers College Press.

Beach, R., Thein, A., & Parks, D. (2006). Students experience of dialogic tensions in responding to multicultural literature. In J. V. Hoffman, et al. (Eds.), *55th yearbook of the national reading conference.* Oak Creek, Wisconsin: NRC.

Beach, R., Thein, A., & Parks, D. (2008). *High school students competing social worlds: Negotiating identities and allegiances in response to multicultural literature.* London: Erlbaum Publishers.

Beach, R., Parks, D. Thein, A., & Lensmire, T. (2007). Working class high school students' discussions of affirmative-action. In J. Van Galen & G. Noblit (Eds.), *Late to class: Social class & schooling in the new economy* (pp. 141–166). Albany: SUNY Press.

Benigni, R. (Director). (1997). *Life is beautiful* [Motion picture]. US: Miramax.

Black, (2003). Teaching about religion. *American School Board Journal, 190*, 50.

Bordwell, D., & Thompson, K. (1990). *Film art: An introduction.* New York: McGraw-Hill.

Bos, P. (2004). Reconsidering Anne Frank: Teaching the Diary in its historical and cultural context. In M. Hirsch & I. Kacandes (Eds.), *Teaching the representation of the Holocaust*, (pp. 348–359). New York: Modern Language Association.

Brabham, B. (1997). Holocaust education: Legislation, practices, and literature for middle school students. *The social studies, 88*(3), 139–142.

Britzman, D. (1999). "Dimensions of a lonely discovery": Anne Frank and the question of pedagogy. In J. Robertson (Ed.), *Teaching for a tolerant world, Grades K-6: Essays and resources*. Urbana, IL: NCTE.

Browning, C. (1992). *Ordinary men: reserve police battalion 101 and the final solution in Poland*. New York: Harper Collins

Bruner, J. (1986). *Acts of meaning*. Cambridge, MA: Harvard University Press.

Burroughs, R. (1999). From the margins to the center: Integrating multicultural literature into the secondary English curriculum. *Journal of curriculum and supervision, 14*(2), 136–155.

Connell, R.W. (1995). *Masculinities*. Sydney: Allen & Unwin.

Connell, R.W. (2001). *The Men and the boys*. Sydney: Allen & Unwin.

Danks, C., & Rabinsky, L. B. (Eds.). (1999). *Teaching for a tolerant world*. Urbana, IL: NCTE.

Dawidowicz, L. S. (1990). How they teach the Holocaust. *Commentary, 9*(6), 25–32.

Donnelly, M. B. (2006). Educating students about the Holocaust: A survey of teaching practices. *Social Education, 70*(1), 51–54.

Dornheim, R. (Director). (2001). *Anne Frank: The whole story*. ABC Miniseries [Videorecording]. New York: ABC.

Dressel, J. H. (2003). *Teaching and learning about multicultural literature: Students reading outside their culture in a middle school classroom*. Newark, DE: International Reading Association.

Dutro, E. (2002). "But that's a girls' book!" Exploring gender boundaries in children's reading practices. *The Reading Teacher, 55*(4), 376–84.

Ellison, J., & Pisapia, J. (2006). The state of Holocaust education in Illinois. *Idea Journal, 11*(1). Retrieved September 10, 2007, from http://www.ideajournal.com/articles.php?id=41

Enciso, P. (1997). Negotiating the meaning of difference. In *Reading across cultures: Teaching literature in a diverse society* (pp. 13–41). New York: Teachers College Press.

Fallace, T. D. (2006). The origins of Holocaust education in American public schools. *Holocaust and Genocide Studies, 20*(1), 80–102.

Fine, M. (1995). *Habits of mind*. San Francisco: Jossey-Bass.

Frank, A. (1952). In B. M. Mooyaart (Trans.), *The Diary of a Young Girl*. New York: Doubleday.

Frank, A. (2001). In O. H. Frank, M. Pressler, & S. Massotty (Eds. & Trans.), *The diary of a young girl: The definitive edition*. New York: Doubleday.

Gee, J. P. (2001). Reading as situated language: A sociocognitive perspective. *Journal of Adolescent & Adult Literacy, 44*, 714–725.

Geertz, C. (1979). *Meaning and order in Moroccan society: Three essays in cultural analysis*. Cambridge, England: Cambridge University Press.

Glanz, J. (1999). Ten suggestions for teaching the Holocaust. *The History Teacher, 3*(4), 547–565.

Glazier, J., & Seo, J. A. (2005). Multicultural literature and discussion as mirror and window? *Journal of Adolescent & Adult Literacy, 48*(8), 686–700.

Goodrich, F., & Hackett, A. (1956). *The diary of Anne Frank*. New York: Random House.

Grant, C. A., & Gomez, M. L. (2001). *Campus and classroom: Making schooling multicultural*. Upper Saddle River, NJ: Merrill/Prentice.

Haas-Dyson, A. (2001). Relational sense and textual sense in a U.S. urban classroom: The contested case of Emily, girl friend of a Ninja. In B. Comber & A. Simpson (Eds.), *Negotiating critical literacies in classrooms* (pp. 3–18). Mahwah, NJ: Erlbaum.

Haynes, C. C., & Thomas, O. (2001). *Finding common ground: A guide to religious liberty in public schools*. Nashville, TN: First Amendment Center.

Hemphill, L. (1999). Narrative style, social class, and response to poetry. *Research in the Teaching of English, 33*(3), 275–302.

Hermans, H., & Kempen, H. (1993). *The dialogic self: Meaning as movement.* San Diego, CA: Academic Press.

Hernandez, A. A. (2004). *Voices of witness, messages of hope: Moral development theory and transactional response in a literature-based Holocaust studies curriculum.* Unpublished doctoral dissertation, Ohio State University.

Hicks, D. (2002). *Reading lives: Working-class children and literacy learning.* New York: Teachers College Press.

Hull, G., & Rose, M. (1990). This wooden shack place: The logic of an unconventional reading. *College Composition and Communication, 41*, 287–298.

Jacobs, W. (2005). *Speaking the lower frequencies: Students and media literacy.* Albany: SUNY Press.

Johnson, C. (1994). Participatory rhetoric and the teacher as racial/gendered subject. *College English, 56*(4), 409–419.

Johnson, L. (2002). "My eyes have been opened": White teachers and racial awareness. *Journal of Teacher Education, 53*, 153–167.

Jones, S. (2006). *Girls, social class, & literacy: What teachers can do to make a difference.* Portsmouth, NH: Heinemann.

Juzwik, M. M. (in press). *The Rhetoric of teaching: Understanding the dynamics of Holocaust narratives in an English classroom.* Cresskill, NJ: Hampton.

Kessler, K. (1991). Teaching holocaust literature. *The English Journal, 80*(7), 29–32.

Klein, G. (1995). *All but my life.* New York: Hill and Wang.

Kopf, H. R. (1997). *Understanding Anne Frank's* The Diary of a young girl*: A student casebook to issues, sources, and historical documents.* Westport, CT: Greenwood.

Lafrance, M. (1991). School for scandal: Different educational experiences for females and males. *Gender & Education, 3*(1), 3–13.

Landau, R. (1994). *The nazi Holocaust.* London: Tauris.

Langer, L. (1975). *The Holocaust and the literary imagination.* New Haven: Yale University Press.

Langer, L. (1998). *Preempting the Holocaust.* New Haven, CT: Yale University Press.

Lesko, N. (1999). *Masculinities at school.* Thousand Oaks, CA: Sage.

Levi, P. (1993). *Survival in Auschwitz: The nazi assault on humanity.* New York: Collier.

Lewis, C. (2000). Limits of identification: The personal, pleasurable, and the critical in reader response. *Journal of Literacy Research, 32*(2): 253–266.

Lewis, C., Ketter, J., & Fabos, B. (2001). Reading race in a rural context. *Qualitative Studies in Education, 14*(3), 317–350.

Lewis, C. (2004). Resituating the self: The pedagogic possibilities of critical discourse analysis. Paper presented at the Critical Discourse Analysis Conference, Indiana University.

Lewison, M., Flint, A., & Sluys K. (2002). Taking on critical literacy: The journey of newcomers and novices. *Language Arts, 79*(5), 382–392.

Lipstadt, D. E. (1995). Not facing history: How not to teach the Holocaust. *The New Republic, 6,* 26–29.

Meisel, E. (1982). "I don't want to be a bystander: literature and the Holocaust." *English Journal 71*(5), 40–44.

Miller, S. (1993). Why a dialogic pedagogy? In S. Miller & B. ScCaskill (Eds.), *Multicultural literature and literacies: making space for difference* (pp. 247–265). Albany: SUNY Press.

Miller, S., & Legge, S. (1999). "Supporting possible worlds: Transforming literature teaching and learning through conversation in the narrative mode." *Research in the Teaching of English, 34*(1), 10–65.

Morris, M. (2001). *Curriculum and the Holocaust.* Mahwah, NJ: Lawrence Erlbaum.

Morrison, T. (1992). *Playing in the dark: Whiteness and the literary imagination.* Cambridge, MA: Harvard University Press.

Novick, P. (1999). *The Holocaust in American life*. Boston: Houghton Mifflin.

Parsons, W., & Totten, S. (1993). *Guidelines for teaching about the Holocaust.* Washington, DC: United States Holocaust Memorial Museum.

Raftery, D., Harford, J., Valiulis, M., & Redmond, J. (2007). "What's comin up in the exam?" A survey of teachers and the delivery of gender-balanced curriculum. *Irish Education Studies, 26*(1), 107–117.

Rochman, H. (1998). Should you teach Anne Frank: The Diary of A Young Girl? *Book Links, 7*(5), 45–49.

Rogers, R. (2004). *An introduction to critical discourse analysis in education.* Mahwah, NJ: Lawrence Erlbaum.

Rosenblatt, L. (1978). *The Reader, the text, the poem: The transactional theory of the literary work.* Carbondale, IL: Southern Illinois University Press.

Schweber, S. (2004). *Making sense of the Holocaust: Lessons from classroom practice*. New York: Teachers College Press.

Schweber, S. (2006). "Holocaust fatique" in teaching today. *Social Education, 70*(1), 44–50.

Schweber, S., & Irwin, R. (2003). "Especially special": Learning about Jews in a fundamentalist Christian school. *Teachers College Record, 105*(9), 1693–1719.

Scollon, S. (2003). Political and somatic alignment: Habitus, ideology and social practice. In G. Weiss & R. Wodak (Eds.), *Critical discourse analysis: Theory and interdisciplinarity* (pp. 167–198). New York: Palgrave.

Seidman, N. (1996). Elie Wiesel and the scandal of Jewish rage. *Jewish Social Studies, 3*, 1–19.

Singer, J. Y., & Smith, S. A. (2003). The potential of multicultural literature: Changing understanding of self and others. *Multicultural perspectives, 5*(2), 17–23.

Spector, K. (2005). *Framing the Holocaust in English class: Secondary teachers and students reading Holocaust literature*. Unpublished doctoral dissertation, University of Cincinnati.

Spector, K. (2007). God on the gallows: Reading the Holocaust through narratives of redemption. *Research in the Teaching of English, 42*(1), 7–55.

Spector, K., & Jones, S. (2007). Constructing Anne Frank: Critical literacy in an 8th grade English classroom. *Journal of Adolescent & Adult Literacy, 51*(1), 36–48.

Spielberg, S. (Director). (1993). *Schindler's list* [Motion picture]. US: Universal Studios.

Spiegelman, A. (1986). *Maus: A survivor's tale, I: My father bleeds history.* New York: Pantheon Books.

Spiegelman, A. (1991). *Maus: A survivor's tale, II: And here my troubles began.* New York: Pantheon Books.

Squire, J. R. (1963). *The responses of adolescents to four short stories*. Urbana, IL: NCTE.

Strom, M. S. & Parsons, W. (1983). *Facing history and ourselves: The Holocaust and human behavior.* Brookline, MA: FHAO.

Stotsky, S. (1999). Academic and pedagogical issues in teaching the Holocaust. In C. Danks & L. B. Rabinsky (Eds.), *Teaching for a tolerant world,* (pp. 194–217). Urbana, IL: NCTE.

Stryker, S. (1968). Identity theory and role performance. *Journal of Marriage and the Family, 30*, 558–564.

Sumara, D. (1996). *Private readings in public*. New York: Peter Lang.

Teichman, M. (1976). Literature of agony and triumph: An encounter with the Holocaust. *College English, 37*(6), 613–618.

ten Boom, C. (1984). *The hiding place*. New York, Bantam.

Thein, A, Beach, R., & Parks, D. (2007). Perspective taking as transformative practice in teaching multicultural literature to white students. *English Journal, 97*(2), 54–60.

Totten, S. (2001). *Teaching Holocaust literature*. Boston: Allyn and Bacon.

Totten, S., & Feinberg, S. (2001). *Teaching and studying the Holocaust.* Boston: Allyn and Bacon.

United States Holocaust Museum and Memorial. (2007). Teaching resources: Guidelines for teaching the Holocaust. Retrieved September 20, 2007, from http://www.ushmm.org/education/foreducators/teachabo/part_2.pdf

University of Cincinnati Evaluation Services Center. (2003). *An assessment of Holocaust education in Ohio, Indiana, and Kentucky*. Cincinnati: University of Cincinnati Evaluation Services Center.
Van Dijk, T., Ting-Toomey, S., Smitherman, G., & Troutman, D. (1997). Discourse, ethnicity, culture and racism. In T. van Dijk (Ed.), *Discourse as social interaction* (pp. 144–180). Thousand Oaks, CA: Sage.
Wegner, G. (1998). "What lessons are there from the Holocaust for my generation today?" Perspectives on civic virtue from middle school youth. *Journal of Curriculum and Supervision*, *13*(2), 167–183.
Weiss, L., & Fine, M. (2000). *Construction sites: Excavating race, class, and gender among urban youth*. New York: Teachers College.
Weiss, L., & Fine, M. (2005). *Beyond silenced voices: Class, race, and gender in United States schools*. Albany: State University of New York Press.
Wiesel, E. (1978). Why I write. In A.H. Rosenfeld & I. Greenberg (Eds.), *Confronting the Holocaust: The impact of Elie Wiesel*. Bloomington, IN: Indiana University Press.
Wiesel, E. (1982). *Night*. New York: Bantam.
Wiesenthal, S. (1998). *The sunflower: On the possibilities and limits of forgiveness*. New York: Schoken Books.
Wyatt, E. (2006, January 17). Next book for Oprah is 'Night' by Wiesel. *The New York Times*, p. E1.

Daryl Parks
Metropolitan State University Minnesota

Karen Spector
University of Alabama

TIBBI DUBOYS

AN EDUCATOR'S VIEW OF RESISTANCE

INTRODUCTION

This chapter stems from my belief, not shared by all educators, that some core aspects of the Holocaust can and should be taught to elementary age pupils. Of the many topics to which we might expose children, I introduce important materials for teaching about Jewish resistance to the Nazi project of mass murder. This essay also presents a greatly expanded understanding of resistance. In the face of a total assault on Jewish existence, I view every struggle to maintain life, individual or organized, spiritual or armed, successful or not, as an act of resistance. It seems to me all but collaborators may be considered resisters in one or another way. *In extremis*, I view even suicide as an act of resistance.

I invite teachers to consider, to question, and to formulate what they think is appropriate for their classrooms. Many of the following examples might be used for lessons in middle and secondary schools. Some, but not all topics in this chapter are suitable for children in childhood education classrooms.

The Holocaust is perhaps the most widely documented complex of events in human history. The enormity and complexity of the time interests scholars from a variety of disciplines, who continue to uncover and interpret new materials, and to create an expanding literature. Teachers cannot possibly read all that has been written about many topics, and our knowledge of the events about which we teach is necessarily partial. Nevertheless, teaching despite partial and inconsistent knowledge is a risk all teachers take on. It is not our goal, however, to present exhaustive magisterial knowledge. Our purpose is more limited and more useful: to expose pupils to important aspects of human experience and encourage them to think with us about some of many questions that we might raise. Even very young children can understand some issues and problems embedded in the Holocaust, and thereby enrich their growing understanding of the world.

I intend this essay neither to delineate all relevant material nor to replace the comprehensive scope, rigorous attention to narrative detail, and analytic precision that are the hallmarks of historians and other social scientists. The interested reader will find a rich literature, and the bibliography points to some major works that respond to such interests. My professional expertise is in teaching and teacher education, and I thus present an approach and raise questions designed to help teachers, including teachers of young children. The focus here is on resistance for its intrinsic importance and interest. I present some stories and events, and examples of questions that invite children to think and talk about the materials in ways that connect with concrete experiences they may have had.

T. Duboys (ed.), Paths to Teaching the Holocaust, 143–164.

Context and Curriculum

Effective educators are mindful of the context of the events about which they teach. Knowledge is complex, and not everything about a topic can or should be discussed with elementary aged children. As creators of curriculum, we know which events preceded those taught in today's lesson, and those to follow tomorrow. We know more than what we present within a given lesson or topic, and how to continue to add to our own knowledge. Teachers of young children are thoughtful about what is taught, and more particularly, about how and when to teach it. We know that material in the future will add to the body of knowledge to which children have already been exposed, creating an ever widening spiral. We know that teaching young children about gas chambers and crematoria would be inappropriate. Our aim, after all, is to educate, not to terrorize.

To their deaths like lambs to the slaughter?

Wherever people are oppressed and victimized, they are likely to attempt to subvert the aims of the enemy. Some efforts might be large and require the collaboration and coordination of numbers of people, such as seen in the 1943 Warsaw Ghetto Uprising (Krall, 1986; Gutman, 1994; Kurzman, 1976) and the November 1944 destruction of crematorium No. 4 in Auschwitz (Rees, 2005; Miller, 2000; Nomberg-Pryztyk, 1985). The work of partisans is another example of sensitive and exacting collaboration. These and other acts of resistance will be discussed in greater detail below.

Abba Kovner, 25 years old in 1942, was Russian-born and educated in a Hebrew high school in Vilna, now called Vilnius. He is generally named the first person to have called for Jewish armed resistance, and urged people "do not go like lambs to slaughter," words he adapted from Jeremiah 51:40. He and some others hid in a Dominican convent, and when they returned to the Vilna ghetto learned that nearly 20,000 people had been murdered in the nearby Ponar woods.

He was a Zionist and formed alliances in the ghetto with Communists, Bundists and others, in an attempt to find a critical mass of young people willing to take up arms. Many partisans were young people, because they could better withstand the ravages of sustained starvation. They were also able to envision a future beyond being hunted, enslaved and murdered. In leaving their families they were making choices that were both deep and painful. They could stay with their community, and, they thought, die with them, or they could strike out with others and attempt to save at least some people.

Ultimately they were not able to rise up in Vilna, and those who supported armed struggle went to the Rudnicki woods to join other partisans under the command of Jurgis, the Soviet commander in the Vilna area. About 600 partisans from Vilna, Kovno, and the surrounding areas, were divided into four groups. What was not known at the time was that Jurgis was the nom de guerre of Israel Zieman, a Jewish member of the Communist Party, and a teacher before the war. He hid his Jewish identity in the forest, because Jews and Jewish partisan groups were sometimes set upon by local nationalists who were also antisemitic (Mais, ed, 2007). Jews were more likely than other partisans to be robbed of their weapons, and were sometimes killed (Draegner, 1996, p.25). For Jews, it was a war within a war.

The image of Jews going to their deaths like sheep to slaughter sometimes stems from opinions formed without knowledge of the context of events. Consider the fact that relatively small numbers of armed Nazi soldiers rounded up residents of a given town. Why were they not overpowered by people who outnumbered those who would conquer them? It is possible to answer that, like lambs, they responded passively; that like lambs they did not know they were about to be killed. Lambs willingly move along together. Lambs do not know the meaning of slaughter or death. Embedded in such a conclusion is the implied assertion of the observer's superior intelligence. The behavior of the lambs was foolish, we think, and perhaps willingly compliant with those who led them to their deaths. Many people, even those of good will, seem unaware of the implications of their judgments. Not only is the judgement being made in the safety of our present environment, we may be unaware we are blaming victims for their own misfortune. We do not, commonly, do so with the humility that is necessary to acknowledge we have only approximate awareness of those events. Such judgements do not take into account the cultural imperatives of either the victims or their oppressors. Many of us have not been victims of hunger, humiliation, of an attempt to denigrate our identities and self-image and to threaten our very existence. We have not had to look back upon our former lives as having taken place in the halcyon days. Perhaps many of us have not heard the deafening noises of war. Most of us have not known occupation by a foreign government. Since most of us have not been in a situation in which our towns have been occupied by outside forces, have we thought about the initial shock of such a takeover? Can any of us predict that the fourth action we take will entangle us more deeply than our third action? The theft, destruction of property, violence and murder of people were unprecedented in scale. Did victims have the information they needed to have behaved differently? To make informed decisions? Do we know if we are correct in our conclusions? If people responded to authority as law abiding citizens, can we conclude they did so willingly?

Raul Hilberg's early work (1961) offers an instructive example. Many people thought his work blamed Jews for complicity with their Nazi oppressors. Some of his readers interpreted his work to confirm their perception that Jews went to death like lambs. However, his work, eventually recognized as authoritative, was about the nature of bureaucracy, and the degree to which murderous actions took place under the cover of its authority. The essence of bureaucracy is the creation of rules. With rules in place, many Jews, like any other citizens, complied with what was requested of them without knowing it would ultimately lead to their death. To learn more about the Holocaust is to see ways in which victims were drawn into the destruction, and as participants, some people conclude their responses were compliant, which would render them, like lambs, unable to think.

Another episode in which Jews became entangled in putting forward National Socialist practices and policies is seen in the well-organized night of terror that took place in Germany on November 9-10, 1938. That night became known as Kristallnacht, after the extensive amount of broken storefront glass that littered many streets in Germany. In October of 1938, many Jews who had immigrated to Germany found themselves stateless. Their status in Germany was no longer recognized, even, in some cases, stripped of the German citizenship they had acquired. Their countries of origin sometimes would not take them back, and with their lapsed passports they became stateless persons. Henryk Grynszpan, a 17-year-old son of Polish immigrants who had gone to Paris to study art, was enraged by the imposed statelessness of his parents. He went to the German embassy hoping to kill their Ambassador to France. Instead he encountered Ernst vom Rath, the 3rd Attache at the Embassy. Grynszpan shot him, and vom Rath succumbed two days later.

Goebbels, the Minister of Propaganda in Germany saw in this the occasion to unleash a carefully orchestrated eruption of violence that, up to that point, was the largest single act of destruction against Jews (Thalmann & Feinermann, 1974). Simultaneously, and throughout Germany, synagogues and Jewish businesses were vandalized, set afire and destroyed. Several thousand Jews were arrested and beaten and more than 90 Jews were killed. Fire fighters and police stood idly by while the destruction was taking place. The next day, glass and material goods littered the streets of cities throughout Germany.

Two days later, on November 12, Hermann Goering, another man highly placed in the Third Reich, called a meeting in which he declared Jews responsible for the destructive acts. While the synagogues were of no consequence to the Reich, the material goods lost or destroyed were needed by the German economy. Therefore, he decided to fine Jews in the amount a billion marks and he demanded that monies collected from insurance companies be turned over to the German government as well. In addition, Jews were forced to clean the mess created by the destruction. The Jews thus compelled to clean the debris were mostly workers or owners of the destroyed shops. Nevertheless, sometimes, the mere fact they were Jews was sufficient reason to force them to participate in the cleanup.

The topic of resistance in France is especially complex, as part of France was politically connected to Germany shortly after the war began by setting up a collaborationist government in Vichy. It should be noted, however, that Grynszpan was not turned over to Germany until 1940 and through a series of bizarre events, he is presumed to have been killed, but his fate is still unknown with certainty.

Individual Acts of Resistance

Although some scholars (Bauer1978, 1982) might not agree, I believe the very struggle to remain alive is an act of resistance. Personal resistance includes maintaining memory and connection to previously lived experience (Karmel, 1969; DeSilva, 1996). Such resistance, found in ghettos and camps, attempted to preserve and strengthen the dignity and humanness that were persistently threatened by oppressors. People who lost close family and friends sometimes formed relationships with others as a way of staying connected to people. When families were no longer alive to care and communicate, friends and especially those who shared similar experiences became most important. Connections with others in such circumstances might involve telling stories of personal histories

(Gotfryd, 2001; Jackson, 1980) hopes and aspirations, and even humor in the most horrifying environments (Lipman, 1991).

Escape as a Form of Resistance

Sometimes people tried to resist by attempting to escape from ghettos or camps. They might separate themselves from their work details in their marches to or from their slave labor sites. While some were successful, most were not. Often a bullet shot by a guard would kill them instantly. Sometimes they were not shot, but captured and beaten to death in the presence of camp inmates forced to witness the murder, and sometimes, to perform the beating (Langbein, 1996; Ka' tzetnik, 1955, 1963).

Few members of my family survived, but the tale of my uncle Herman bears telling. Before the war, he owned a photography shop in a small city not far from Lvov. When the ghetto in Lvov was liquidated, he, my aunt and a niece were taken to the Janowska Road Camp that was not far from the city. My uncle became the "camp photographer" and was convincing in his argument he could do his best work if he had two workers whose specialties might enhance his photos and help him be more productive. Thus, he was able to save his wife and his niece. He photographed some key personnel of the camp as instructed, and when undetected, took a variety of photos that might have cost his life had they been discovered. He took pictures of a kind of steamroller that crushed the bones of heaps of dead people, to flatten the pile into which they'd been tossed. He took a photo of a man, not yet dead, whose skin was being removed from his body.

One day, he was told to go into town to get the supplies he needed for his work. He was unaccompanied, and used the opportunity to get a shovel, and to break off the stem and handle. When he returned to camp, the supplies he had gone for were searched. Fortunately, his person was not searched, and he was able to carry the spoon of the shovel into the camp, tucked into his armpit. He began to dig under the electrified fence, but found he was too weak and emaciated to accomplish very much. He was in his thirties at the time. He found a young man, new to the camp, who had not yet lost much weigh and was stronger. My uncle told him of his plan to escape, and to take some others with him. The young man (whose name was never told to me) would be included if he were willing to dig an escape route under the fence. When the mission was completed at last, my uncle had my aunt and cousin go to the men's barracks that night. He made sure to plan their escape at the new moon, because it offered the cover of darkness. Sixteen men and two women left the camp. Some were immediately set upon by the guard dogs and killed instantly. A few others, unfamiliar with their surroundings, went in circles, and decided to return to the camp where they too were murdered. At the time of their liberation in 1944, my relatives and three of the men who had escaped with them were the only members of that group still alive. My uncle had buried some glass negatives that were in use at the time, and developed the pictures later. Several albums of his work are now in the collection of the United States Holocaust Memorial Museum in Washington, D.C. and in other places as well (Herman Lewinter 1996; Unpublished conversation).

Suicide as an Act of Resistance

It is not my intention to present a view of suicide as an act of resistance universally. I offer this argument within the context of the Holocaust and other genocides. I well understand and empathize with a person who might choose to die under such conditions.

Some people who could not continue to endure the tortures they had to undergo, committed suicide, which I view as an act of resistance for two reasons. It gave the person control over her or his life in a setting in which the prisoners had little. In addition, it thwarted the possibility of further inhumane treatment to which they had been subjected.

Even in such final decisions, available means were limited. In ghettoes, where people had been stripped of most personal belongings, some people had access to such items as cyanide capsules which they carried about on their persons, and used when they no longer saw hope for themselves. In concentration or work camps, some decided to end their lives by running toward the electrified fences that surrounded the camps. Some died of gunshot wounds delivered by a guard even before they reached the fences.

Some camp inmates became Mussulmen, the camp word for those who no longer tried to keep themselves clean, who no longer felt the intense hunger so prominent in the memory of those who survived such places of cruelty, illness and death (Levi, 1973). Mussulmen (Frister, 1999) developed distended abdomens and vacant stares that marked them as the living dead. Those with such an appearance would, others recognized, die in a very short time, since they had given up hope and the struggle to survive. They were more vulnerable than others, since they stopped listening to the orders and commands upon which their lives depended, and were thus more likely to commit an infraction for which they might be killed. They seemed to have opted out of existence. I do not know if that was the result of a conscious choice.

It was one of the central goals of the Nazis to turn Jews into objects of humiliation, torture and annihilation. In committing suicide people reclaimed themselves as subjects, not objects, and became the authors of how and when they would die.

Religious or Spiritual Resistance

Some people who were religiously observant tried to continue ritual practice even in environments that forbade such observance. (Eliach, 1988, pp13-15). There are stories of people who scooped out the inside of a potato, and used threads from their own sparse clothing to fashion a wick, thus creating the semblance of a Chanukah candle. Yet others would forego their meager rations on the Day of Atonement, when fasting is part of one's obligation of observance. Sometimes that was the only way in which they could observe, since long periods of prayer were not possible on a day that might consist of 12 hours of work. (Langbein, 1994). It is more than a little ironic that Jews in camps, who were never given enough food to keep them alive for very long, were sometimes severely punished if they chose not to eat that food on a particular day. Eliach, 1988, pp.103-105).

Cultural Resistance

Famous examples of cultural resistance within a community may be seen in both Warsaw and Theresienstadt. The clandestine classes offered by teachers in the Warsaw Ghetto have been described (Kaplan, 1965). So too have some activities that were created in Theresienstadt and engaged in by prisoners to try to keep mind and spirit active. The activities included (Friedlander, 1968) clandestine classes held in a loft by Rabbi Baeck, the creation and performance of an opera, and a number of concerts. A group of adolescent boys published a magazine, *Vedem,* for two years (Krizkova *et al.*, 1995). Art classes were offered by Friedel Decker Brandeis who encouraged children to draw from memory, rather than to recreate the squalor that was before them. *I Never Saw Another Butterfly* is a compilation of the work of children. A group of starving women created a cookbook that is not really a cookbook. *In Memory's Kitchen* was created by people who thought they were faithfully recreating the dishes that had graced their tables in the past. Many failed to remember all of the ingredients, or all of the steps necessary to create the delicacies they loved most. The material was given to Mina Pachter, who gathered the recipes for her grandson. She died of starvation before the material could be presented to him, (DeSilva, 1996), and it surfaced many years later.

Armed Group Efforts and Cooperation

Large and organized acts of resistance, e.g. Warsaw Ghetto Uprising, and blowing up crematorium # 4 in Auschwitz, or the revolts at Sobibor, (Rashke,1982) and Treblinka (Steiner, 1966) took great effort by numbers of people who, under the most hideous of circumstances had to trust each other, and had to communicate when contact with others was forbidden and often punished when detected, since they were under nearly constant scrutiny. Thus, communication, it seems to me was also an act of resistance.

The Warsaw Ghetto Uprising was an incredible feat, a David and Goliath story in which David did not ultimately prevail. Central to the story are the misery and endemic conditions of hunger, disease and general hopelessness that impelled some of its prisoners to rebel.

Jews comprised approximately 10% of the prewar population of Warsaw, Poland's largest city. Warsaw was also the site of the largest ghetto in Europe when Germany began to incarcerate Jews in them. A great deal has been written about this ghetto, various acts of resistance within it, and the armed uprising that began on April 19, 1943. (Levin, 1968; Gilbert, 1993; Katz, 1970; Heydecker, 1990; Rotem, 1994).

Mordechai Anielewicz was a twenty-two-year-old incarcerated in the Warsaw ghetto. Like others, he witnessed great horror in the forms of illness, despair, hunger and deportations. He thought young people had to attempt to defend the ghetto, since many older people were unable to do so for a variety of reasons. He and colleagues who led the Warsaw Ghetto Uprising did so after communication with members of different groups within the ghetto. They brought people together who had not previously shared the same ideas. Religious Zionists, socialists, communists, and unaffiliated people whose dire circumstances, from which they saw no surcease, impelled them to collaborate in ways they had not previously done. Anielewicz became the leader of the **zob**, the Jewish Fighting Organization. A number of problems had to be surmounted. There was a fragile alliance between the various groups and a grave shortage of weapons. Anielewicz and his friends had tried for some time to gather weapons and to increase the size of their group. They held no illusion they would do great damage against the German forces, but thought that if they were bound to die, they would do so with dignity (Kermish, Ed., 1986) and with the knowledge they had done all they could for themselves, and for others in the ghetto as well. When they learned of the impending liquidation of the ghetto, they struck. Their efforts lasted far longer than most people would have imagined, and surprised and angered the Germans so they were forced to increase their military presence in response to the ongoing attack by ghetto fighters. Ultimately, the Germans burned the houses in the ghetto one at a time, often forcing those in hiding within them to try to escape. Many were shot when they emerged. Some very few escaped through the sewers of Warsaw. Of those, some became partisans. Few ghetto fighters survived. Anielewicz was not among those who did.

Intellectual and Spiritual Resistance

Even in the most adverse circumstances, people who did not engage in armed resistance contributed their skills and expertise to efforts led by others to document the terrible conditions. In the Warsaw Ghetto, Dr. Israel Milejkowski, responsible for Public Health, organized a group of medical specialists to document their clinical experience (Winick, 1979). Dermatologists, ophthalmologists internists, among others, studied the long range effects of malnutrition. They had little medicine to treat people who came to them, or journals with the most recent innovations in their medical specialties. The doctors who so metriculously documented their work were suffering from the same maladies as thier patients. The resulting manuscript was smuggled to a Christian colleague on the Aryan side of Warsaw. At the end of the war, very few of the twenty-eight doctors who had participated in the work were still living. Dr. Milejkowski committed suicide, but the book that came of their work, entitled *Hunger Disease*, remains in use and is widely known by doctors as the most exhaustive study of the long range effects of starvation on various organs and body functions. An additional legacy is found in Milejkowski's words:

> My beloved colleagues and companions in misery. You are a part of all of us. Slavery, hunger, deportation, those death figures in our ghetto were also your legacy. And you by your work could give the henchmen the

> answer "*Non omnis moriad,*" "*I shall not wholly die.*" (Milejkowski 1942, cited in Winick, 1979, p.5)

To chronicle, to record, to analyze (Lewin, 1988) lived experience is a powerful tool of resistance. Emmanuel Ringelblum was a well known and respected figure in prewar Warsaw. He held a doctorate in history, and was a teacher and writer. He gathered a group of people who agreed to document what they were seeing so those in the future would know what had been lived in the past. (Kaplan, 1965). Some were teachers in the Yehudia School, the premier gymnasium for Jewish girls in Warsaw. Ringelblum's contributors taught various disciplines, to children of various ages. He also recruited journalists, poets, novelists, theatrical performers, musicians, and intellectuals from a wide spectrum of disciplines. Each had few materials with which to write. Paper, ink, pencils were scarce, and had to be smuggled into the ghetto. This group became known as the Oneg Shabbos group, named for the Sabbath gathering of people who enjoy fellowship and refreshments after religious services. This is ironic since there were many ideas, but no refreshments among these Yiddish, Hebrew and Polish writers. Ringelblum gathered their work and buried the contributions in milk cans and other metal containers. It is estimated there were more than 21,000 documents (Roskies, 1984). At this time, only some have been found, and a mere fraction translated into English.

Although Ringelblum escaped from the ghetto at the time of the uprising, he was murdered by the Nazis in 1944 with his wife and young children. He was in his early forties at the time of his death and had already written a scholarly work about Polish-Jewish relations during the war. His death and the loss of other work he might have created if he had lived longer are lamentable.

Decades after the end of the war, some Polish children were preparing the ground for a spring garden in an area of Warsaw near where the ghetto had been enclosed. Their digging was interrupted by a metallic sound. The metal box they uncovered was yet another of many in which documents written by people long dead, had been stored.

Educators might consider and teach about the generosity and brilliance of a person who began a vast undertaking he might not see to completion. What of the others who contributed to this effort? Did they know they would not personally live to see these works published? In what ways are these contributors heroes? Resisters? What might have happened to them if their work were discovered? What can we learn from intellectual protest and resistance? Spiritual?

Jewish Partisans

When some people drive past a thickly wooded area they are reminded of material they have read, or experiences they had during their childhoods (Klajman, unpublished conversations, 2007). They ask themselves if that would be a good place to hide. Are there people in hiding there at this moment? Why are they in hiding? How do they manage to survive? What sounds might they be hearing at this very moment? What light do they see during the day? How many people are there? How are they connected to one another? Whom can they trust? Who are their enemies?

Each of these questions might have been asked by partisans whose "home base" were the woods, but other partisans, in their role as resistance fighters, were not in the woods at all. (Mais, 2007, pp 86-90). Couriers who brought news of Jews, (Vladka Meed, 1979) of impending Nazi plans, and who tried to educate people as they went from one ghetto to another, played an important role in bringing hope to people who had little contact with the world outside, even if the news were not good (Draegner, 1996).

This section focuses upon a group of Jewish partisans who operated in Byelorussia. This focus offers a better understanding of the specific problems faced by Jewish partisans. Their problems were distinct from those they shared with other heroes, subverting the Nazi occupation of their country. For Jews, this was only one part of their work. The other part, the work of partisans, was complicated because not all non-Jewish partisan groups accepted or even tolerated Jews. In some groups (Mais, 2007), people hid their Jewish identity, because Jewish resistance fighters had sometimes been killed by non-Jews (Tec, 1993). For all who did this work, there was a struggle for food, for weapons, and the hope they would succeed in their missions and thwart Nazi aggression in their country. They all faced danger, but for Jews there remained an additional question about how they would be received by their Christian brothers.

A widely researched partisan group was led by the Bielski brothers (Tec, 1993, Duffy, 2003), who saved the lives of about 1200 Jews in the Naliboki forest in Byelorussia. Tuvia and his brothers led this group to the successes they achieved. The Bielski brothers, tall people who stood out, were accomplished horseback riders who knew the area very well. Having witnessed the brutality to which Jews had been subjected, their primary reason for forming a community in the forest was to save the lives of Jews. As more people joined them, more skills were available, but it was also increasingly difficult to feed such a great number of people. They had dug shelters underground, had a bakery, a tailor shop and an infirmary and thus engaged people who were not armed fighters.

They forged an alliance with a Russian partisan group led by Victor Panchenko (Tec, 1993, pp73-75) who was at first hostile to the Jewish partisans. Sometimes this was due to antisemitism, and in this case both partisan groups clearly needed more weapons and ammunition, and had the problem of feeding those in their own group.

The Bielski brothers' group were guided by the principle of saving as many Jews as possible more than by a desire to inflict harm even on their enemies, (Tec, 1993, p.131). It should be noted the Bielski group almost never turned away someone who asked for their help and protection. Precisely that principle led them, from time to time, to inflict deadly violence. A group of ten Bielski partisans on a mission, accepted an offer of food and shelter by a farmer named Bilous. While they slept, he betrayed them to the police who rounded up the group and killed nine of them, mistakenly believing they had killed the tenth as well. The survivor appeared before the peasant's family and promised to avenge the death of his group. He was murdered with an axe by one of the peasant's sons.

Despite their own hatred of killing, the Bielski group vowed to annihilate the Bilous family for two reasons. They thought not doing so would give permission for other peasants to behave in the same way. Farmers were subject to two competing groups who wanted food from them. There were the Nazi occupiers on the one hand, and the partisans on the other, and farmers wondered what would be left for them and their families. To discourage such betrayal in the future, the Bielski partisans needed to be known as a serious force that would punish those who harmed them. In addition, the loss of ten people, very important to the survival of the community, provided a strong motive for vengeance.

Teachers might raise questions about the daily lives of those who lived in the community. How did they get food? Weapons? How was labor divided? What voice did residents have in the life of the community? What part did residents play in the governance of the group?

Resistance Within the Ghetto

At the outset, when Jews were forced into ghettos from larger and more prosperous environments, they were able to bring only some of the things they valued. The first ghetto residents had no way of knowing the conditions under which they would be living. They brought things that had been important to them in the context of the lives they had led before the war. An observant family might have been sure to bring candlesticks and candles into the ghetto (Marshall, 1991), while a musician would have thought of an instrument; writers and teachers would have thought of books, paper, pencils. In the early days of the ghetto, such goods were used for their normal purposes. Nevertheless, as time passed, they became scarce commodities, sometimes useful to barter for food (Lewin, 1988).

Resistance can take the form of breaking rules, for the symbolic implications of doing so. It is a small power indeed, but carries a certain dignity and control of one's own life. Such small acts of resistance, sometimes life sustaining, sometimes less vital in nature, are often not sufficiently considered as acts of resistance by those who accuse the victims of participating in their own murder. Each person who was out after curfew, each who went into the street without the armband or patch of cloth that identified them as Jews, was resisting in some measure. Not all were able to return home alive if they were caught during such an infraction, but for those who did succeed, life had a little victory with which to reward them. (Laird, 1989).

In the early days of ghetto imprisonment, teachers would gather a few children in their quarters, and give them instruction. Since classes were illegal, (Kaplan, 1965) these were mobile schools at best. So scarce were materials that teachers taught from memory. In exchange for their work, they might have gotten bread or a potato, or another bit of food that would keep them or their families from starvation. As food became ever more scarce, families had less to barter in payment to teachers. Children's formal education ended as teachers became increasingly unable to support themselves and their families. In time, children themselves became less available for instruction of an academic nature, as they were called upon to play a vitally important and risky role in the survival of their families.

Eastern European ghettos were surrounded by high walls. Their hasty construction left holes in some places so small that only children could go through them. Thus, children would cross into the Aryan (Christian) world, to barter or sell one of the last remaining family possessions in exchange for food. Sometimes children fell victim to a gang or gangs of Polish youth who preyed upon them, beating them and stealing the food they were bringing back for their families. Many children trying to reenter the ghetto were caught by guards, and, much more often than not, were shot instantly. Despite such great dangers, some children successfully made many trips out of and back to the ghetto, and thus enabled the survival of their families. (Dwork, 1991).

Many questions might be considered by teachers. Some seem to flow directly from the experiences of children. Why, when facing mortal dangers, would people worry about the education of their children? (Flinker, [1958] 1976). In a culture based in hierarchy and respect for the authority of parents, teachers and elders, what dynamics were set in motion by empowering children? What happened to parents, and children, when roles were reversed and parents lost their status as protectors and providers for their children? (Dwork, 1991). Childhoods are always lost to the stresses and demands of war. In this war, many children, willingly or not, became resisters. In leaving an environment in which they were to be permanently imprisoned, they confronted a series of dangers in the world outside. The food they could bring back was also a tool of resistance, as those who were no longer employed, no longer had the work cards necessary to receive rations. They were in danger of starving to death, and many did.

Hidden Children

Throughout Europe, Jewish parents, in their increasingly grave circumstances feared for the lives of their children. Their responses to imminent danger and the scope of possibilities narrowed as the war spread and progressed. Some parents began to understand they had little chance to survive, but as an act of love and resistance sent their children to what they hoped would be a more secure environment. Such a decision is heart rending and added, in the uncertainty of their children's whereabouts, yet other layers of worry, concern, fear and ambiguity. Parents hoped people could be found who would offer shelter and safety to their children. The hunt for and restrictions against Jews in Western Europe, while broadening and terrifying, still enabled some contact with people in the Christian community. In Eastern Europe, however, by the time Jews were herded into ghettoes, high walls prevented even minimal contact with the non-Jewish population. As the noose tightened around the necks of the victims and conditions became ever more dangerous for survival, some parents tried to arrange to have their children sent elsewhere. More than one family went through the sewers of Eastern European cities (Halter, 1989; Eliach, 1988; Marshall, 1991). Arrangements were made for their children to find shelter with Christian families who were either personally known to the parents, or who were found by members of the Resistance.

Sometimes children went to orphanages operated by the Church. (Roth-Hano, 1989). In such cases, often only one or two of the nuns knew the child's true identity and reason for being there. Hidden children had to memorize their new names, and other facts concerning their identity. They had to learn how to bless themselves, and received rapid instruction in the Catechism. This is an example of resistance by some members of the Church.

Sometimes, urban children were sent to rural families where they had to learn new ways of living. Some children were treated warmly and welcomed. Nevertheless, others were enslaved, molested, and otherwise abused. Dwork (1991) found that children were best off with families most like their families of origin, but such placements were rare.

Some children who could pass for Aryan took new identities and publicly lived the life of Christians. Their sudden appearance in a community forced their rescuers to invent a story to account for their presence. They might describe the child as a family member whose father had died in the war, and whose mother died in an accident. Other children living with new families were hidden from view because it was thought they "looked Jewish."

In either situation, it is difficult to imagine the sense of abandonment, isolation and loneliness children separated from their families experienced. Sometimes, they did not know where their parents were, or if they were still alive. (Klarsfeld, 1984). Idleness, boredom and terror were constant companions for children in hiding, as they were permitted few activities for fear of being discovered. (Vos, 1996). Many memoirs describe conditions and experiences that force us to consider how strong an act of resistance it was to survive in such circumstances. (Roth-Hano, 1989, Klarsfeld, 1984, 1996).

Children hidden with their own families

The following story illustrates some aspects of the life of a child who was hidden for about two years, but who had the good fortune to be with her parents, sisters, and some members of her extended family. (Frishberg (no date) - unpublished conversations). It is offered to afford teachers the opportunity to see that details in stories enable us to think of people as real even if we do not know them, and to help children identify with the experiences of others.

A farmer, who lived near her home in Poland, had been a good friend to her late grandfather. Her family agreed to give the farmer their furs in exchange for hiding them. In all, the farmer hid 14 people in the loft of his barn. Unfortunately, her infant brother was killed, because an infant might endanger the entire group by crying in ways that could not be controlled. Such noises might betray the whereabouts of those in hiding. Other instances in the literature describe the same actions (Eliach, 1988, Swanzger, 1990).

At the time of their liberation, they all had to learn to speak again, since they had not used their voices except to whisper to each other. The loft did not offer much space in which to walk, and a great deal of time was spent sitting or lying. They had to relearn to use their lower extremities.

How did the people spend their time? How did they handle issues of privacy? One wonders about their hunger, their feeling cold in winter, and heat they experienced in summer. What was the effect of sustained deprivation of light and air? How did the farmer feed all those people? How and when did he carry their waste away? Who helped him? From whom did he keep his activities secret?

After their liberation, the family came to America, where my friend married and had children, as did her sisters. She became a teacher, and for many years taught a Holocaust program in the high school in which she worked. In her professional work she would draw upon lived experience. While her sisters spoke of their experiences little, or not at all, one of their daughters, a film maker, was interested in the family's history of survival. She accompanied my friend, her husband and their two children to Poland. The trip resulted in a documentary film *Voices From the Attic.* The film depicts heartwarming and painful scenes. The farmer was long dead, but his wife, grown children, and several neighbors gathered to meet this American family. One neighbor said she thought the farmer must have been hiding Jews, since his was the only barn in the area that was not snow covered. The number of people in the loft warmed the pitched roof and melted the snow. Fortunately, that neighbor never discussed her observation with others, or the barn might have been searched.

On a more terrible note, we see a scene in which my friend and her family twice walk past her childhood home. It seemed, at first glance, to be a house much like others. After her presence in the area was known, a huge red swastika was painted on the house and the words "Jews die!" Such an unconscionable act in the 1990's, provokes many questions. Who would do this in an area where Jews no longer lived? At least some, we know, thought Jews might be hidden, but never betrayed them or the family that had offered them shelter. It is well known that other Jews in hiding were betrayed. Why do some people help, while others betray even their close neighbors? For at least some people in Poland, antisemitism persists even without Jews.

The Resister as Hero

Some acts of resistance give birth to heroes whom one would wish to emulate. Janusz Korczak was born Henryk Goldszmit to an assimilated professional family. His grandfather was a doctor and his father a lawyer. Korczak, too, trained as a physician, and was a veteran of The Russo-Japanese War, having been conscripted in 1905. His work in education was progressive and forward looking. He viewed children as people in the present, rather than as becoming people only in the future.

He opened an orphanage in Warsaw long before the war and was assisted by Stefania Wilczynska (Madame Stefa; Laird, 1989, Lifton, 1988) who remained with him until the end in 1942. Contrary to thinking quite common then, Korczak believed the work of the orphanage was to socialize children, and to teach them to live in the world, whereas other orphanages emphasized learning a trade so the children could earn a living in the future. The stress in Korczak's orphanage was on social skills. Children would meet regularly with the adults in a kind of town hall meeting. At such times, each person present had one vote. Thus children of 10 had only one vote, as did Stefania and Korczak. The orphanage was a community in which people knew, and depended upon others and learned to respect their rights.

At the time the ghetto was formed in Warsaw, Korczak's first orphanage was within its walls. Although he was offered safe conduct to the Aryan side, he refused to go. It is said (Laird, 1989) he was the only person in the ghetto who did not wear the armband or the cloth marking him as a Jew. As he went about the streets of the ghetto, perhaps to the Judenrat (Jewish council) to try to get enough food for the children, he was seen in his military uniform, which may have been his personal act of resistance. While in the ghetto he kept a diary (Korczak, 1978), which recorded his increasing despair caused by the difficulties in trying to feed the children and protect them from the tragedy that surrounded them. Stefa and Korczak's shielding children from the gravity of their environment seem to me to be an act of resistance. They thus created hope for the future. On Aug. 6, 1942, the entire orphanage was ordered to go to the Umschlagplatz (a gathering place) where they were to board trains for 'relocation to the east'. Korczak, again offered safety on the Aryan side, said the children needed him more than ever. As they left the orphanage, he had them march in an orderly fashion that publicly showed their good manners and discipline. Some of the older children carried or held the hands of younger ones. He carried one child and held the hand of another as they went to the gathering place as ordered. They were all murdered at Treblinka when they arrived there two days later. At the time of his death, he was 62 years old. Korczak's work is a legacy of resistance, personal heroism and dignity. While suffering privately during the war years, he gave the children hope for a future they were not permitted to see.

Resistance by Diplomats

While most individual acts of heroism and resistance were conducted in private, a few diplomats, acting under the flags of their countries, worked in public. In each instance, they paid dearly for their life saving activities.

Aristide de Sousa-Mendes was a Portugese diplomat in southern France who was responsible for granting about 10,000 transit visas for Jews to enter Portugal. He was recalled by his government, which was officially neutral, and dismissed from diplomatic service. He died in abject poverty in 1954. In 1995, his career was posthumously restored and he was honored with a medal. His family has yet to receive the salary that was due to him.

The work of the Swedish diplomat Raoul Wallenberg has been widely documented (Skoglund, 1997; Lester, 1982; Yahil1969), and after his capture by the Soviets, he seems to have disappeared from view. To date his fate is not known.

What follows is a detailed story of Chiune Sugihara, the most enigmatic of the diplomats who aided Jews. I offer it in greater detail than those mentioned above because I hope it will help teachers to see the personal, living aspects of interactions between people who, under different circumstances, might never have met. It illustrates that some who resisted, who aided total strangers, did so because they thought it was the right thing to do.

Chiune Sugihara was Japanese Vice-Consul in Kaunas, (Kovno) Lithuania in 1940. His country was an ally of Germany, and his granting many transit visas to Jews in contravention of his government's orders, caused them great embarrassment.

Sugihara, born in 1900, was long practiced in doing what he thought was right. He deliberately failed his college exams, so that he was not accepted as a medical student, which had been his father's wish for him. His father would pay for no other education. He wanted to be an English teacher, so he went to Harbin, China, where he studied languages. He also converted to Christianity there. It appears he was a brilliant linguist. (Levine, 1996). It was said of him, many years later, he sounded like a native Russian speaker. Nevertheless, in that fateful summer of 1940, he was a little-known diplomat.

One morning, a Jewish artist from Poland went to his Consulate to ask for a transit visa to Japan. He sought help, he explained, because of the untenable conditions for Jews in Poland. The diplomat, saddened by the artist's account of what he had witnessed, granted him a transit visa. As a diplomat he was empowered to do so without seeking the permission of his government. The next day, however, about 200 people stood outside the Consul's home/office/consulate. (Sugihara, 1993). The young man shared the news of his good fortune with members of his community, and they came to get visas as well. Sugihara knew he needed the consent of his government if he were to grant so many visas, so he cabled Tokyo for permission. In a few days, the answer came: he was not to grant transit visas to Jews. Yet the Jews kept coming, and Sugihara was so moved when he learned of their experiences, he continued to grant them visas.

At that time, it took 22 days to cross Russia where ships could be boarded for Japan. He arranged with the Russians to grant permission to this group of travelers. He reasoned that 22 days, and the 30 days they would be permitted in Japan would give the Jews time to find some nation on earth that would accept them. At the time, a single visa covered an entire family, so it is not known how many people were directly helped by him and his assistants.

The consulate in Kovno was scheduled to close, and he was reassigned to Konigsberg, Germany. Sugihara signed visas in the hotel lobby in which he stayed while awaiting transfer. He continued to sign blank visas (Sugihara, 1993) and threw several hundred of them from the train window as he sped away to what was ultimately his diplomatic undoing. In 1946, he and his family were incarcerated by the Russians in Romania. When they returned to Japan in 1947, he expected to be made an ambassador. Instead, he was dismissed from diplomatic service. One would have to know Japanese culture to understand the power of such disgrace.

Years later, when Jews inquired about Sempo Sugihara, an informal name of affection by which he was known to them, the Foreign Service claimed to have no record of him. It took nearly 20 years, and the untiring research of some people whose lives he had saved, to learn what had happened to him.

After his dismissal from government service, he was unable to find suitable work, so he sold light bulbs door-to-door to support his family. After a time, he found work in a company that had offices in Russia. During that period in his life one of his sons died, and another was born to him and his wife. He remained in Russia for 15 years, until he returned to Japan to retire.

When he was finally found by some Israelis who were among those who were recipients of the visas he had signed more than 20 years earlier, his son was offered an education in an Israeli university. His youngest son, trained in gemology, lives there part of the year to this day. Sugihara was ultimately honored in 1985 by Yad Vashem, as a Righteous Gentile, but he was too ill to attend (Levine, 1996).

One may imagine the surprise of his neighbors, who, at the time of his death, visited his home to pay their respects to his family, and found more than 100 Chasidim, ultra orthodox Jews, who had come for the same reason. Sugihara, ever modest, had never spoken of his deeds.

Some concluding thoughts

The will to subvert an oppressor's intentions and to survive is essential to resistance by victims. An examination of resistance helps us learn about decency, courage, and survival in conditions over which victims had little control or information. Resistance motivated the actions of people who tore a book apart by chapters and, having read the pages, passed them along to others. Resistance is embedded in the words of witnesses who left us with some idea of the evil and cruelty they were experiencing. Resistance (Tec, 1993) is evident when people, after the murder of those closest to them, formed groups with whom they shared thoughts, ideas, concerns and feelings (DeSilva, 1996).

The motives and actions of those who struggled to survive raises a number of questions. Did they do so to thwart the aims of their captors? (Szwajger, 1990) Did they struggle to survive in the hope of a better future? (Walshaw and Walshaw, 1991; Goldenberg and Goldenberg, 1988). Did they struggle simply to live even under the oppressive conditions in which they found themselves? (Frister, 1999). In teaching about resistance, we might focus on helping learners see that acts of resistance take many forms and entail various kinds of activities. In what ways do we personally resist? Whom are we resisting? Why?

Care should be taken not to glorify resistance for its own sake. Rather, we can probe with students the difference between the legitimate use of power and its unjustified use to oppress and destroy. It is as distorting to romanticize those who did resist, as it is to judge negatively, those whose actions seem less heroic to us. It has been my argument that resistance is seen in the acts of trying to remain alive, in working cooperatively with others, in maintaining the dignity and humanness oppressors attempt to annihilate. Resistance has been presented in various ways and as readers, our knowledge is only approximate. An imaginative approximation is, fortunately, the nearest most of us can come to grasping the realities of living with exhaustion, confusion, anxiety, fear and hunger as constant companions, as well as feelings of impotence in the face of adversity.

We cannot claim with certainty we would act in ways more moral or less passive than those we judge. It is simplistic and limiting to find resistance only in the grand heroic gesture, or the dramatic violent confrontation that successfully ends with the physical destruction of the enemy. Despite the best attempt to resist, resistance is not always crowned with success.

NOTES

[1] Even today in many parts of the world, teachers of younger children go to teacher's colleges, but are not university-educated. In gymnasia, teachers are university educated, and not infrequently hold doctoral degrees. Secondary teachers in Europe are sometimes referred to as "Professor," a title that carries great esteem and respect.

REFERENCES

Adelson, A. (Ed.). (1996). *The diary of Dawid Sierakowiak.* New York: Oxford.

Adler, D.A. (1995). Illustrated by Ritz, K. *Child of the Warsaw Ghetto.* New York: Holiday House.

Appelman-Jurman, A. (1988) *Alicia, my story.* New York: Bantam.

Arad, Y. (1979). *The partisan.* New York: Holocaust Library.

Aroneanu, E. (compiler) (1996). *Inside the concentration camps: eyewitness accounts of life in Hitler's death camps.* Westport, CT: Praeger.

Bachrach, S. (1994). *Tell them we remember.* U.S. Holocaust Memorial Museum & Little, Brown & Co.

Baker, L. (1978). *Days of sorrow and pain: Leo Baeck and the Berlin Jews.* New York: Macmillan.

Bartoszewski, W. (1987), *The Warsaw Ghetto - A Christian's testimony.* Boston: Beacon Press.

Bauer, Y. (1978). *The Holocaust in historical perspective.* Seattle, WA: University of Washington Press.(1982). *A history of the Holocaust.* New York: Franklin Watts.

Bitton-Jackson, L. (1997) *I have lived a thousand years: growing up in the Holocaust.* New York: Scholastic.

Blatter, J., & Milton, S. (Eds.). (1998) *Art of the Holocaust.* New York: Routledge Press.

Bondy, R. (1989). *"Elder of the Jews": Jakob Edelstein of Theresienstadt.* New York: Grove Press.

Bor, J. (1963, 1978). *The Terezin requiem.* New York: A Bard Book/Avon.

Bridenthal, R., Grossman, A., & Kaplan, M. (Eds.). (1984) *When biology became destiny: Women in Weimar and Nazi Germany.* New York: Monthly Review Press.

Brostoff, A. (Ed.). with Chamovitz, S. (2001). *Flares of memory: stories of childhood during the Holocaust.* New York: Oxford University Press.

Capelluto, L. (n. d.). Compiled by Delfini, L. J. *My life in Auschwitz and Bergen-Belsen.* Sponsored by Bridges for Peace.

Cargas, H. J. (1992) *Shadows of Auschwitz: A Christian response of the Holocaust* originally published in 1981 as *A Christian response of the Holocaust.* New York: The Crossroad publishing Co.

Cholowski, S. (1980). *Soldiers from the ghetto.* San Diego, CA: A.S. Barnes.

Colodner, S. (1964). *Jewish education in Germany under the Nazis.* New York: Jewish Education Committee Press.

Crome, L. (1988). *Unbroken: resistance and survival in the concentration camps.* New York: Schocken.

Cross, R. (1994) *Children and war. World War II.* New York: Thomas Learning.

Crowe, D. (2004) *Oskar Schindler.* Cambridge, MA: Westview Press.

Czarnecki, J. P. (1989) *Last traces: the lost art of Auschwitz.* New York: Atheneum.

Czech, D. (1989). *Auschwitz Chronicle 1939-1945. From the archives of the Auschwitz Memorial and the GermanFederal Archives.* New York: An Owl Book: Henry Holt and Co.

David K. (1989). *A Child's War: World War II Through the eyes of children.* New York: Four Walls Eight Windows.

De Silva, C. (Ed). (1996) *In Memory's Kitchen. Imperfect cookbook by the starving women of Terezin.* London: Jason Aronson.
Donat, A. (Ed.) (1979). *The Death Camp Treblinka.* New York: Holocaust Library.
Draenger, G. D. (1996) *Justyna's Narrative.* Amherst, MA.: University of Massachussetts Press.
Duboys, T. (2006) Should the Holocaust be taught in urban schools? In J. Kincheloe, K. Hayes, K. Rose, & P. Anderson (Eds.), *Handbook of urban education.* (pp 112–121). New York: Praeger.
Duffy, P. (2003) *The Bielski brothers.* New York: Harper Collins Publisher.
Dwork, D. (1991) *Children with a star.* New Haven, CT: Yale University Press.
Eliach, Y. (1988). *Hasidic Tales of the Holocaust.* New York: Vintage.
Elkes, J. (1997, 1999) *Dr. Elkhanan Elkes of the Kovno Ghetto.* Brewster, MA: Paraclete Press.
Epstein, H. (1979). *Children of the Holocaust. Conversations with sons and daughters of survivors.* New York: Bantam.
Faber, D.. Kitchen, J. D. (1997) *Becaise of Romek.* El Cajon, CA: Granite Hills Press.
Ferencz, C. (1979). *Less than slaves.* Cambridge, MA: Harvard University Press.
Flinker, M. (1958, 1976). *Young Moshe's diary:The spiritual torment of a Jewish boy in Nazi Europe.* Jerusalem: Yad Vashem.
Friedlander, A. H. (1968). *Leo Baeck: teacher of Theresienstadt.* New York: Holt, Rinehart and Winston.
Frishberg, S. (n. d.). Unpublished conversation.
Frister, R. (1993, 1999). *The Cap: The price of a life.* New York: Grove Press.
Geier, A. (1993). *Heroes of the Holocaust.* New York: Berkeley Books.
Geve, T. (1958). *Guns & barbed wire: A child survives the Holocaust.* Chicago: Academy Chicago Pub.
Gold, A. (2003) *Fiet's vase: stories of survival.* (Uncorrected proof). New York: Putnam.
Goldenberg, S., & Goldenberg, A. (1988) *Whispers in the darkness.* New York: Shengold Publishers.
Gotfryd, B. (2001) *Anton the dove fancier and other tales of the Holocaust.* Baltimore: Johns Hopkins Press.
Greenfeld, H. (1993). *The hidden children.* New York: Ticknor & Fields.
Grossman, M. (1977). *With a camera in the ghetto: 70 photos from the Lodz ghetto.* New York: Schocken Books.
Gutman, I. (1994). *Resistance: the Warsaw Ghetto uprising.* Houghton Mifflin in association with United States Holocaust Memorial Museum.
Hallie, P. (1979). *Lest innocent blood be shed: The story of the village of Le Chambon and how goodness happened there.* New York: Harper Torchbooks.
Halter, M. (1989). *The jester and the kings: a political auto-biography.* New York: Arcade, Little, Brown & Co.
Hart, K. (1982). *Return to Auschwitz.* New York: Atheneum.
Hendel, T. (compiler and editor) (1996) *Life with death: drawings and life stories by child Holocaust survivors.* Bethesda, MD: Create Expressive Arts Press.
Heilman, A. (2001). *Never far away: The Auschwitz chronicles of Anna Heilman.* Calgary, Alberta Canada: U. Of Calgary Press.
Heydecker, J. J. (1990). *The Warsaw Ghetto.* London: I. B. Tauris.
Hilberg, R. (1961). *The destruction of European Jewry.* New York: Qadrangle.
(1996) *The politics ofmmemory: The journey of a Holocaust historian.* Chicago, IL: Ivan R. Dee.
Hirshaut, J. (1982). *Jewish martyrs of Pawiak.* New York: Holocaust Library.
Holliday, L. (1995). *Children in the Holocaust and World War II: Their secret diaries.* New York: Pocket Books.
Hyams, J. (1968). *A field of buttercups.* Englewood Cliffs, NJ: Prentice-Hall.
Jackson. L. B. (1980). *Elli: coming of age in the Holocaust.* New York: Times Books.
Kallen, S. A. (1994). *The Holocaust: the faces of resistance.* Edina, MN: Abdo & Daughters.
Kamenetsky, C. (1984). *Children's literature in Hitler's Germany.* Athens, OH: Ohio University Press.
Kantor, A. (1987). *The book of Alfred Kantor. facsimile of his Holocaust drawings.* New York: Schocken Books.
Kaplan, C. (1965) *Scroll of agony. Warsaw Ghetto diary.* New York: Macmillan.
Ka'tzetnik 135633. (1955). *House of dolls.* New York: Simon & Schuster.
(1963) *Atrocity at Auschwitz.* New York: Kensington Books.

Kermish, J. (Ed.). (1986). *To live with honor and die with honor: selected documents from the Warsaw Ghetto underground archives (Oneg Shabbat)*. Jerusalem: Yad Vashem.
Kern, A. (1988) *Tapestry of hope: Survivor of Auschwitz and Bergen-Belsen*. Portland, OR: Author.
Klajman, G. (2007). Unpublished conversation.
Klarsfeld, S. (1984) *The children of Izieu: A human tragedy* New York: Harry N. Abrams.
(1996). *French children of the Holocaust: A Memorial*. New York: New York University Press.
Kogon, E. (1975). *The theory and practice of hell: The German concentration camps and the system behind them*. New York: Berkeley.
Korczak, J. (1978). *Warsaw diary*. New York: Holocaust Library.
Kovaly, H., & Kohak, E. (1973). *The Victors and the Vanquished: memoir of a Czech survivor of Auschwitz*. New York: Horizon.
Krall, H. (1986). *Shielding the Flame*. New York: Holt.
Krizkova, R., Kotouc, K. J., & Zdenek O. (1995). *We are children just the same: VEDEM, The secret magazine by the boys of Terezin.*. Translated from the Czech. Philadelphia: The Jewish Publication Society.
Kubar, Z. (1989). *Double Identity*. New York: Hill & Wang.
Kulka, E. (1986). *Escape from Auschwitz*. Westport, CT: Bergin & Garvey.
Laird, C. (1989). *Shadow of the wall*. New York: Greenwillow.
Lang, B. (2000). *Holocaust representation:Art within the limits of history and ethics*. Baltimore: Johns Hopkins Press.
Langbein, H. (1996). In Z. Harry (Trans.), *Against all hope: Resistance in Nazi concentration camps 1938-1945*. New York: Continuum.
Langer, L. (1995). *Art from the ashes: A HolocaustaAnthology*. New York: Oxford Press.
(1998) *Preempting the Holocaust*. New Haven, CT: Yale University Press.
Laska, V. (1985). *Nazism, resistance & Holocaust in W. W. II. A bibliography*. Metuchen, NJ & London: Scarecrow Press.
Le Chene, E. (1971). *Mauthausen - The History of a death camp*. London: Methuen and Co.
Lengyel, O. (1947). *Five Chimneys:The Story of Auschwitz*. Chicago, IL: Ziff-Davis Publishing.
Lester, E. (1982). *Wallenberg, the man in the iron web*. New York: Prentice-Hall.
Levi, P. (1973). *Survival in Auschwitz*. New York: Collier Macmillan.
(1979) *Moments of reprieve*. New York: Summit.
Levine, H. (1996). *In search of Sugihara*. New York: Free Press.
Lewin, A. (1988). *A cup of tears. A diary of the Warsaw Ghetto*. Oxford, England: Basil Blackwell.
Lewinter, H. (1996). Unpublished conversation.
Lifton, B. J. (1988). *The king of children.- A biography of Janusz Korczak*. New York: Farrar, Strauss.
Lipman, S. J. (1991) *Laughter in hell: The use of humor during the Holocaust*. New York: Aronson.
Mais, I. (Ed.) (2007). *Daring to resist/Jewish defiance in the Holocaust*. New York: Museum of Jewish Heritage - A Living Memorial to the Holocaust.
Mark, B. (1975). *Uprising in the Warsaw Ghetto*. New York: Schocken.
Marks, J. (1993). *The hidden children - The secret survivors of the Holocaust*. New York: Fawcett Columbine/Random House.
Marshall, R. (1991). *In the sewers of Lvov: A heroic story of survival from the Holocaust*. New York: Chas. Scribner's.
Mazor, M. (1955, 1993). *The vanished city A first person account of the Warsaw Ghetto*. New York: Marsilio Publishers.
Meed, V. (1979). *On both sides of the wall*. New York: Holocaust Library.
Miller, J. E. (2000). *Love carried me home: Women surviving Auschwitz*. Deerfield Beach. FL: Simcha Press.
Millu, L. (1947, 1991). *Smoke over Birkenau*. Philadelphia & New York: Jewish Publication Society.
Neimark, A. E. (1986). *One man's valor. Leo Baeck and the Holocaust*. New York: Lodestar Books. E. P. Dutton.
Nicholas, L. (2005). *Cruel world. The children of Europe in the Nazi web*. New York: Alfred A, Knopf.
Nieuwsma, M. (Ed.). (1998). *Kinderlager/An oral history of young Holocaust survivors*. New York: Holiday House.

(1998). *Surviving Auschwitz: Children of the Shoah.* New York: ibooks Distributed by Simon and Schuster.

Nomberg-Przytyk, S. (1985). *Auschwitz: True tales from a grotesque land.* Chapel Hill, NC: University of North Carolina Press.

Paley, V. G. (1992) *You can't say you can't play.* Cambridge, MA: Harvard University Press.

Panchyk, R. (2002) *World War II for kids. A history with 21 activities.* Chicago, IL: Chicago Review Press.

Perl, L., & Lazan, M. B. (1996). *Four perfect pebbles.* New York: Avon/Camelot:Greenwillow, a div. Of William Morrow.

Petit, J. (1993). *A place to hide: True stories of Holocaust rescue.* New York: Scholastic.

Read, A., & Fisher, D. (1989). *Kristallnacht.* New York: Random House.

Rees, L. (2005). *Auschwitz: A new history.* New York: Public Affairs.

Reiss, J. (1972). *The Upstairs room.* New York: Scholastic.

Richman, S. (2002). *A wolf in the attic: The legacy of a hidden child of the Holocaust.* Binghamton, NY: The Haworth Press.

Richter, H. P. (1987). *Friedrick.* New York: Puffin.

Ringelblum, E. (1974). *Notes from the Warsaw Ghetto/The journal of Emmanuel Ringelblum.* New York: Schocken Books.

(1974). *Polish-Jewish relations during the Second World War.* Jerusalem: Yad Vashem.

Ritvo, R. A., & Plotkin, D. M. (1998). *Sisters in sorrow: Voices of care in the Holocaust.* College Station, Texas: Texas A & M. University Press.

Rosenberg, B. (1993). *To tell at last: Survival under false identity 1941-1945.* Chicago, IL: University of Illinois Press.

Roskies, D. G. (1984). *Against the apocalypse: Responses to catastrophe in modern Jewish culture.* Cambridge, MA: Harvard University Press.

Roskies, D. G. (Ed.). (1989). *The literature of destruction: Jewish responses to catastrophe.* Philadelphia: Jewish Publication Society.

Rotem, S. (Kazik). (1994) *Warsaw Ghetto fighter: the past within me.* New Haven, CT: Yale University Press.

Roth-Hano, R. (1989). *Touch wood.* New York: Puffin.

Rovit, R., & Goldfarb, A. (Eds). (1999). *Theatrical performance during the Holocaust: Texts, documents, memoirs.* Baltimore, MD: The Johns Hopkins Press.

Rubin, S. G. (2000) *Fireflies in the dark: The story of Friedl Dicker-Brandeis and the children of Terezin..* New York: Scholastic.

Schwab, G. (1990). *The day the Holocaust began: The odyssey of Herschel Grynszpan.* New York: Praeger.

Schweber, S. (2004). *Making sense of the Holocaust: Lessons from classroom practice.* New York: Teachers College Press.

Schwarberg, G. (1982) *In the Ghetto of Warsaw: Heinrich Jost's Photographs.* Germany: Steidl.

Skoglund, E. (1997). *A quiet courage/Per Anger, Wallenberg's co-liberator of Hungarian Jews.* Grand Rapids, MI: Baker Books.

Stein, A. (1994). *Hidden children: Forgotten survivors of the Holocaust.* New York: Penguin.

Steinbacher, S. (2005). In W. Shaun (Trans.), *A history of Auschwitz.* New York: HarperCollins.

Steiner, J. F. (1966). *Treblinka.* London: Weidenfeld & Nicholson.

Stroop, J. (1979). *The Stroop Report: The Jewish Quarter of Warsaw is no more! (facsimile of the official Nazi report).* New York: Pantheon.

Sugihara, K. (1995). *Visas for life.* San Francisco: Edu-Comm Plus.

Suhl, Y. (Ed.). (1967). *They fought back.* New York: Schocken.

(1975). *On the other side of the gate.* New York: Franklin Watts.

Szwajger, A. B. (1990). *I remember nothing more - The Warsaw Children's Hospital and Jewish resistance.* New York: Pantheon.

Tec, N. (1993). *Defiance: The Bielski partisans.* London: Oxford University Press.

Tedeschi, G. (1992). *There is a place on earth: A woman in Birkenau..* New York: Pantheon Books (Random House).

Thalmann, R., & Feinermann, E. (1974). *Crystal Night. 9-10 November, 1938.* New York: Coward, McCann & Geoghegan.
Tillion, G. (1975). *Ravensbruck.* New York: Anchor/Doubleday.
Treseder, T. W. (1990) *Hear O Israel/A story of the Warsaw Ghetto.* Atheneum and United States Holocaust Memorial Museum.
Volavkova, H. (Ed.). (1994) *I never saw another butterfly... Children's drawings and poems from Terezin, 1942-44.* expanded second edition by U.S. Holocaust Memorial Museum. Schocken Books.
Vos, I. (1981). *Hide and seek.* New York: Scholastic.
(1996). *The key is lost.* New York: Scholastic.
Walshaw, R., & Walshaw, S. (1991) *From out of the firestorm.* New York: Shapolsky.
Warren, A. (2001) *Surviving Hitler: A boy in the Nazi Death Camps: The story of Janek Mandelbaum.* New York: Harper Collins Publishers.
Wdowinski, D. (1963). *And we are not saved.* New York: Philosophical Library.
Weinstein, F. S. (1985). *A hidden childhood: A Jewish girl's sanctuary in a French convent, 1942–45.* New York: Hill & Wang.
Weintraub, J. D. (1994) *Jacob's ladder: From the bottom of the Warsaw Ghetto to the top of New York's art world.* Lanham, MD: Madison Books.
Weiss, A. (2001). *The last album: Eyes from the ashes of Auschwitz-Birkenau..* New York: W.W. Norton and Company.
Winick, M. (1979). *Hunger disease: Studies by the Jewish physicians in the Warsaw Ghetto.* New York: John Wiley.
Wyszogrod, M. (1999) *A brush with death/ An artist in the Death Camps.* SUNY Press.
Yahil, L. (1969). *The rescue of Danish Jewry: Test of a democracy.* Philadelphia: Jewish Publication Society.
(1990) *The holocaust - the fate of European Jewry, 1932-1945.* New York: Oxford University Press.
Zapruder, A. (Ed.). (2002). *Salvaged pages. Young writers' diaries of the Holocaust.* Yale University Press.
Zuckerman, A. (1991). *Memories of a teenager saved by Schindler.* Stamford, CT: Longmeadow Press.

Tibbi Duboys
School of Education
Brooklyn College of the
City University of New York

ABOUT THE AUTHORS

Helen Bond is an Assistant Professor in the School of Education at Howard University in Washington, D.C. She earned a Bachelor of Science degree with Distinction in Education from Ohio State University, a Master of Arts degree from West Virginia University, and a Ph. D. in Human Development from Virginia Polytechnic and State University. She teaches courses in Social Foundations of Urban Education and Integrated Methods for Social Studies. Her primary research interests are peace education, the use of technology as an instrument of peace, and the study of genocide. She has completed a contribution to Jones, A. (Ed.). *Evoking genocide* titled You and I We Must change the World.

Tibbi Duboys is an Associate Professor in the School of Education at Brooklyn College of the City University of New York. She earned a Bachelor of Arts degree in Classics from Brooklyn College, an M.S. from Hunter College, and a Ph. D. in Counselor Education from Fordham University. She has taught undergraduate and graduate courses about the Holocaust, and is currently teaching student teachers. Her primary research interests involve the legacy of oppression in the lives of children, academic unionism and academic freedom. She is affiliated with Axe 6 of the Social Science laboratory at the Sorbonne. She has spoken widely about the Holocaust, and has published in journals. She contributed an entry, **Should the Holocaust be Taught in Urban Schools?** published in *A Handbook of Urban Education (*Praeger, 2006).

Lloyd Duck is an Associate Professor of Education at George Mason University in Fairfax, Virginia. He earned a Bachelor of Arts degree in history/music from the College of William and Mary, and an MAT degree and Ph.D. from the University of Virginia. He teaches graduate courses in Foundations of Education and in Social Studies methodology. His major research interests include teaching and learning styles, teacher retention, and character and moral education. He is the author of two books published by Chatelaine Press. He received the George Mason University Alumni Association's Distinguished Faculty Member of the Year Award in 2002.

Jesus Garcia is a Professor in the Department of Curriculum and Instruction at the University of Nevada, Las Vegas. He teaches undergraduate and graduate courses in social studies education and multicultural education. His research interests include his course work as well as the representation of diverse groups in textbooks. He is the co-author of *American History* published by McDougal Littell.

Jan LaBonty is a Professor at the University of Montana at Missoula. She earned a Bachelor of Arts degree in elementary education from the University of Montana, an M.Ed. in reading/language arts from Northern Montana College, as well as a Ph.D. from the University of Nebraska. She teaches courses in elementary language arts and reading at both undergraduate and graduate levels and graduate courses in Children's Literature. Her research interests include reading and writing methodology, poetry, and integrating literature into the curriculum. She has publicly spoken about the Holocaust, and published a paper subsequent to a professional conference.

Marian McKenna is Professor of Literacy Studies at the University of Montana. She earned a B.S. in Child Studies and Child Psychology from Purdue University. Her subsequent degrees, an M.A. and Ph. D. in Literacy Education and Cognitive Psychology were awarded by the University of Colorado at Boulder. She teaches Content Literacy Strategies, Social and Cultural Foundations of Literacy, and a graduate course in Young Adult Literature. Her current research interests involve academic service learning, and using young adult literature to teach concepts in the content areas. Her most recent publication (2007), **Breaking Boundaries with Global Literature: Celebrating Diversity in K-12 Classrooms,** was published by the International Reading Association.

Daryl Parks is an Assistant Professor of English Education in the Urban Teacher Program at Metropolitan State University in Minnesota. He received a Bachelor of Arts degree in English (summa cum laude), and subsequent degrees, M. A. in Education and a Ph.D. in Literacy from the University of Minnesota. He teaches courses in language and culture, urban education teaching methods, and reading and writing in urban secondary schools. His research interests are at the intersections of literacies, identities and teaching/learning. He is co-author of *High school students' Competing Social Worlds: Negotiating identities and allegiances in response to Multicultural Literature* published by Erlbaum.

Elizabeth Spalding is an Associate Professor in the Department of Curriculum and Instruction at the University of Nevada Las Vegas. Her Ph. D. was awarded by Indiana University-Bloomington. She teaches undergraduate and graduate courses in English Education and secondary education. Her research interests include the impact of cross-cultural experiences on pre-service and in-service teachers and the teaching of writing. Her most recent publication with E. Savage and J. Garcia is: **The March of Remembrance and Hope: Teaching about diversity and social justice through the Holocaust.** *Teachers College Record,* 109 (6), 1423-1456.

Karen Spector is an Assistant Professor at the University of Alabama who has studied and practiced critical English education in diverse educational settings. She earned a Bachelor of Arts in English, and an M.Ed. in English Education from the University of Florida. Her doctorate in Literacy was awarded by the University of Cincinnati. Her teaching and research interests include Holocaust literature, identity and critical literacy. Her dissertation concerned students reading Holocaust literature. She has published on students' religious responses to the Holocaust in *Research in the Teaching* *of English.* In addition, a critical literacy article about how students constructed Anne Frank in an English class was published in *The Journal of Adolescent & Adult Literacy.*

Leah Stambler earned a Bachelor of Arts degree from Hunter College, where she majored in History and had a minor in Political Science. A Master of Arts degree in History was awarded by Stanford, and a Ph.D. by the University of Connecticut. Her wide range of expertise enables her to teach undergraduate, Masters' and Doctoral level students. Some of the courses she has taught are in foundations and history of education, methods of teaching elementary social studies, secondary methods of teaching and adolescent development. Her research interests are in women's history, civic and character education and Holocaust education. Her work on teaching Holocaust Studies through literature and character education has been presented regional, national and international conferences. She is also the co-author of an article about The Canonization of Sister Teresa Benedicta (nee Edith Stein).

TRANSGRESSIONS: CULTURAL STUDIES AND EDUCATION

Volume 1
An Unordinary Death...*The Life of a Suicide Bomber*
Khalilah Christina Sabra
Paperback ISBN 90-77874-36-4
Hardback ISBN 90-77874-37-2

Volume 2
Lyrical Minded *The Critical Pedagogy of Hip-Hop Artist KRS-ONE*
Priya Parmar, City University of New York, USA
Paperback ISBN 90-77874-50-X
Hardback ISBN 90-77874-64-X

Volume 3
Pedagogy and Praxis in the Age of Empire *Towards a New Humanism*
Peter McLaren & Nathalia Jaramillo
Paperback ISBN 90-77874-84-4
Hardback ISBN 90-77874-85-2

Volume 4
Dewey and Power *Renewing the Democratic Faith*
Randall Hewitt, University of Central Florida, USA
Paperback ISBN 90-77874-92-5
Hardback ISBN 90-77874-93-3

Volume 5
Teaching, Learning and Other Miracles Grace Feuerverger, Ontario Institute for Studies in Education, University of Toronto, Canada
Paperback ISBN 978-90-8790-000-7
Hardback ISBN 978-90-8790-003-8

Volume 6
Soaring Beyond Boundaries *Women Breaking Educational Barriers in Traditional Societies*
Reitumetse Obakeng Mabokela (ed.), Michigan State University, USA
Paperback ISBN 90-77874-97-6
Hardback ISBN 90-77874-98-4

Volume 7
Diasporic Ruptures *Globality, Migrancy, and Expressions of Identity*
Volume I
Alireza Asgharzadeh, *York University, Canada,* Erica Lawson, *The University of Nevada, Las Vegas, USA,* Kayleen U. Oka, *University of Toronto, Canada and* Amar Wahab (Eds.), *University of Toronto, Canada*
Paperback ISBN 90-8790-050-3
Hardback ISBN 90-8790-051-1

Volume 8
Diasporic Ruptures *Globality, Migrancy, and Expressions of Identity*
Volume II
Alireza Asgharzadeh, *York University, Canada,* Erica Lawson, *The University of Nevada, Las Vegas, USA,* Kayleen U. Oka, *University of Toronto, Canada and* Amar Wahab (Eds.), *University of Toronto, Canada*

Volume 9
The Politics of Education *An Introduction*
Tony Monchinski, *City University of New York, USA*
Paperback ISBN 90-8790-037-6
Hardback ISBN 90-8790-038-4

Volume 10
Language, Capital, Culture *Critical Studies of Language and Education in Singapore*
Viniti Vaish, S. Gopinathan and Yongbing Liu, *Centre for Research in Pedagogy and Practice, National Institute of Education, Nanyang Technological University, Singapore*
Paperback ISBN 978-90-8790-122-6
Hardback ISBN 978-90-8790-123-3

Volume 11
The Great White North? *Exploring Whiteness, Privilege and Identity in Education*

Paul Carr, *Youngstown State University, USA* and Darren Lund (Eds.), *University of Calgary, Canada.*
Paperback ISBN 978-90-8790-142-4
Hardback ISBN 978-90-8790-143-1

Volume 12
Education Under Occupation *The Heavy Price Of Living On A Neocolonized And Globalized World*
Pierre Orelus, *University of Massachusetts-Amherst, USA.*
Paperback ISBN 978-90-8790-145-5
Hardback ISBN 978-90-8790-146-2

Volume 13
The Ethics of Caring *Bridging Pedagogy and Utopia*
Tammy A. Shel
Paperback ISBN 978-90-8790-209-4
Hardback ISBN 978-90-8790-210-0

Volume 14
Disrupting Privilege, Identity, and Meaning *A Reflective Dance of Environmental Education*
Alison Neilson
Paperback ISBN 978-90-8790-182-0
Hardback ISBN 978-90-8790-183-7

Volume 15
Girls in a Goldfish Bowl *Moral Regulation, Ritual and the Use of Power amongst Inner City Girls*
Rosalyn George *Goldsmiths, University of London, UK*
Paperback ISBN 978-90-8790-185-1
Hardback ISBN 978-90-8790-186-8

Volume 16
Leornado's Vision *A Guide to collective Thinking and Action*
Valerie A. Brown *Australian National University*
Paperback ISBN 978-90-8790-134-9
Hardback ISBN 978-90-8790-135-6

Volume 17
Expanding Waistlines *An Educator's Guide to Childhood Obesity*
David Campos *University of the Incarnate Word, USA*
Paperback ISBN 978-90-8790-206-3
Hardback ISBN 978-90-8790-207-0

Volume 18
Harry Potter: *Feminist Friend or Foe?*
Ruthann Mayes-Elma
Paperback ISBN 978-90-8790-081-6
Hardback ISBN 978-90-8790-082-3

Volume 19
Intellectual Advancement through Disciplinarity: Verticality and Horizontality in Curriculum Studies
William F. Pinar *University of British Columbia, Canada*
Paperback ISBN 978-90-8790-236-0
Hardback ISBN 978-90-8790-237-7

Volume 20
Symbolic Movement: *Critique and Spirituality in Sociology of Education*
Philip Wexler, *The Hebrew University of Jerusalem, Israel*
Paperback ISBN 978-90-8790-273-5
Hardback ISBN 978-90-8790-274-2

Volume 21
Rasists Beware: *Uncovering Racial Politics in the Post Modern Society*
George J. Sefa *Dei, University of Toronto, OISE, Canada*
Paperback ISBN 978-90-8790-276-6
Hardback ISBN 978-90-8790-277-3

Volume 22
Paths to Teaching the Holocaust
Tibbi Duboys *School of Education Brooklyn College of the City University of NewYork*
Paperback ISBN 978-90-8790-382-4
Hardback ISBN 978-90-8790-383-1

www.ingramcontent.com/pod-product-compliance
Lightning Source LLC
LaVergne TN
LVHW010605110826
845149LV00003B/772

* 9 7 8 9 0 8 7 9 0 3 8 2 4 *